QUILTING step by step

Maggi Gordon

DK

LONDON, NEW YORK, MUNICH,
MELBOURNE, DELHI

DK INDIA

Project Editor Charis Bhagianathan
Editor Manasvi Vohra
Assistant Editor Swati Mittal
Art Editors Prashant Kumar, Mahua Sharma
Assistant Art Editors Rohit Walia, Mansi Nagdev
Managing Editor Glenda Fernandes
Managing Art Editor Navidita Thapa
DTP Manager Sunil Sharma
DTP Designers Manish Upreti, Anurag Trivedi

DK UK

Project Editor Laura Palosuo
Project Art Editor Pamela Shiels
Managing Editor Penny Smith
Managing Art Editor Marianne Markham
Senior Jacket Creative Nicola Powling
Production Editor Sean Daly
Senior Production Controller Seyhan Esen
Creative Technical Support Sonia Charbonnier
Publisher Peggy Vance

This edition produced for The Book People Ltd,
Hall Wood Avenue, Haydock, St Helens, WA11 9UL

First published in Great Britain in 2012
by Dorling Kindersley Limited,
80 Strand, London WC2R 0RL

Penguin Group (UK)
2 4 6 8 10 9 7 5 3 1
001 – 178865 – Jan/2012

A CIP catalogue record for this book
is available from the British Library.

ISBN 978-1-4093-8414-4

Colour reproduction by Media Development & Printing Ltd
Printed and bound in Singapore by Tien Wah Press

Discover more at www.dk.com

CONTENTS

INTRODUCTION

Although quilts, defined as textiles consisting of layers held together by stitching, have been made specifically as bed covers for only a few hundred years, the techniques used to create them and countless other quilted items, from garments to tent walls, have been employed in almost every civilization throughout the history of humankind. Quilt making, once viewed as a make-do-and-mend necessity, has become a creative outlet for practitioners around the world, and *Quilting Step by Step* will help you learn the skills you need to join their ranks.

The book covers the important techniques associated with making quilts, wall hangings, and other quilted items. Beginning with the essential tools, materials, and design principles, it moves to Patchwork, which involves cutting fabric into strips or shapes and joining them with seams; Appliqué in which fabric shapes are applied to a background with invisible or decorative stitching; and Quilting, the stitching that holds the layers – top, padding, and back – together. Separate chapters provide instructions, hints, and tips on finishing and embellishing projects, and the information throughout the book is detailed in clear, easy-to-follow step-by-step photographs. In addition there is a Gallery of popular patchwork block patterns and a Glossary, as well as information about caring for quilts.

I hope it will provide inspiration and be a valuable reference tool, so that you, too, can experience the pleasure that I find in creating quilts and other quilted items.

Maggi Gordon

TOOLS AND MATERIALS

ALTERNATING SQUARES

Squares can be cut with scissors or rotary equipment (pages 23 and 37) and assembled into rows or blocks (pages 57–60), then turned on point (page 154) to create an under-and-over pattern.

Tools and materials

Making a quilt does not require a lot of equipment. If you are a beginner, you probably won't need more than needles and thread or a sewing machine, scissors, pins, ruler or measuring tape, a pencil, and a thimble. There is, however, a huge selection of specialized tools that have been designed to make the process easier.

General sewing equipment

For quiltmaking you will need a set of hand-sewing needles – both "sharps" and "betweens". Both types come in several lengths, thicknesses, and eye sizes. Needles are sized by number: the higher the number, the finer the needle. Pins are essential for pinning the layers of a quilt together while you work (see page 168). Always press seams as you go, with an iron or by fingerpressing.

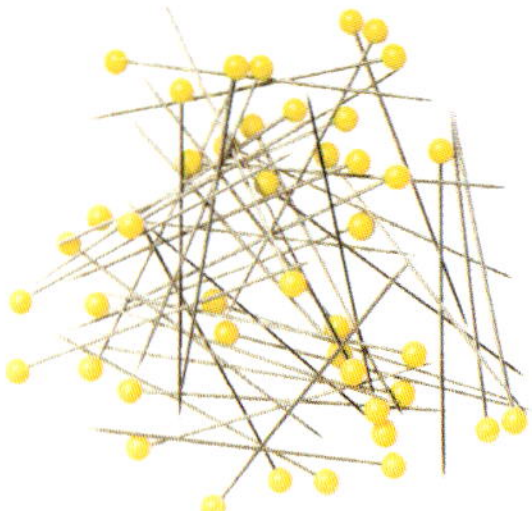

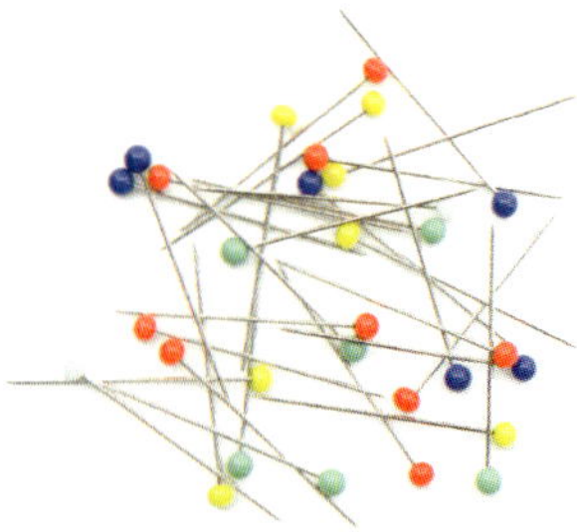

Quilters' pins ↑
Long quilters' pins with a decorative motif such as a small paper flower on top, make them easy to spot in the fabric.

Glass quilters' pins ↑
These extra-long pins are easy to handle. Extra-short pins called appliqué pins are also available to secure pieces as you stitch.

Glass-headed straight pins ↑
Ordinary dressmaking pins are used to hold pieces together during hand piecing.

Safety pins ↑
If the layers of the quilt are not too thick, you can use ordinary safety pins to hold them together.

Hera ↑
A plastic, blade-like device for fingerpressing. A little wooden iron with a flat, chisel-shaped edge can also be used.

← Thimble
Thimbles are made from metal, leather, plastic, and even ceramic, and are designed to protect both the sewing finger and the hand underneath in quilting.

Pin cushion ↓
Pin cushions range from traditional sawdust-filled felt shapes to magnetic pin-catchers. Magnetic types can interfere with the smooth operation of computerized sewing machines.

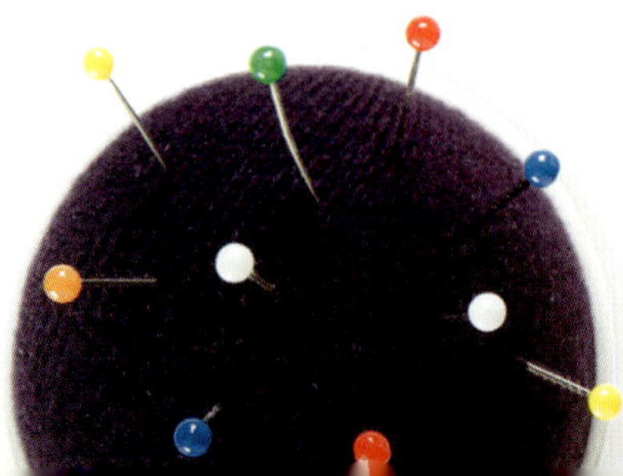

Needles and threaders

Using the correct pin or needle for your work is so important, as the wrong choice can damage fabric or leave small holes. Needles are made from steel and pins from steel or occasionally brass. Look after them by keeping pins in a pin cushion and needles in a needle case – if kept together in a small container they could become scratched and blunt.

Sharps

A general-purpose hand-sewing needle, with a small, round eye. Available in sizes 1 to 12. For most hand sewing use a size 6 to 9.

Crewel

Also known as an embroidery needle, a long needle with a long, oval eye that is designed to take multiple strands of embroidery thread.

Milliner's or straw

A very long, thin needle with a small, round eye. Good for hand-sewing and tacking as it doesn't damage fabric. A size 8 or 9 is most popular.

Betweens or quilting

Similar to a milliner's needle but very short, with a small, round eye. Perfect for fine hand stitches and favoured by quilters.

Beading

Long and exceedingly fine, to sew beads and sequins to fabric. As it is prone to bending, keep it wrapped in tissue when not in use.

Darners

A long, thick needle that is designed to be used with wool or thick yarns and to sew through multiple layers.

Bodkin

A strange-looking needle with a blunt end and a large, fat eye. Use to thread elastic or cord. There are larger eyes for thicker yarns.

Self-threading needle

A needle that has a double eye. The thread is placed in the upper eye through the gap, then pulled into the eye below for sewing.

Wire needle threader

A handy gadget, especially useful for needles with small eyes. Also helpful in threading sewing-machine needles.

Automatic needle threader

This threader is operated with a small lever. The needle, eye down, is inserted and the thread is wrapped around.

Sewing machine

All the main manufacturers have sewing machines designed with the quiltmaker in mind, with numerous attachments available. For machine quilting, you will need to be able to drop the feed dogs. Machine needles in sizes 70–90 universal are recommended for quiltmaking. This machine is an example. Others may be configured differently.

Machine features
Before you buy a machine, decide which features will be most useful to you and, if you're planning to quilt, make sure it's sturdy enough to be able to stitch through the quilt top, wadding, and backing fabric.

Threading guides
Markings to help guide you in threading the machine.

Tension dial
To control the stitch tension on the upper thread, i.e. how fast the thread feeds through the sewing machine.

Automatic needle threader
A pull-down gadget to aid threading the machine needle.

Needle
The machine needle. Replace it regularly to ensure good stitch quality (see page 16).

Presser foot
To hold the fabric in place while stitching. Various feet can be used here to aid different sewing processes (see pages 16–17).

Removable free arm
This section of the machine will pull away to give a narrow work bed. It also contains a useful storage section.

Feed dogs
These metal teeth grip the fabric and feed it through the machine.

Shank
To hold the various feet in place.

Needle plate
A removable cover reveals the bobbin. This plate is gridded to help stitch seams of various widths.

Speed control
A slide, to control the speed of your machine.

Spool holder
To hold your sewing thread in place.

Bobbin winder
Winds the thread from the spool on to the bobbin, keeping it under tension (see page 16).

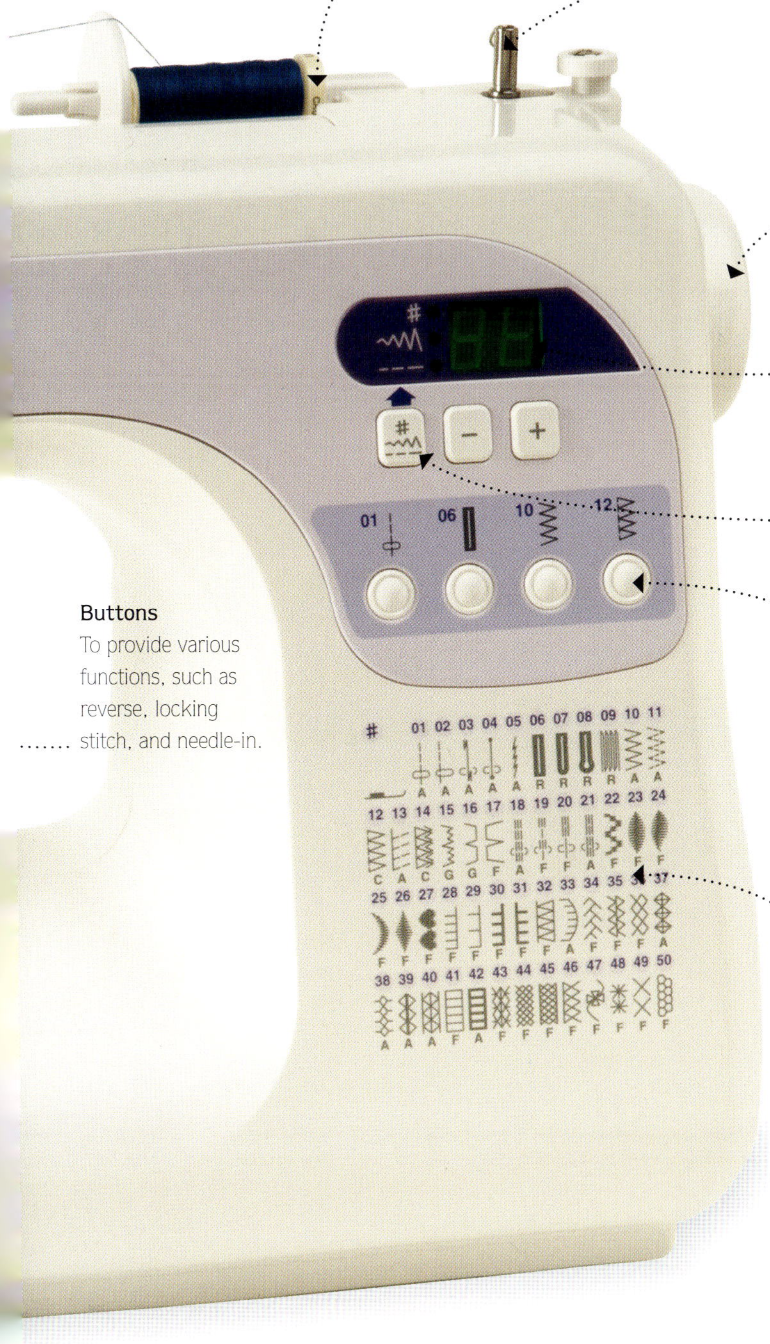

Balance wheel
This can be turned towards you to move the needle up or down manually.

LCD screen
An illuminated screen that indicates which stitch you are using.

Touch buttons
Use these to change the type of stitch you are using and to increase and decrease size and width of stitch.

Buttons
To provide various functions, such as reverse, locking stitch, and needle-in.

Touch buttons
These quickly select the most popular stitches such as zigzag and buttonhole.

Stitch library
All the different stitches this machine can stitch. You just have to key in the number.

Sewing-machine accessories

Many accessories can be purchased for your sewing machine to make certain sewing processes so much easier. There are different machine needles not only for different fabrics but also for different types of threads. There is also a huge number of sewing-machine feet, and new feet are constantly coming on to the market. Those shown here are some of the most popular.

PLASTIC BOBBIN

The bobbin is for the lower thread. Some machines take plastic bobbins, others metal. Always check which sort of bobbin your machine uses as the incorrect choice can cause stitch problems.

METAL BOBBIN

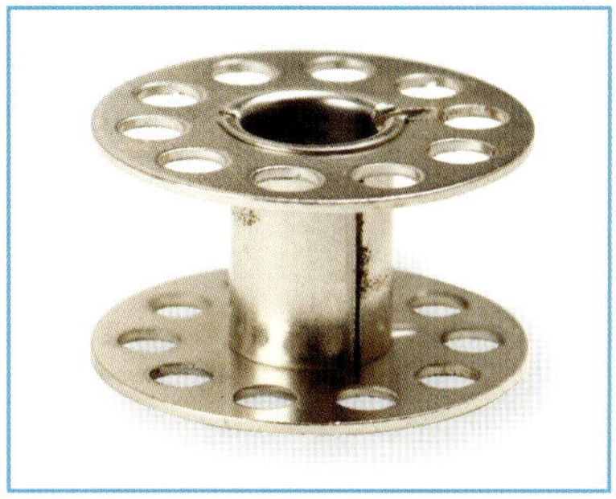

Also known as a universal bobbin, this is used on many types of sewing machines. Be sure to check that your machine needs a metal bobbin before you buy.

FREE EMBROIDERY OR DARNING FOOT

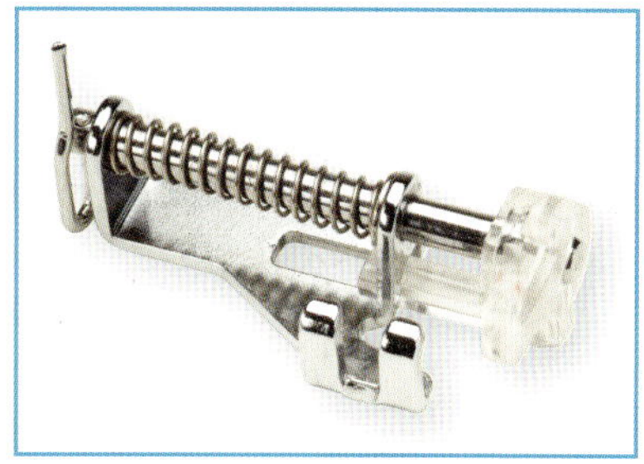

A foot designed to be used when the feed dogs on the machine are lowered. This enables a free motion stitch to be worked.

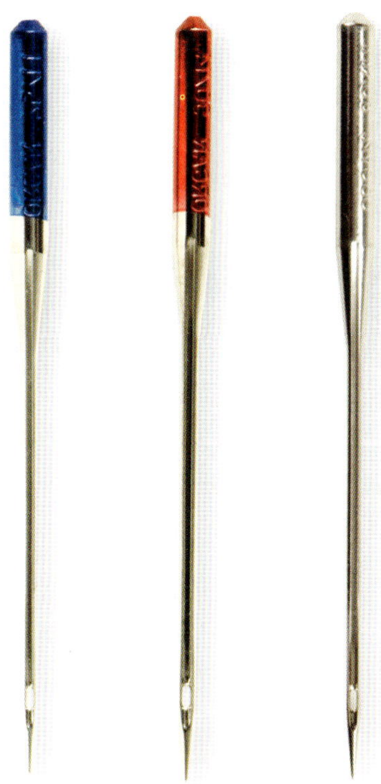

OVEREDGE FOOT

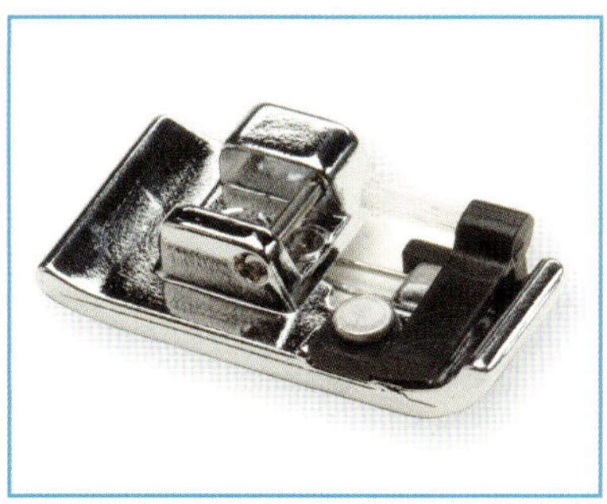

A foot that runs along the raw edge of the fabric and holds it stable while an overedge stitch is worked.

EMBROIDERY FOOT

A clear plastic foot with a groove underneath that allows linear machine embroidery stitches to pass under.

MACHINE NEEDLES

There are different types of sewing machine needles to cope with different fabrics. Machine needles are sized from 60 to 100, a 60 being a very fine needle. There are special needles for machine embroidery and also for metallic threads.

WALKING FOOT

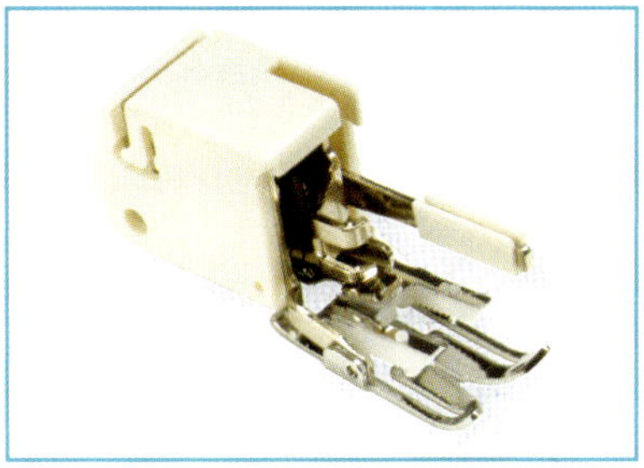

This foot "walks" across the fabric sandwich so the upper layer doesn't push forward. Great for machine quilting and for working on difficult fabrics.

ZIP FOOT

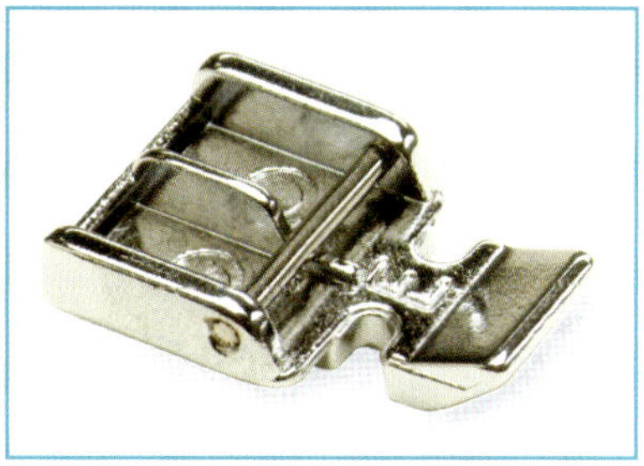

This foot fits to either the right or left-hand side of the needle to enable you to stitch close to a zip.

CONCEALED ZIP FOOT

A foot that is used to insert a concealed zip – the foot holds open the coils of the zip, enabling you to stitch behind them.

ROLLED HEM FOOT

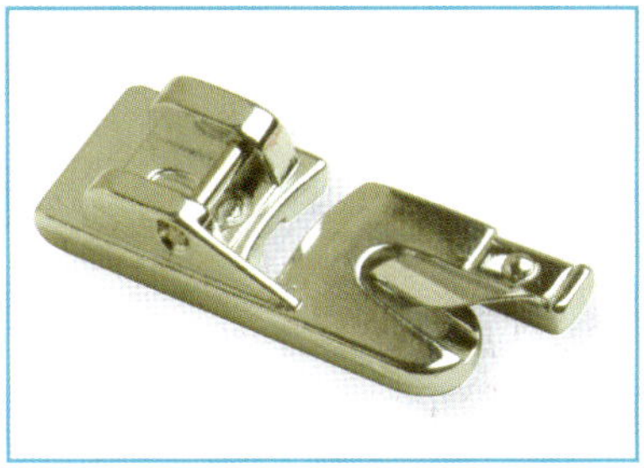

This foot rolls the fabric while stitching with a straight stitch or a zigzag stitch.

PIPING FOOT

A deep groove in this foot allows a piping cord to fit underneath, enabling close stitching to the cord.

RIBBON FOOT

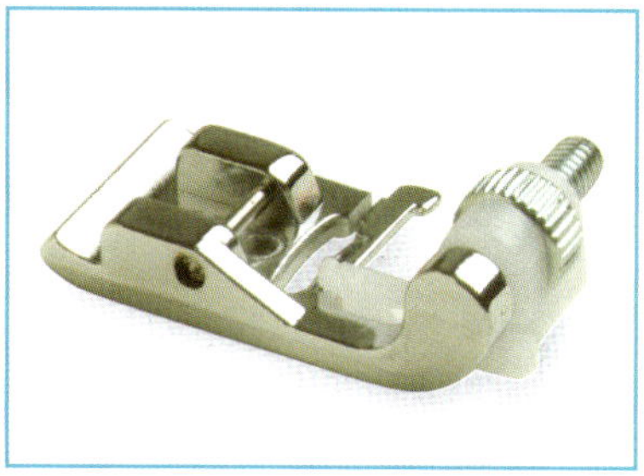

A foot that will feed either one or two ribbons evenly under the machine needle to ensure accurate stitching.

BEADING FOOT, NARROW

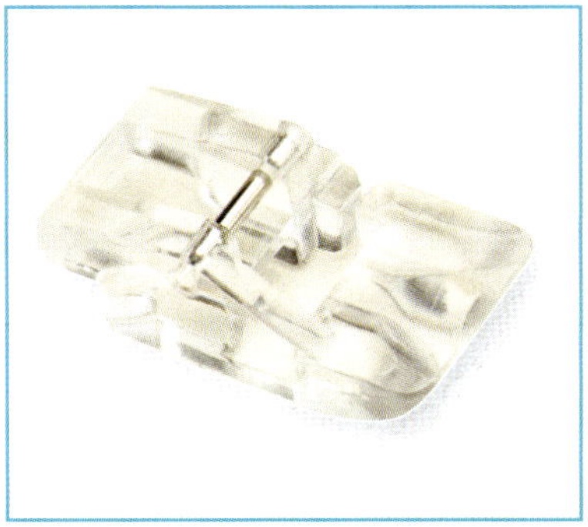

This foot has a narrow groove and is used to attach small beads or decorative cords.

FEET FOR PATCHWORK

All sewing machines come with a standard presser foot as well as a selection of specialized feet for various purposes. Among the most useful for quiltmaking are:

¼-inch foot: Designed to measure a seam of exactly ¼in (5–6mm), rather than the ⅜in (10mm) presser foot that is standard in dressmaking.

Open-toe foot: Useful for appliqué and quilting.

Free-style quilting foot: "Floats" on a spring mechanism for free-motion quilting.

Twin-needle foot: Gives interesting textured effects.

Threads

There are many threads available and knowing which ones to choose can be confusing. There are specialist threads designed for special tasks, such as machine embroidery or quilting. Threads also vary in fibre content, from pure cotton to rayon to polyester. Some threads are very fine while others are thick and coarse. Failure to choose the correct thread can spoil your project and lead to problems with the stitch quality of the sewing machine or overlocker.

Cotton thread ↓

A 100% cotton thread. Smooth and firm, this is designed to be used with cotton fabrics and is much favoured by quilters.

Quilting thread ↓

Quilting thread is heavier than sewing thread and is waxed to prevent breaks.

Silk thread ↓

A sewing thread made from 100% silk. Used mainly for hand appliqué and sewing on delicate silk fabrics. Also useful for tacking in areas that need to be pressed as it can be removed without leaving an imprint.

Top-stitching thread ↓

A thicker polyester thread used for decorative top-stitching and buttonholes. Also for hand sewing buttons on thicker fabrics and some soft furnishings.

Polyester all-purpose thread ↓

A good-quality polyester thread that has a very slight "give", making it suitable for sewing all types of fabrics and soft furnishings. The most popular type of thread.

Overlocker thread ↓

A dull yarn on a larger reel designed to be used on the overlocker. This type of yarn is normally not strong enough to use on the sewing machine.

Embroidery thread ↓

Often made from a rayon yarn for shine. This is a finer thread designed for machine embroidery. Available on much larger reels for economy.

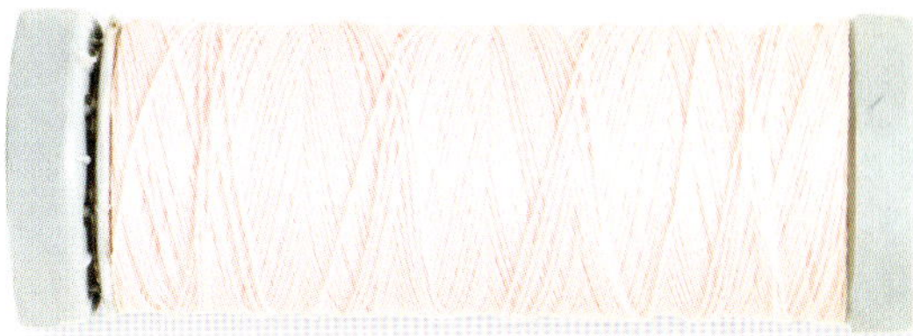

Metallic thread ↓

A rayon and metal thread for decorative machining and machine embroidery. This thread usually requires a specialist sewing-machine needle.

Measuring tools

Most of the basic measuring and marking tools that a quiltmaker needs are standard items in a home office or workshop. Some can be found in a general sewing kit or a desk drawer.

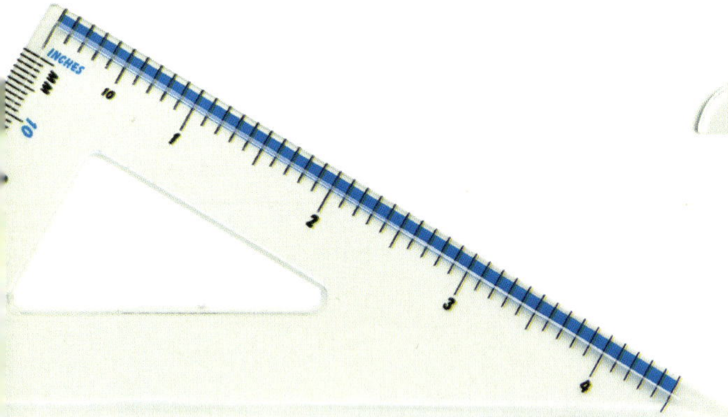

Set square ↑
Useful for measuring and guiding square corners on quilt blocks and for cutting individual pattern pieces.

← T-square
Useful for squaring corners and measuring.

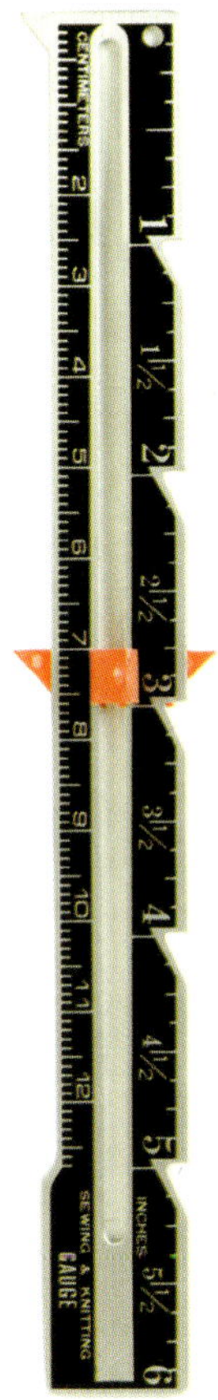

← Seam gauge
Very useful for measuring and marking off seam allowances.

Tape measure ↑
An essential item for quiltmaking and patchwork, for measuring fabric widths and template sizes.

Rotary ruler ↓
Useful for drafting patterns and templates, as well as for determining seam allowances.

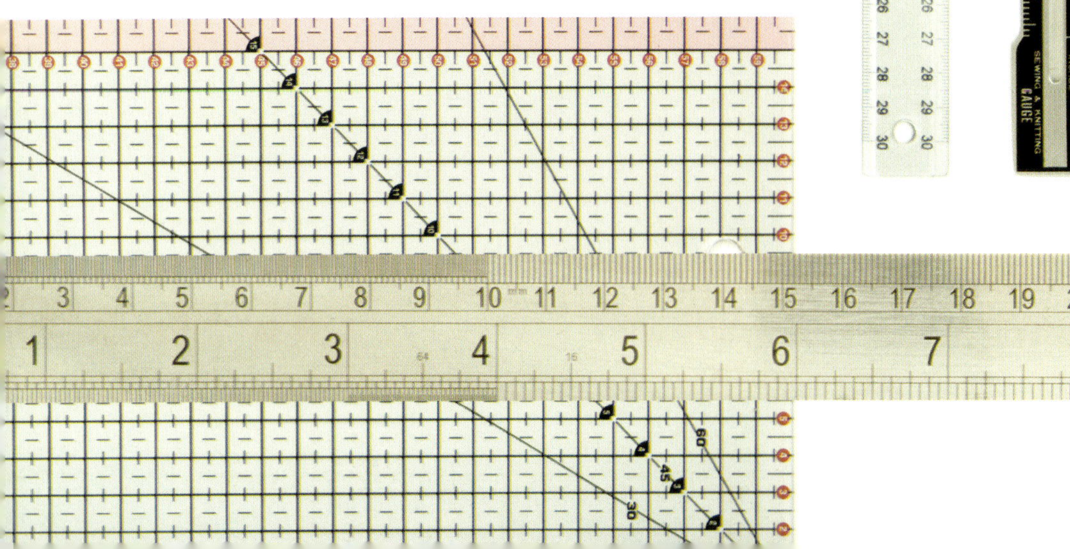

← Ruler
A metal or plastic ruler is useful for measuring and drawing straight lines.

Marking tools

Various kinds of pencils and pens are used to draw designs and mark seam allowances on both paper and fabric. Some markers, such as tailor's chalk and washaway pen, are non-permanent.

¼-inch masking tape →
This tape can be used as an easily removable quilting guide.

Tailor's chalk ↑
The white line of tailor's chalk shows clearly on most fabrics and can be removed easily.

Pencils →
A selection of coloured pencils can be used to mark clearly on fabric when tracing or transferring patterns or designs.

Blue washaway pen →
A water-soluble pen can be used for transferring patterns or drawing around templates.

Fine-point lead pencil →
A sharp point is essential for drawing designs and templates.

Templates and stencils

Templates and stencils are more durable if they are cut from translucent template plastic, rather than card. Cut using a sharp scalpel to ensure accuracy. Freezer paper (see page 136) can also be used to create templates and is especially useful in some appliqué work.

Tracing paper ↓
This is essential for tracing motifs or pattern pieces onto template plastic, or card, before cutting out.

Freezer paper ↓
A good option for appliqué templates, freezer paper can be ironed onto the fabric and removed later.

Card
Stiff card can be used to make templates but will not be as long lasting as plastic.

Ready-made window template →
Made from sturdy template plastic or metal, a window template is used to mark both the outline and the seamline without the need for two templates.

Ready-made quilting stencil →
A quilting stencil can be used to transfer a pattern onto the fabric. Trace the stencil design with a non-permanent marker pen.

Miscellaneous items

Other useful items for quiltmaking can include graph paper, dressmaker's carbon paper, slivers of soap, flexible curves, drawing compasses, protractors, and erasers, which can all help with designing and transferring pattern pieces or motifs.

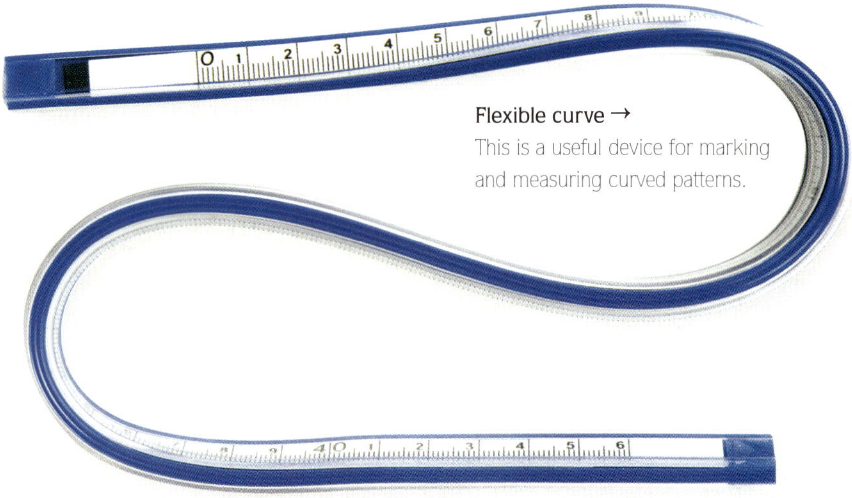

Flexible curve →
This is a useful device for marking and measuring curved patterns.

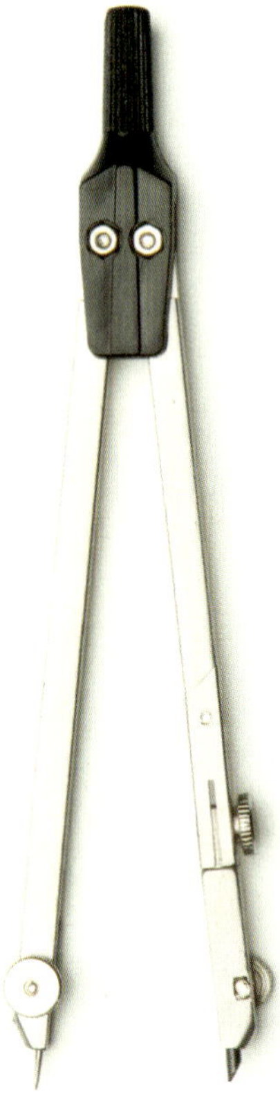

Eraser ↑
A useful item to have on hand when drawing or tracing designs.

Dressmaker's carbon paper ↓
This is a permanent method of transferring designs to the wrong side of the fabric, using a marking wheel or pencil.

Drawing compass ↑
A compass is very useful for drafting curved templates or drawing circular appliqué motifs.

Graph paper
This is useful for designing, transferring or scaling designs.

Cutting equipment

Scissors are absolutely essential in quiltmaking and you should have at least three pairs: one dedicated to cutting fabric; one for paper and wadding; and a small, sharp pair for snipping threads. A rotary cutter speeds up quiltmaking.

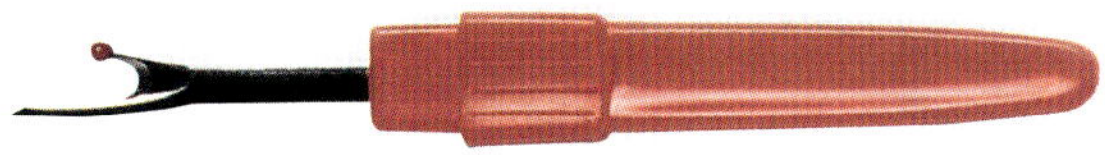

Seam ripper ↑
Used for removing stitching that has gone awry and for "reverse sewing".

Rotary cutter ↑
Cutters come in numerous shapes and several blade sizes, as well as decorative-edge cutting blades.

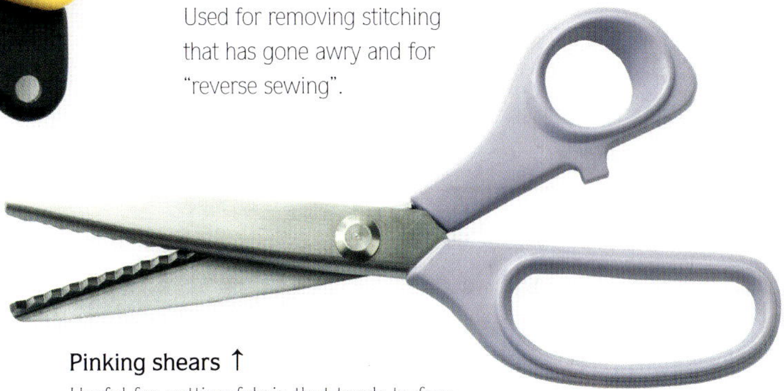

Pinking shears ↑
Useful for cutting fabric that tends to fray.

Small sharp scissors →
Use for snipping thread ends, clipping seams, and trimming and grading seam allowances. A specialized version of small scissors called appliqué scissors can be helpful in appliqué work. The blades are curved to protect layers that are not being trimmed from being damaged by sharp points, but they should not be seen as a replacement for your ordinary pair of small scissors.

Rotary ruler →
With measurements broken into 3mm (1/8in) segments and angled lines for measuring 45- and 60-degree angles, rotary rulers can be square, rectangular, or triangular.

Craft knife →
This is invaluable for cutting stencils from template plastic.

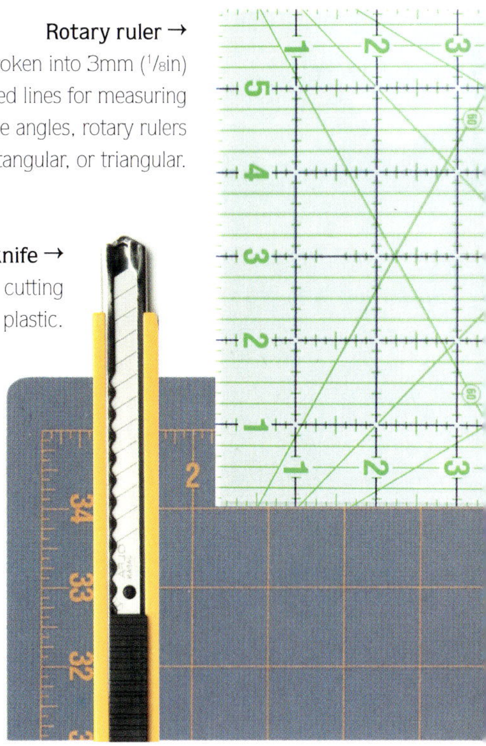

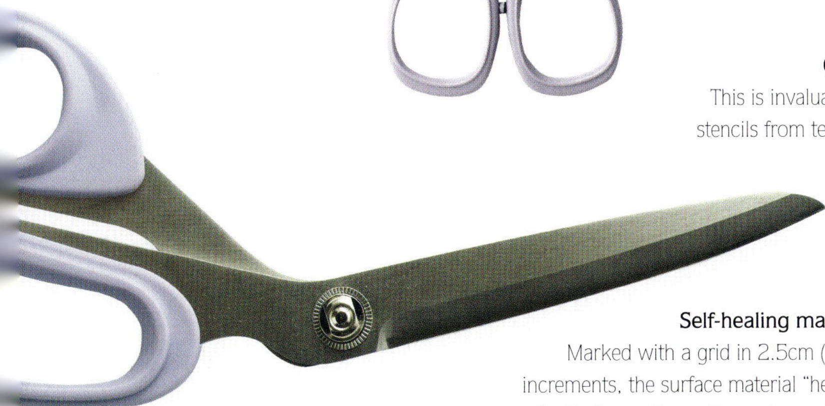

Fabric scissors ↑
These have bent handles, which allow the fabric to lie flat on the surface while you are cutting out your pieces.

Self-healing mat →
Marked with a grid in 2.5cm (1in) increments, the surface material "heals" itself after cutting with a rotary cutter, leaving it smooth again without slits or grooves to catch the cutter next time you cut. Do not cut the top surface with a craft knife.

Fabric and wadding

The standard quilting fabric is 100 per cent cotton, which comes in a vast range of colours, patterns, and weaves and is easy to work. Wadding is used as the filling between the quilt layers. Use large frames or hoops to hold the layers in place while you quilt.

← Plain cotton fabrics
Plain fabrics are often used for the foundation of quilt designs and borders, and for the quilt backing.

← Wadding
Wadding is the soft middle layer between the quilt top and the backing. It is available in polyester, cotton, or a combination of the two. Wool and silk wadding is available for specialized work.

Printed fabrics ↓
Traditional patchwork quilts are constructed with printed fabrics, and small-scale prints work well together.

Check fabric →
Checks work well combined with plains for simple patchwork or quilting designs.

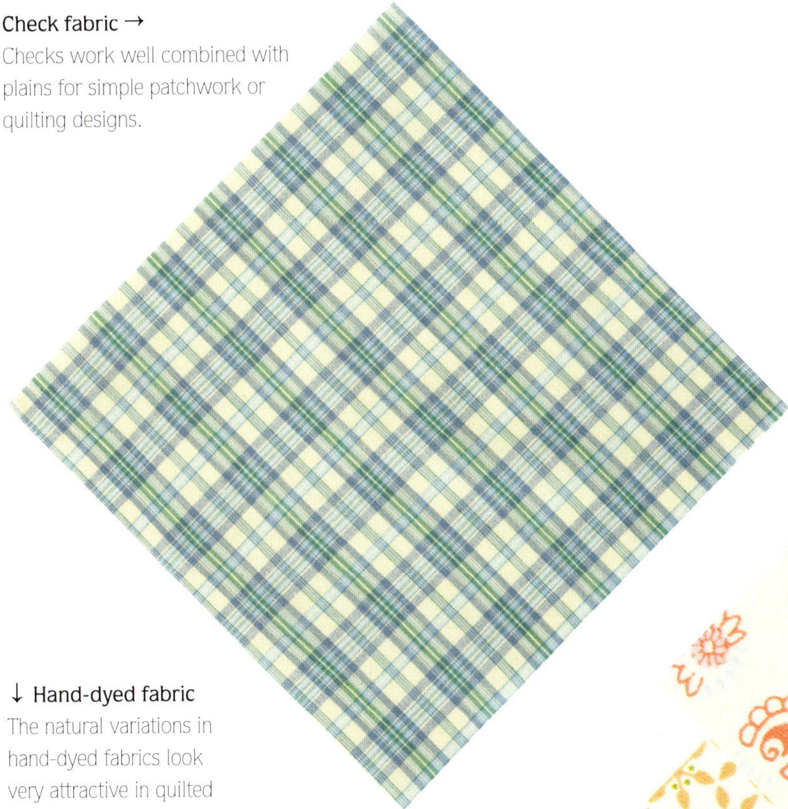

Medium-scale prints →
Ideal for patchwork, medium-scale prints can be successfully combined with plain fabric and small-scale prints for texture and interest.

↓ Hand-dyed fabric
The natural variations in hand-dyed fabrics look very attractive in quilted or patchwork projects.

↓ Large-scale prints
Large-scale prints work best in large-size blocks. Individual motifs can be cut out and used in appliqué, or fussy cut for patchwork.

Pressing aids

Successful patchwork and appliqué rely on successful pressing. Correct pressing equipment can make all the difference in achieving a neat professional finish.

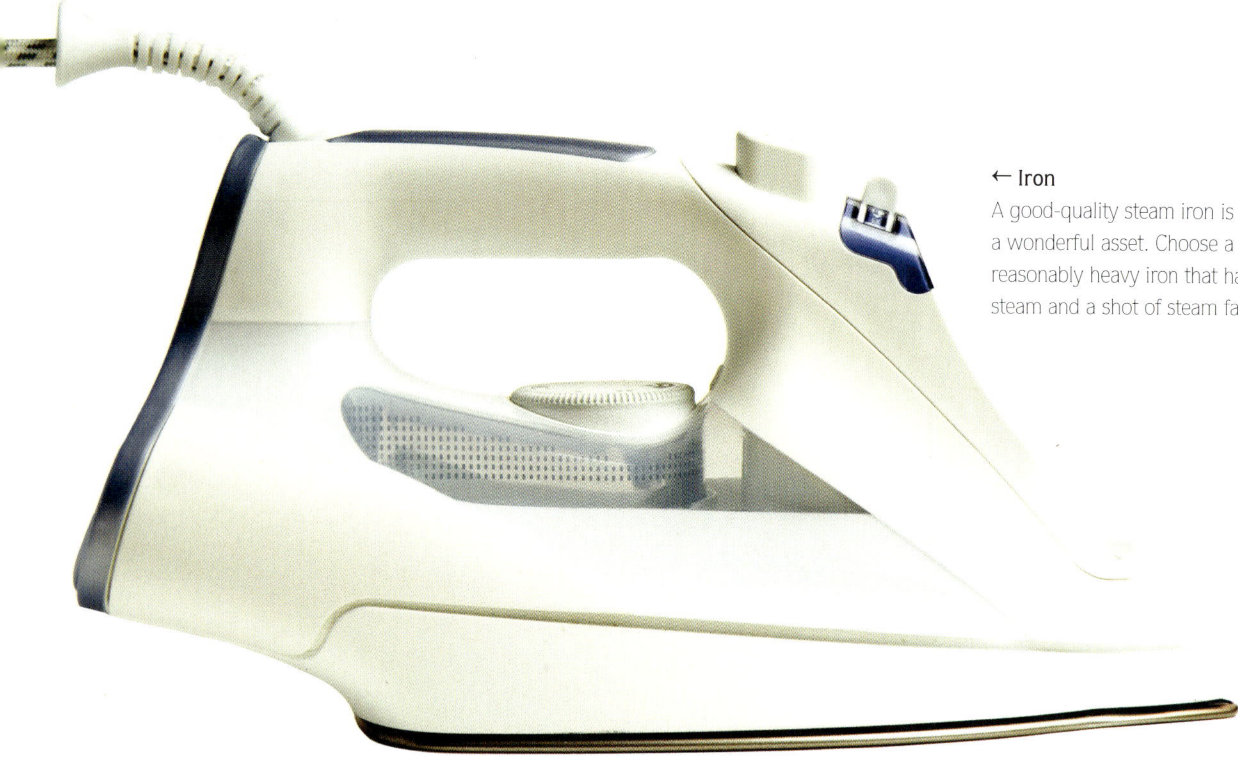

← Iron

A good-quality steam iron is a wonderful asset. Choose a reasonably heavy iron that has steam and a shot of steam facility.

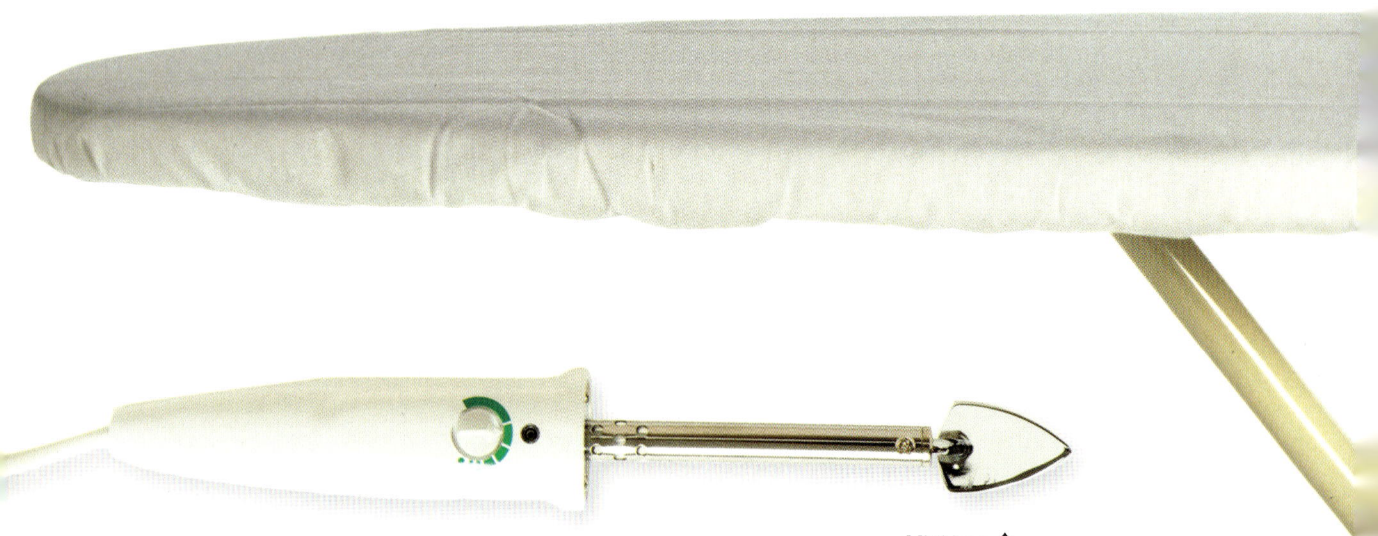

Mini iron ↑

Useful for some appliqué techniques and for getting into small corners. Use in conjunction with the pressing mat.

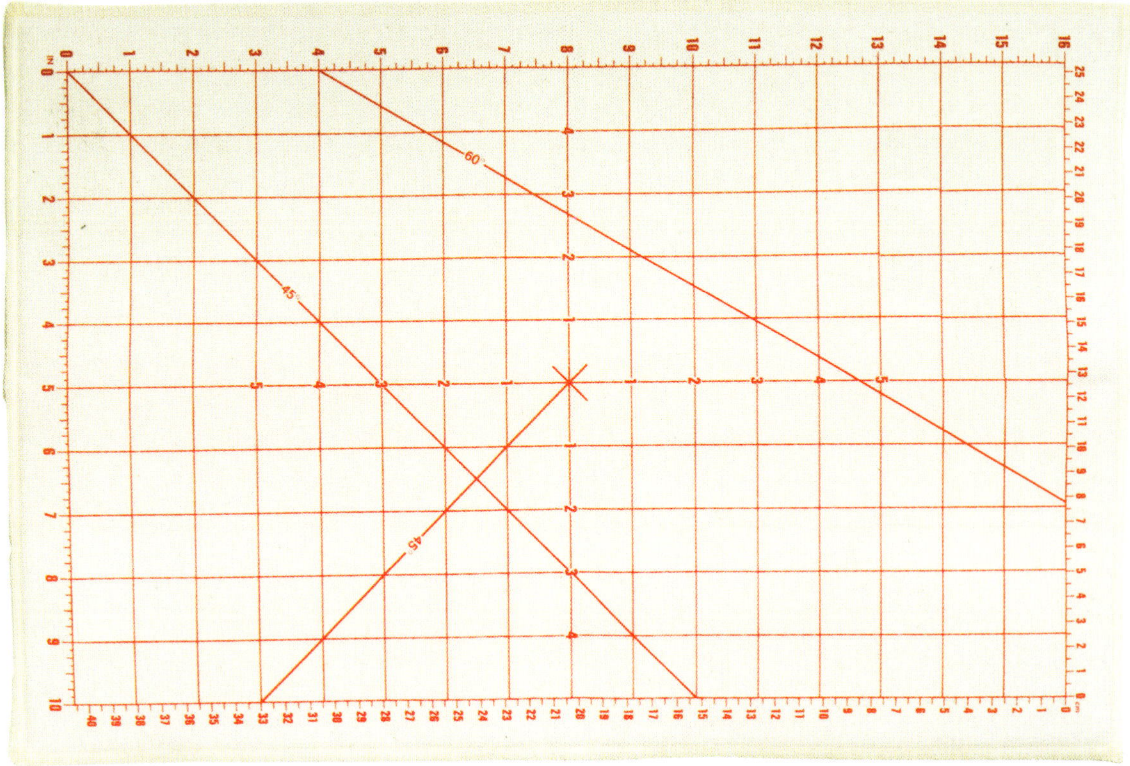

Pressing mat ↑
A heat-resistant mat for pressing small items and single blocks. Often backed with a small cutting mat.

Ironing board ↑
Essential to iron on. Make sure the board is height-adjustable.

Pressing cloth →
Choose a cloth made from silk organza or muslin as you can see through it. The cloth will stop the iron marking fabric and prevent burning delicate fabrics.

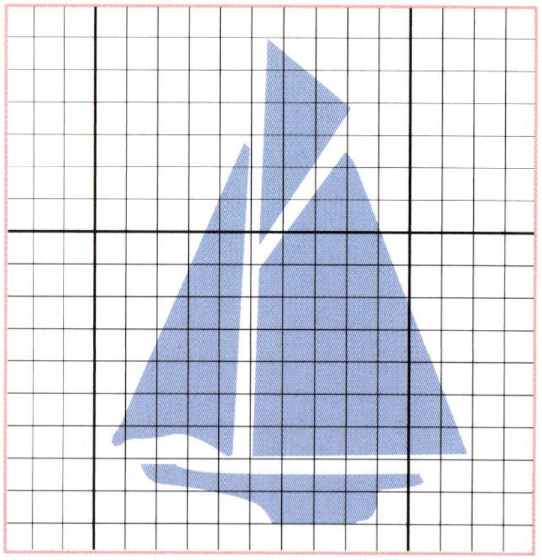

DESIGN PRINCIPLES AND GENERAL TECHNIQUES

PINWHEEL PATTERN

Identical half-square triangle patches (pages 61–63) have been alternated and combined with simple squares to make a lively Pinwheel Star that takes the eye across the work.

Design principles

Most patchwork and many appliqué quilts are based on patterns comprised of blocks – that is, squares made following the same pattern, which are then assembled to make the quilt top. This means that they can be broken down into working units that are easier to cope with than a large overall design. There are literally hundreds of existing blocks that you can make in fabrics and colours of your own choice but, once you understand the basic principles, it's fun to come up with patterns of your own.

Planning your own blocks

The main patchwork block categories are four-patch (see pages 67–69), nine-patch (see pages 70–71), five-patch and seven-patch (see pages 72–75). Each one lends itself to certain finished block sizes. Four-patch patterns can always be divided by even numbers, while nine-patch blocks are easiest to work with if the finished size is divisible by three. Five-patch and seven-patch patterns are more limited; they are multiples of 5 x 5 and 7 x 7 units (or patches) per block respectively.

If you want to design your own block pattern, start by deciding what size you want your finished block to be and draw it on paper, sub-dividing it into the relevant number of patches. Further sub-divide each patch into strips, triangles, smaller squares, or rectangles to create your design. When you are satisfied, transfer each element to another piece of paper and add a seam allowance to each side of each separate element.

With appliqué patterns, enlarge or reduce the pattern if necessary (see page 36) and copy it onto tracing paper. Decide which elements should be cut as separate pieces and trace them individually onto another piece of tracing paper so they can be cut out and used as patterns.

Many blocks can be super-sized by dramatically increasing the dimensions of a single block, making quilts of an ideal size for baby quilts. Combining several of these bigger blocks allows the quick creation of a full-size quilt.

Patchwork block

Appliqué block

Using templates

Some elements require templates, which are copies of the pieces of the pattern. Ready-made templates are available from quilt stores and online. Find out if the seam allowances have been added. Elements to be machine pieced must include the exact seam allowances, while appliqué patterns and those for hand piecing do not need a precise allowance, but are generally cut larger than the finished shape. Many templates are cut with a "window" that shows the area of fabric you will finish up with; this also enables you to mark the seamline and the cutting line without moving the template. Alternatively, you can make your own long-lasting or limited-use templates following these instructions.

Limited-use templates using freezer paper: Trace the pattern pieces onto freezer paper and cut them out. Iron onto the wrong side of the fabric and then cut out around the shape.

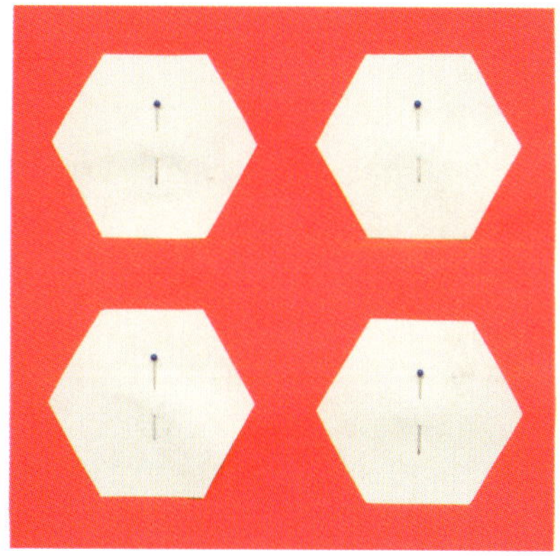

Limited-use templates using tracing paper: Pin the template in place and cut out the shape, again adding the seam allowances by eye.

Durable templates using heavy card: Draw the shapes on paper or tracing paper. Cut them out and draw around them on heavy card. Add the seam allowances and cut them out. Or glue the shapes to card, add allowances and cut out.

Durable templates using template plastic: Trace the shapes directly on to the template plastic or cut them from paper and glue them to the plastic sheet. Cut them out with a craft knife or paper scissors.

Fabric: prints and plains

The scale: The size of the image – its scale – is an important factor when working with print fabrics. A large-scale pattern is generally more difficult to work with, but it can be used successfully, especially in bigger blocks. Try combining large prints with plain fabrics, especially conversation prints with themed motifs. These are useful for making quick-and-easy baby and children's quilts. Medium-scale prints can be fussy-cut (see page 41) quite effectively, and small-scale patterns are usually simple to use as they can be cut into small units that have a consistent look. There are also hand-dyed fabrics (or fabrics printed to look as if they have been hand dyed) and tone-on-tone fabrics that have tiny motifs printed on a background of the same colour that look almost like plain colours from a distance. These give more visual texture than a solid plain colour and can really help to bring a design to life.

Geometric-patterned fabrics: Fabrics like stripes, checks, and tartans can make fascinating secondary patterns when they are cut and re-assembled. Widely used in country-style quilts, they need careful handling to be most effective. Stripes, in particular, can be set in different directions to create visual movement within a block, while checks and plaids can be combined with each other or with plain fabrics to great effect.

Borders and sashing: A plain colour can act as a foil to a busy print, giving the eye somewhere to rest and providing the keen quilter with a place to show off skills. Plain sashing (see page 156) can direct a viewer to the block pattern within, and while borders can be patterned and pieced, plain borders frame and contain a quilt in a special way. Balance – between prints and plains, lights and darks, warmth and coolness – is key to any successful design, and the more quilts you look at, and make, the better your judgment will become. One way to work is to choose a main print first and then coordinate the plains and other prints around it.

Creating a design wall: Working on a design wall is a good way to test how fabrics will look as it allows you to step back and view options from a distance. Hang a plain white sheet over a door to make a temporary version, or fashion a moveable one from foam board covered with white flannel over a layer of wadding. If you have room for a permanent version, mount cork or foam board on a wall in your sewing area.

PRINTS

Gingham

Madras

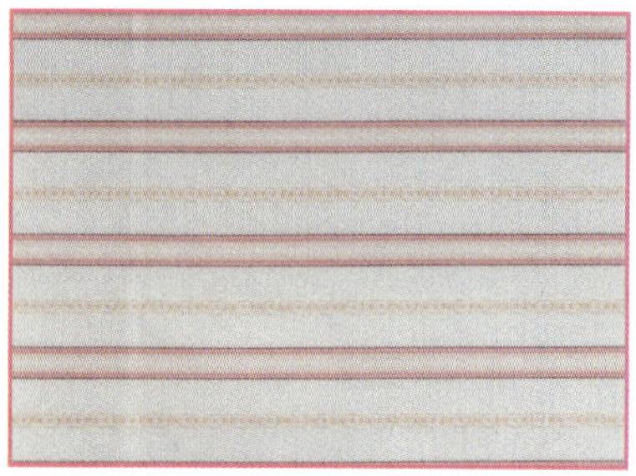

Shirting

PLAINS

Calico

Dupion

Dress-weight linen

Understanding colour

Understanding the basic principles of colour theory is crucial to designing a successful quilt. Even a simple design gains impact from good colour choices. The three primary colours, red, yellow, and blue, can be placed side by side to create a colour wheel. When two adjacent colours are combined, they create "secondaries". Red and yellow make orange, yellow and blue make green, and blue and red make purple. Intermediate colours called tertiaries occur when a secondary is mixed with the nearest primary.

Colour wheel

Complementary colours: Colours that lie opposite one another on the wheel, such as red and green, or yellow and violet, are called complementaries. They provide contrasts that accent design elements and make both colours stand out. Don't forget black and white, the ultimate opposites.

Colour temperature: Colour has a visual "temperature", with some colours being perceived as "warm" and others as "cool". Many people tend to think of blue and its adjacent colours as being cool, while the reds and yellows are warm, but in fact there are warm and cool versions of all the primaries; think, for example, of a warm, azure blue and a cold, icy blue. Colour temperature is an important element in whether a colour recedes or advances – that is, in whether it stands out from or blends in with the background and surrounding colours.

Colour tone: Tone, or value, is the relative lightness or darkness of a particular colour. While some fabrics are obviously dark or light in value, others take their value from the colours surrounding them. Almost all successful quilts rely on contrasting values. These are not necessarily just differences in their qualities of lightness and darkness, but in how the colours react to each other. A quilt made entirely of middle values, even if the colours themselves are quite different, will lack impact and eye appeal.

Monochromatic designs: These use different versions of the same colour. So a quilt based on greens will not stray into the red section of the colour wheel, but might have shades and tints of yellow and blue mixed in, which can then become "harmonious" combinations of colours that are next to each other on the colour wheel. These "adjacent" colours can also be combined to great effect, as long as there are differences in value between them.

General techniques

Quiltmaking involves different stages and different techniques, but some aspects of making a quilt, whether it is pieced or appliquéd, are the same. The skills outlined in this section will help you, whichever type of quilt you choose to make.

Altering the size of a design or pattern

The easiest way to alter the size of a motif is to photocopy it. To enlarge take the size you want the motif to be and divide it by the actual size of the template. Multiply by 100% and set the copier to that number on the enlargement side. To reduce, divide the desired size of the motif by the actual size, multiply by 100%, and set the copier on the reduction side.

1 For non-geometric designs, trace the outline onto gridded paper. To make a pattern twice the size of the original, double the grid on another piece of paper. If you trace on 1cm (½in) squares, for example, increase the size of each square in your new grid to 2cm (1in).

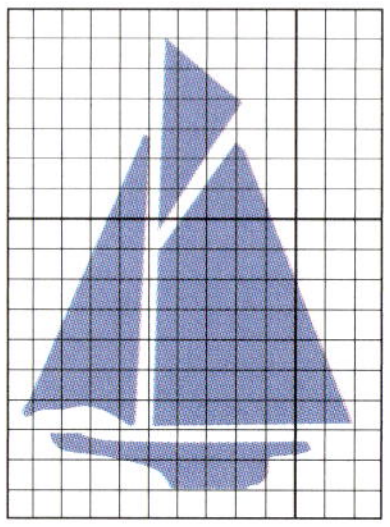

The original motif traced onto paper gridded into 1cm (½in) squares

2 Transfer the lines within each square to correspond to the original image. Trace the pattern again to smooth out any distortions.

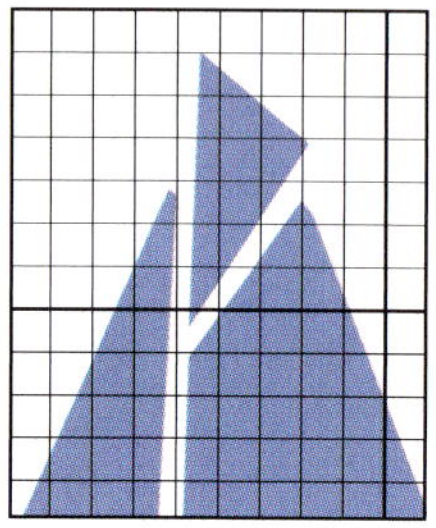

The motif enlarged onto a 2cm (1in) grid

Preparing fabric

All cotton fabrics shrink a little during the first wash. Shrinkage is usually minimal, but it can distort the finished quilt. Using fabrics that have been washed with those that haven't can cause seams to pucker. Always test fabrics for colour fastness, especially dark ones. Before you start to cut, iron each piece and make sure the straight of grain is true by checking against the selvedge.

Fabric has three grains: the lengthways grain (warp); the horizontal grain (weft); and the diagonal grain (bias). The rigid edge on each side is called the selvedge. The bias should be handled carefully as it stretches easily, which can lead to distortions.

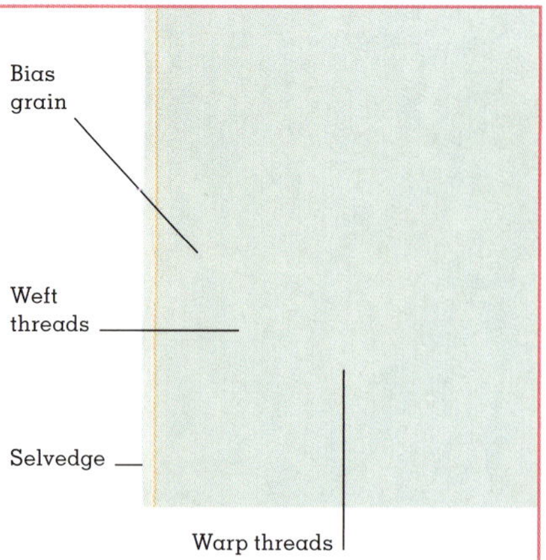

TIPS

- **If you think colour may bleed,** test it by pressing a small damp piece of white fabric on the fabric to be used.
- **When prewashing fabric,** snip off a small triangle at each corner to prevent fraying. Washing small pieces of fabric in a lingerie bag will help prevent fraying.
- **Cut borders on the lengthways grain** to minimize stretching.
- **To find the lengthways grain,** pull it gently along both straight grains. The stretch will be greater along the weft, or widthways, grain.
- **Try to position bias edges** away from the edges of a block to minimize stretching and keep the size of the block accurate.

Rotary cutting

Many of the most popular patterns can be rotary cut. You will need a rotary cutter, transparent plastic ruler, and a self-healing mat. When cutting a square into other shapes, such as right-angled triangles, start with a square that is larger than a simple square in the same size block, to allow for a seam allowance on bias seams.

BASIC ROTARY CUTTING

1 Fold washed and pressed fabric to fit on the mat. Place the ruler over the fabric that you intend to use. Level off the end of the fabric by cutting away from your body. Keep the hand holding the ruler steady and away from the cutter.

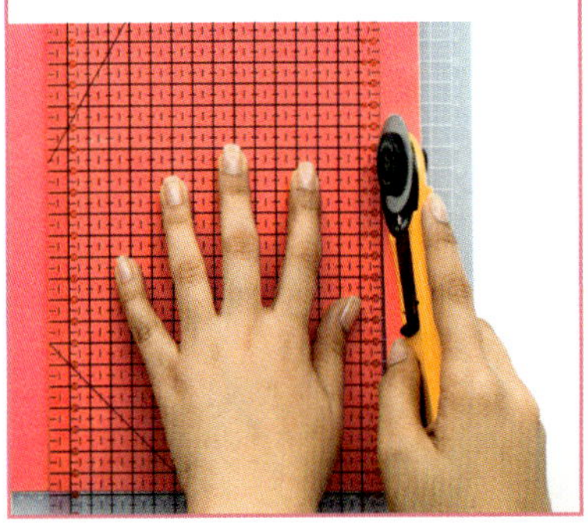

2 Turn the mat so as not to disturb the newly cut edge and place the ruler over the area that you want to use. Align the correct measurement on the ruler carefully along the vertical cut edge and line up the folded edge with a horizontal mark. Cut a strip of the desired width along the grain.

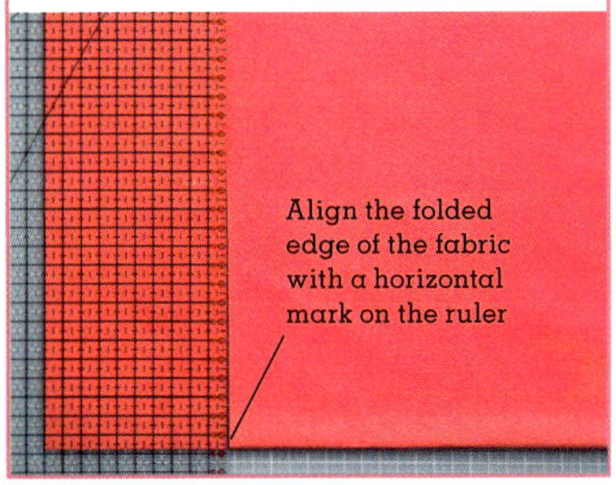

3 To cut strips into smaller units, position the cut strip horizontally on the mat and measure as before.

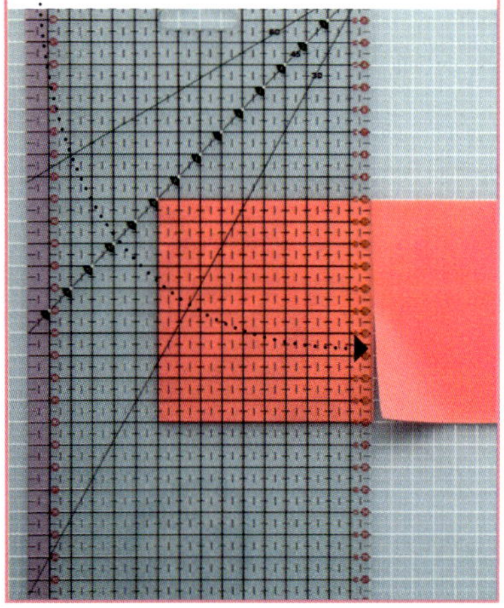

CUTTING SQUARES AND RECTANGLES

Squares and rectangles can also be cut using a square rotary ruler, which has a guideline marked across the diagonal from corner to corner. Add 2.25cm (⅞in) seam allowance for right-angle triangles and 2.75cm (1⅛in) for quarter-square triangles.

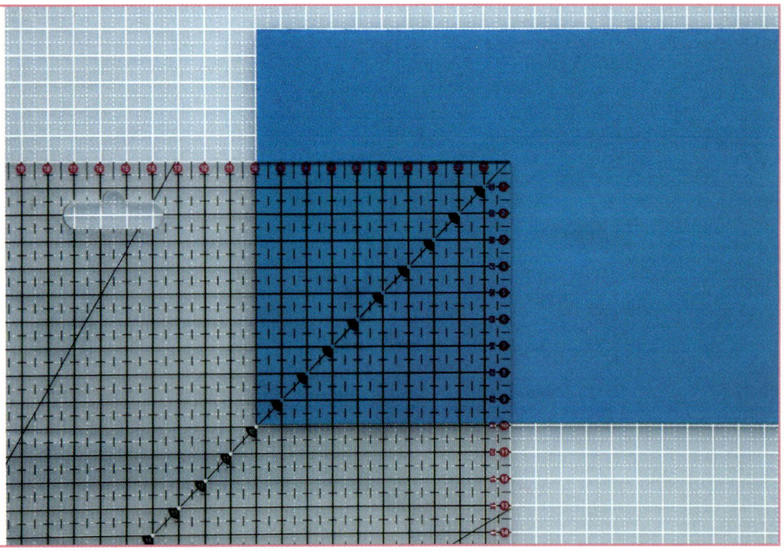

CUTTING PIECED STRIPS

Press the strip and place it right side up horizontally on the mat. If necessary, level the strip at one end, as in Step 1 of basic rotary cutting (see page 37). Turn it, cover the "good" fabric with the ruler, and cut pieced strips of the desired size.

CUTTING PIECED STRIPS ON THE BIAS

Trim one end of the pieced strip at a 45-degree angle, using the line marked on the ruler. Cut strips of the desired width at the same angle by measuring along the straight edge of the ruler.

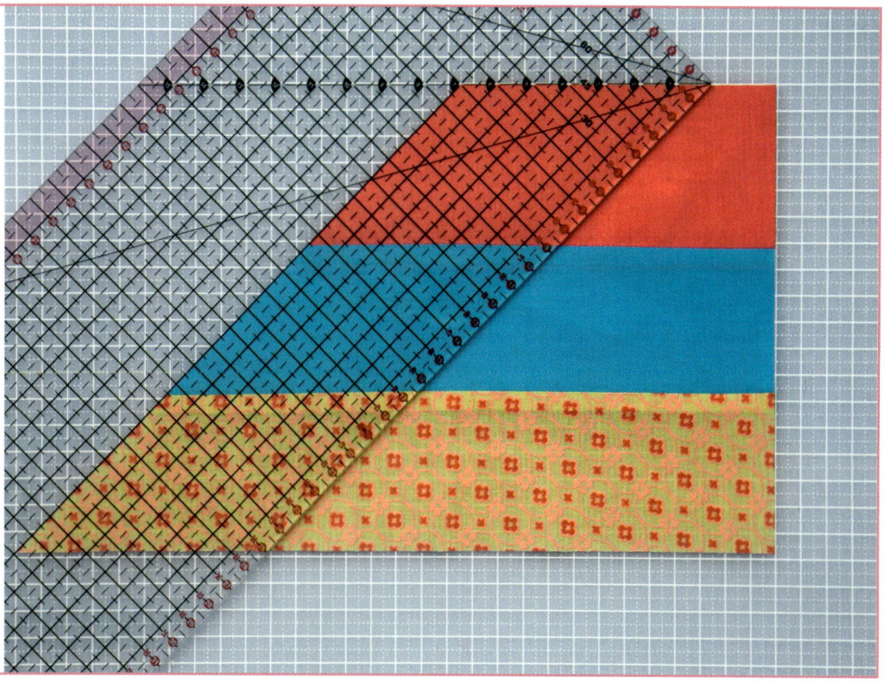

CUTTING TRUE BIAS STRIPS

1 Level the straight grain as in Step 1 of basic rotary cutting (see page 37). Measure a 45-degree angle at the top levelled corner, and cut a short bias edge as a guideline.

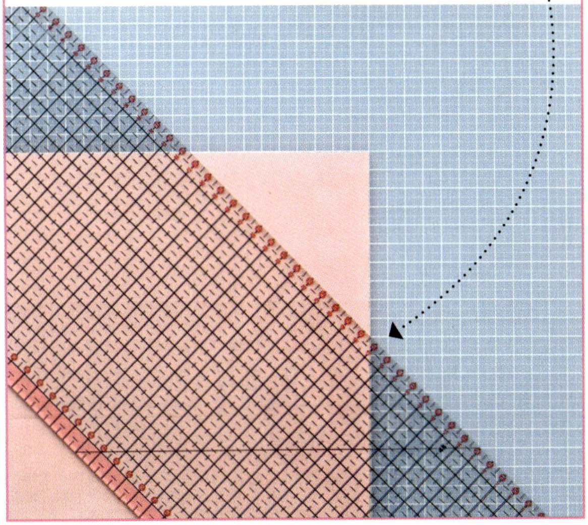

2 Cut strips, as in Step 2 of basic rotary cutting (see page 37).

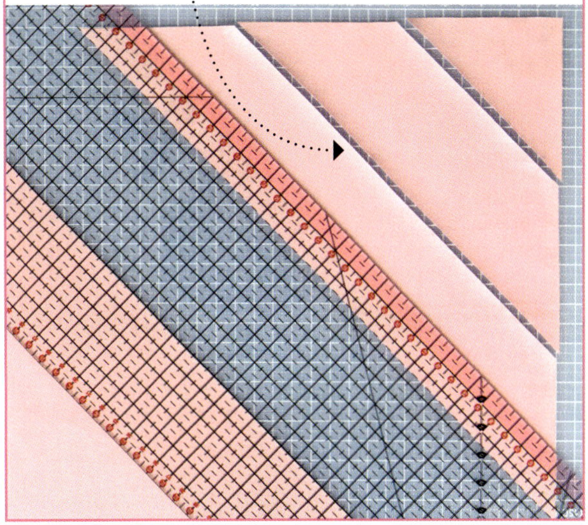

CUTTING HALF-SQUARE TRIANGLES

Cut half-square triangles across the diagonal of a square, taking particular care when cutting the sides that are not on the straight of grain.

CUTTING QUARTER-SQUARE TRIANGLES

Cut diagonally from each corner to create four quarter-square triangles.

CUTTING IRREGULAR TRIANGLES

Cut a rectangle across the diagonal to create two irregular long triangles. For a matching pair, cut another rectangle starting at the opposite corner. Triangular rotary rulers are also available.

CUTTING 45-DEGREE DIAMONDS

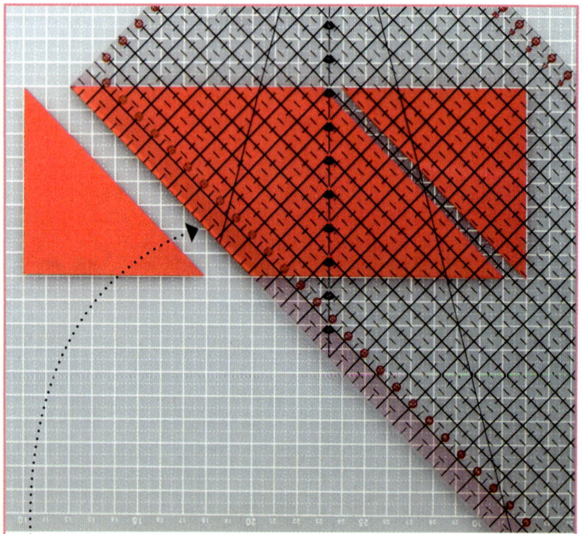

Cut a strip the desired width of the diamond. Cut a 45-degree angle at one end of the strip and use the same measurement to cut the diamond shape.

CUTTING CURVES

Gentle curves can also be rotary cut, but it is advisable to use a small blade.

Cutting by hand

Quiltmakers generally cut with scissors if the pieces are small, or intricate, or have unusual angles or shapes. Appliqué motifs are almost always best cut by hand. You should keep at least one pair of good-quality sharp dressmaker's scissors dedicated to cutting only cloth. Paper, template plastic, wadding, and the like should not be cut with the same pair. Most quiltmakers have several pairs of scissors in different sizes.

CUTTING WITHOUT A PATTERN

1 Mark the outline of the shape to be cut on the wrong side of the fabric and add a seam.

2 Using fabric scissors, cut out the shape along the marked cutting line – or cut a short distance away if only the stitching line is marked.

CUTTING WITH A PATTERN

Patterns made from paper are familiar to dressmakers, and sometimes they provide an easy way for quiltmakers to cut a few similar shapes. Pin the pattern to the fabric and cut around it, adding the seam allowance if necessary.

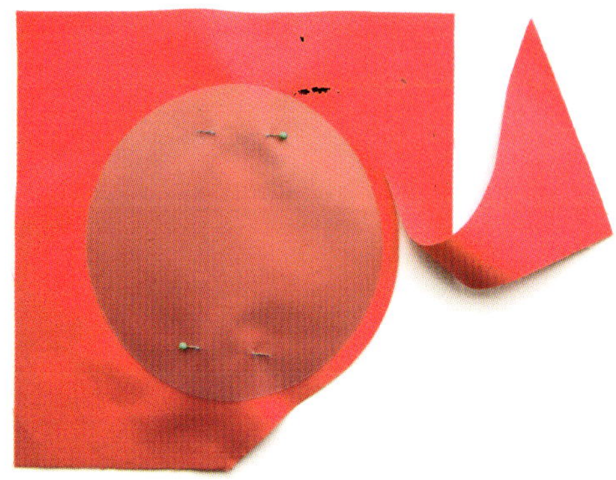

FUSSY CUTTING

This is a method of isolating particular motifs in printed fabric and cutting them to show as a feature in a block of patchwork or appliqué. It can seem wasteful of fabric, but the results are usually worth it. It is easier to delineate the desired area if you cut a window template to the finished size and shape.

Unpicking seams

Everyone makes mistakes and sometimes seams must be removed; moreover, some patterns depend on taking out seams during construction. It is vital that the ripping-out process does not stretch the fabric edges. Unpicking works best on seams that haven't been pressed. Never use scissors to unpick a seam.

METHOD 1

1 Hold the seam open and insert the point of the unpicker between the layers to break the thread.

2 Pull the seam apart gently as you work to the end of the seam.

METHOD 2

1 Hold the seam taut and insert the point of the unpicker into every third or fourth stitch, breaking the thread as you work your way along the seam.

2 Hold the bottom strip flat and pull gently on the top strip to separate the layers. Do not use this method on bias seams.

Starting and finishing

Securing the thread at the beginning and end of any stitching is, of course, essential. Traditional hand sewing begins and ends with a knot at the end of the thread, but knots can interfere with quilting and sometimes show on the quilt top. There are several knots that are useful for quiltmaking, including quilters' knots (see page 170). Backstitched loops have almost no depth to them and are a secure way of tying off.

THREADING A NEEDLE

1 Thread the end of the thread that comes off the reel through the eye of the needle, then cut the desired length. Working in the same direction as the spinning process that wraps the thread around the reel means that it is less likely to knot and tangle as you work.

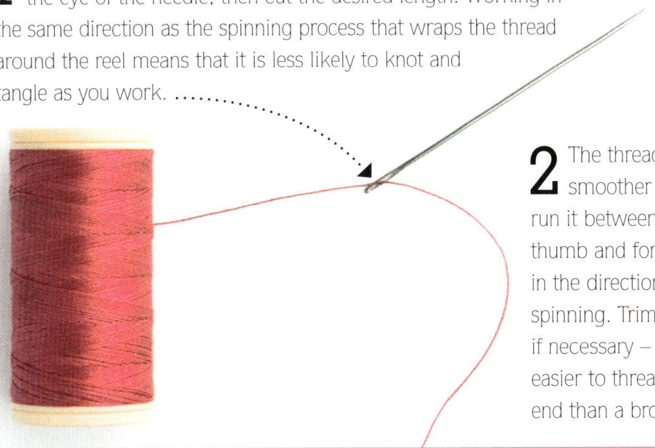

2 The thread will feel smoother if you run it between your thumb and forefinger in the direction of spinning. Trim the end if necessary – it is easier to thread a cut end than a broken one.

TIPS

- **Thread weight:** Use a thread weight appropriate to the needle size and a needle size appropriate to the weight of the fabric.
- **Thread length:** Keep the thread length to no more than 50cm (20in) long, as it is less likely to kink and fray.
- **Needle threader:** Use a needle threader if you have difficulty getting the thread through the eye.
- **Cutting direction:** Cut away from your body whenever possible.
- **Knot size:** Knots make a lump wherever they occur, so make sure that they are small so that they can be hidden easily.

WRAPPED KNOT

1 For a knot that is suitable in quiltmaking, wrap the end of the thread around the shaft of the needle three times, leaving a 10mm (½in) tail. (For a bigger knot, use more wraps.)

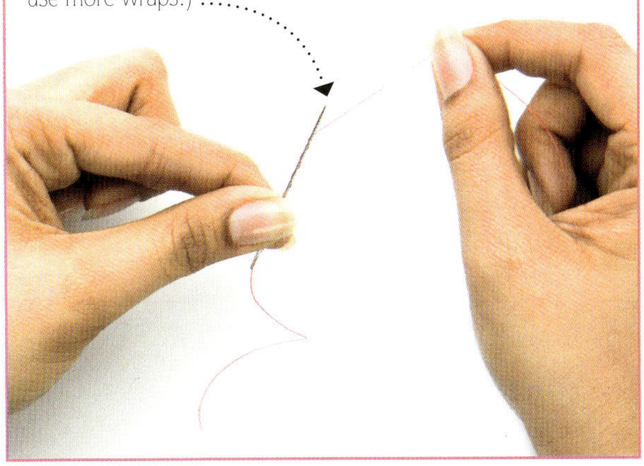

2 Anchor the wraps with your thumb and forefinger, and pull the needle through gently with your other hand. Hold the wraps until the knot is tight at the end of the thread.

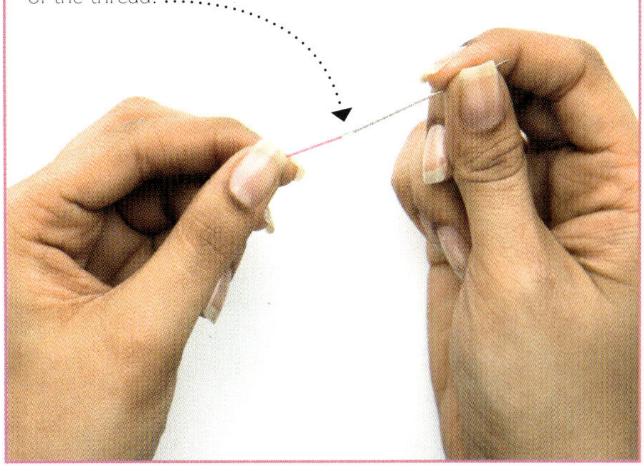

BACK-STITCHED LOOP

1 This method doesn't have the bulk of a knot but is secure. Back stitch once at the end of a line of stitching, and pull the needle through; do not pull the thread taut, but leave a small loop of thread.

2 Take the needle through the loop and pull the thread tight.

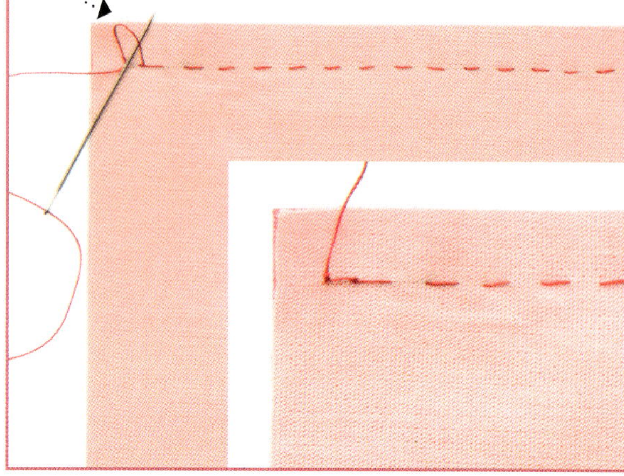

DOUBLE BACK-STITCHED LOOP

1 This method is even more secure. Back stitch once at the end of a line of stitching, leaving a small loop of thread as in Step 1 of the back-stitched loop (above). Insert the tip of the needle through the loop and pull it through to form a second loop, creating a figure of eight.

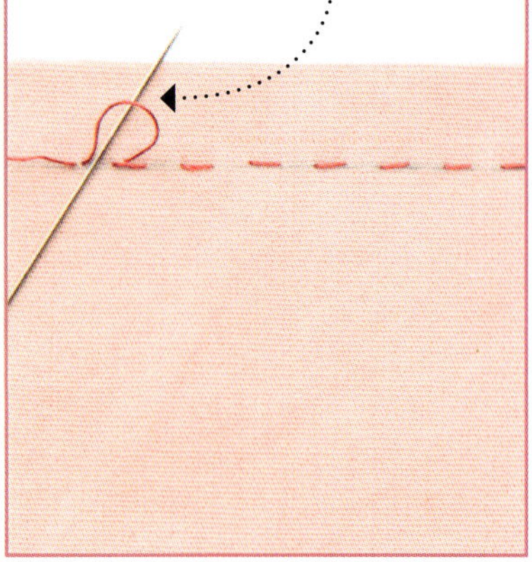

2 Insert the tip of the needle through the second loop.

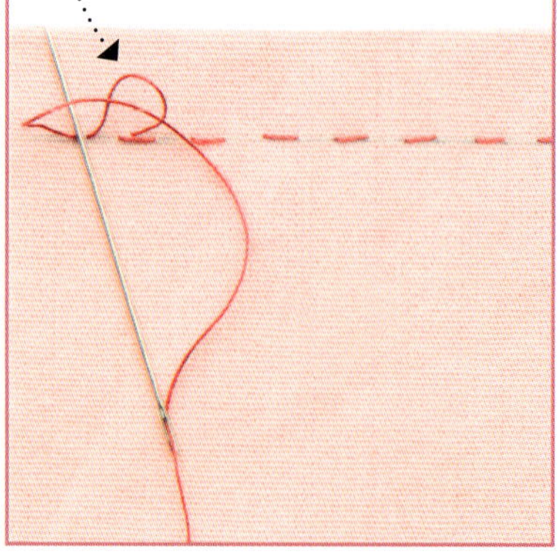

3 Pull the thread taut to form a knot.

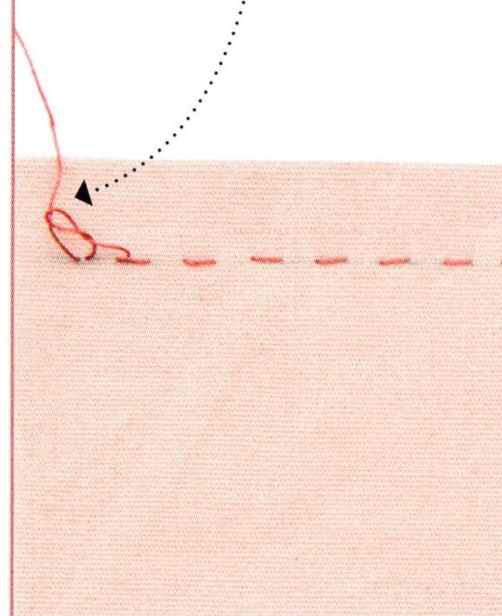

Tacking stitches

Each of the many types of tacking stitches has its own individual use. Basic tacks hold two or more pieces of fabric together. Long and short tacks are an alternative version of the basic tacking stitch, often used when the tacking will stay in the work for some time. Diagonal tacks hold folds or overlaid fabrics together, while slip tacks are used to hold a fold in fabric to another piece of fabric.

BASIC TACKS

Start with a knot and, using single thread, make straight stitches that are evenly spaced.

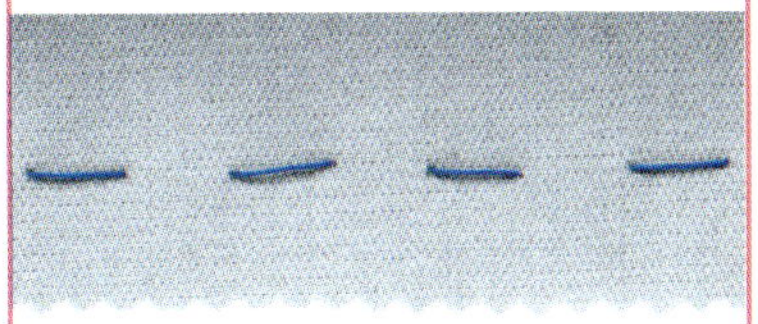

LONG AND SHORT TACKS

Make long stitches with a short space between each one.

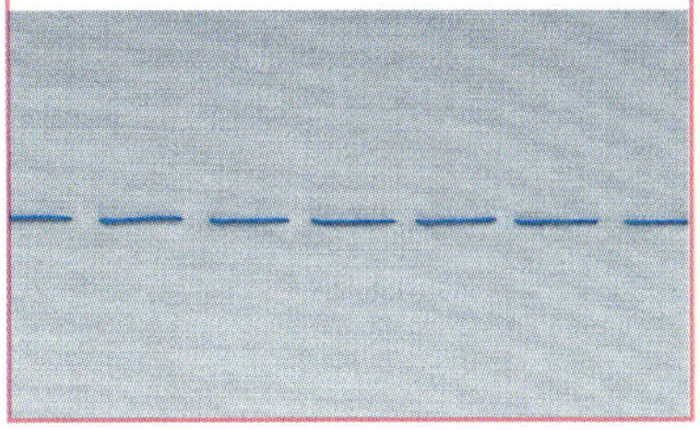

DIAGONAL TACKS

Work vertically, taking horizontal stitches.

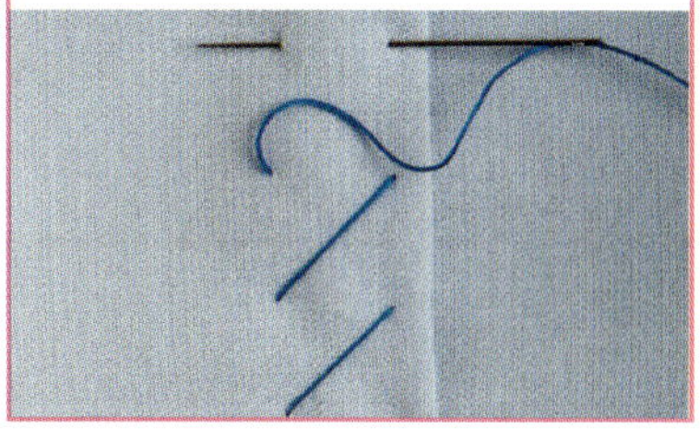

Securing the thread

The ends of the thread must be secured firmly, especially if the hand stitching is to be permanent. A knot is frequently used and is the preferred choice for temporary stitches. For permanent stitching a double stitch is a better option.

DOUBLE STITCH

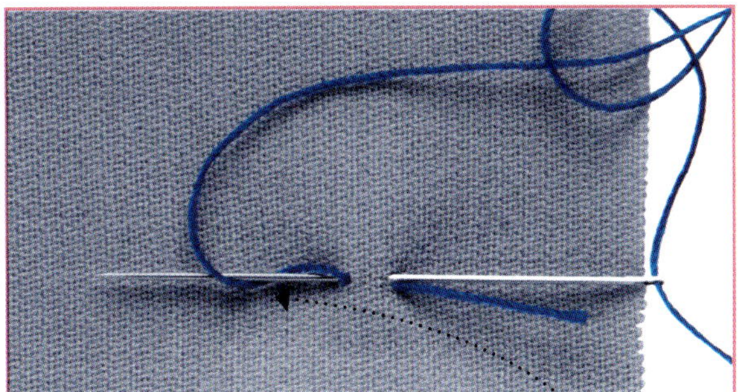

1 Take a stitch.

2 Go back through the stitch with the thread wrapped under the needle.

3 Pull through to make a knot.

BACK STITCH

Make two small stitches in the same place.

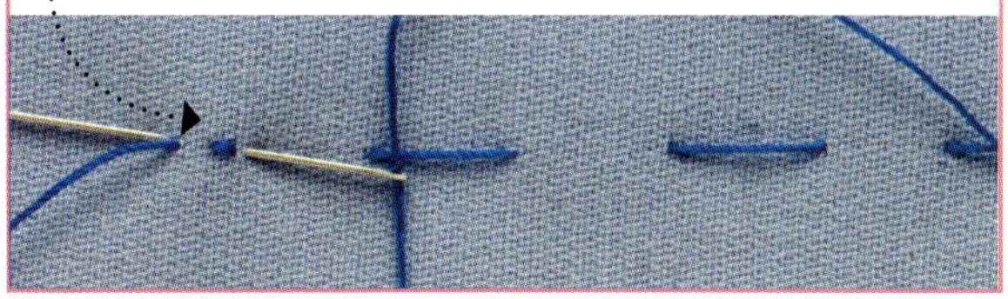

LOCKING STITCH

Start the stitching with a knot and finish by working a knot at the end.

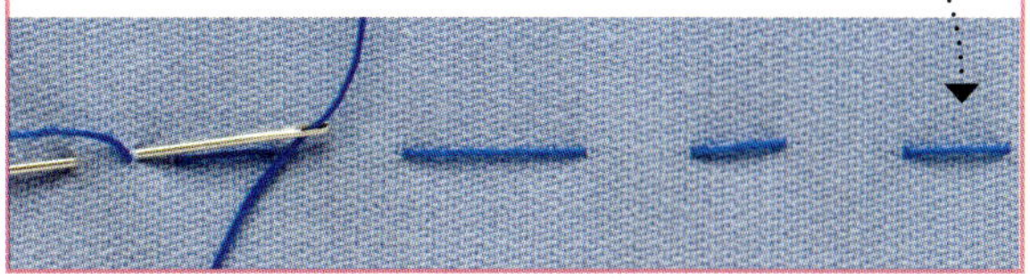

Hand stitches for quiltmaking

Although most quilts today are made on a machine, there are a number of techniques that are hand sewn and it is important to choose the correct stitch for the best result.

RUNNING STITCH

This is the most common stitch for hand piecing. Take the needle in and out of the fabric several times, taking small, evenly spaced stitches. Pull the needle through gently until the thread is taut, but not tense. Repeat to the end of the seam.

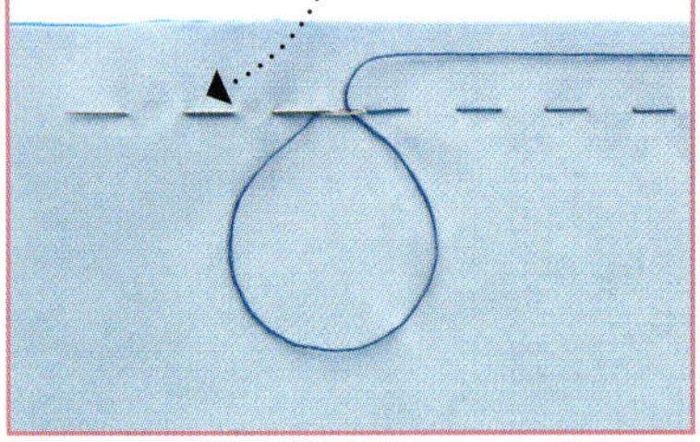

STAB STITCH

This stitch is useful for sewing several layers or thick fabrics and is popular for quilting.

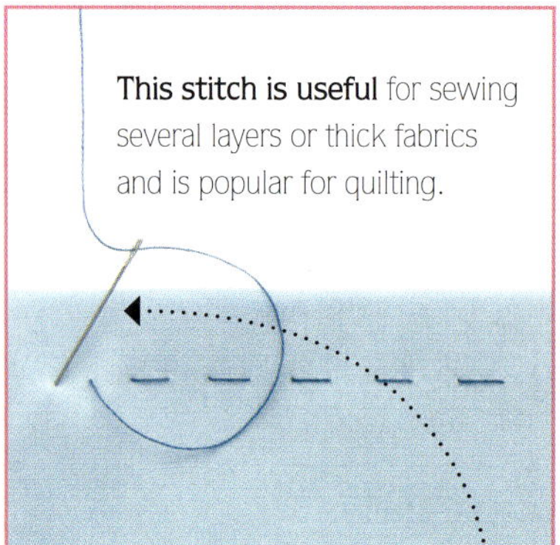

1 Take the needle vertically through the fabric layers from the top and pull until the thread is taut but not tense.

2 Reverse the next stitch, coming up vertically from the bottom. Continue sewing to the end of the seam.

BACK STITCH

Back stitch can be used instead of running stitch to join units; it is also recommended as single stitches to make seams more secure. Bring the needle through all the layers to the right side, then insert it a short distance behind the entry point. Bring it up to the right side of the fabric again, the same distance in front of the point from which it first emerged. Repeat to the end of the seam.

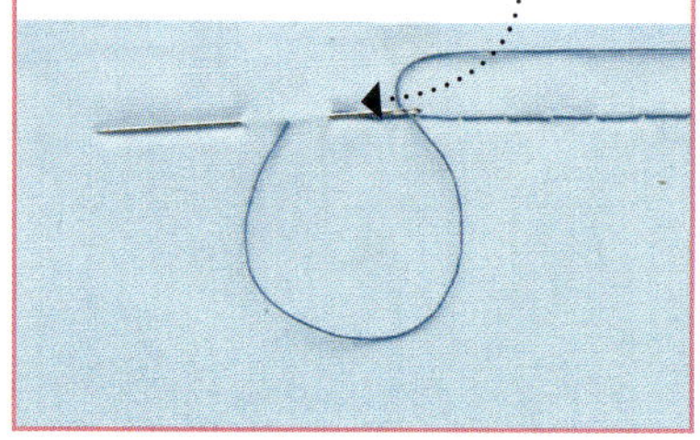

OVERSEWING

Also known as whipstitch and overcasting, oversewing is used to join two edges with an almost invisible seam. Bring the needle through the back edge to the front, picking up a few threads from each side. Pull gently and repeat.

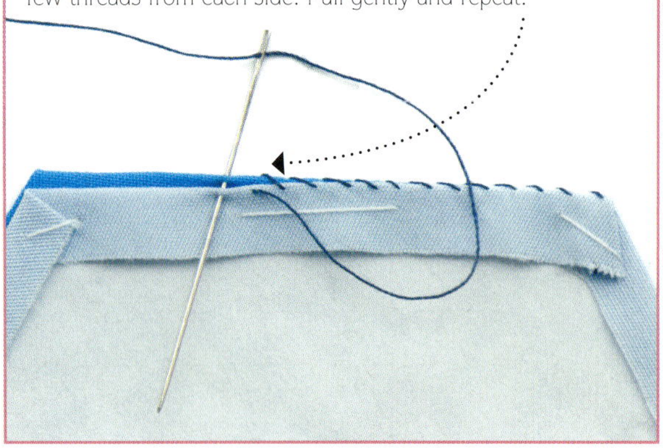

SLIP STITCH

Used mainly in appliqué, slip stitch makes an invisible line of stitching. Knot the thread and hide the knot in the folded edge of the top piece. Pull the needle through and pick up a thread or two on the back piece. Take the needle through the top piece next to this stitch and slide it along the fold in the fabric a short distance. Repeat, catching a few threads on each piece with each stitch.

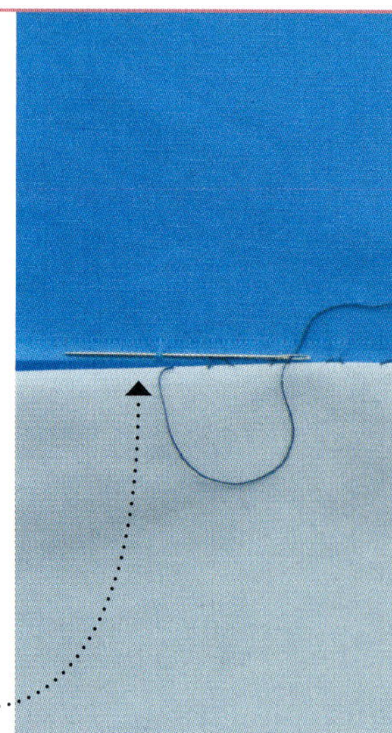

Securing the thread on a machine

Machine stitches need to be secured at the end of a seam to prevent them from coming undone. This can be done by hand, tying the ends of the thread, or using the machine with a reverse stitch or a locking stitch, which stitches three or four stitches in the same place.

TIE THE ENDS

1 On the back side of the work, pull gently on the bobbin thread. This will pull up a loop, which is the top thread.

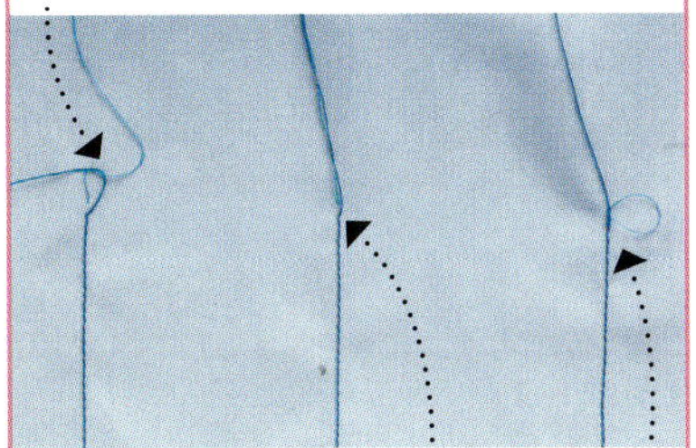

2 Pull the loop through.

3 Tie the two threads together to secure them tight against the stitching line.

REVERSE STITCH

1 When starting, stitch a couple of stitches forward, then hold in the reverse button and reverse over them. Continue forward again.

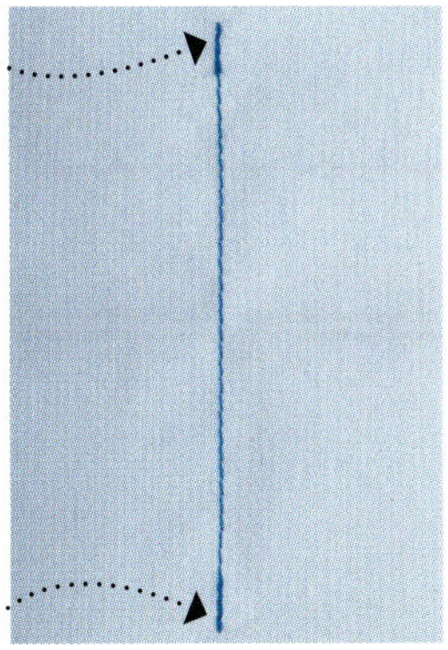

2 At the end of the seam, reverse again to secure the stitches.

LOCKING STITCH

1 Set the stitch length to "0" and take several stitches in place, then adjust the length and stitch normally.

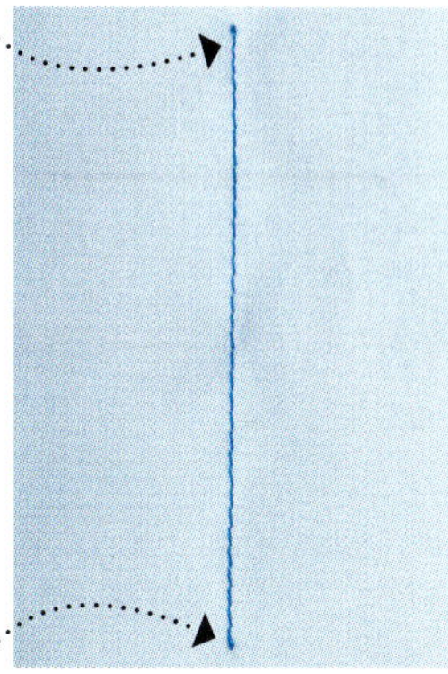

2 At the end, set the length to "0" again and stitch in place.

Stitches made with a machine

Unless you are embroidering or embellishing with decorative stitches, the machine stitches you will need in quiltmaking are straight stitch and occasionally zigzag.

STRAIGHT STITCH

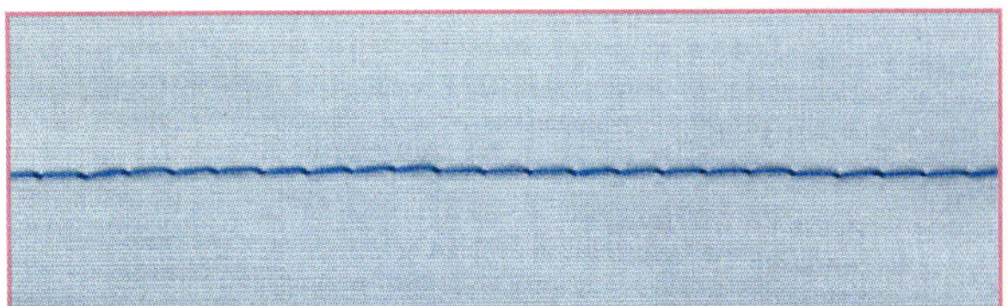

Used for most applications, the length of the stitch can be altered from 0.5 to 5.0 on most sewing machines.

ZIGZAG STITCH

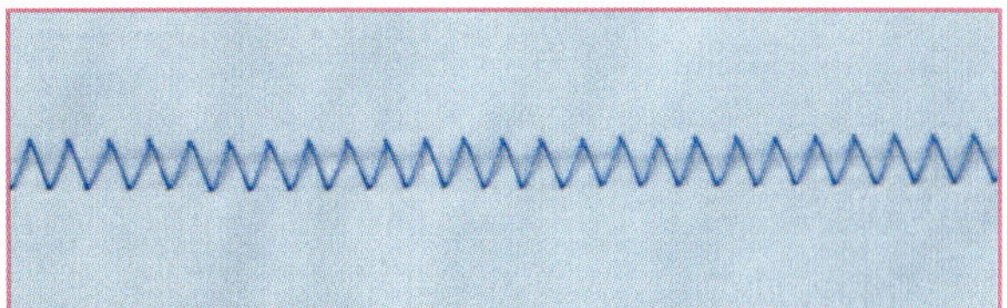

To neaten seam edges and for securing and decorative purposes. Both the width and the length of this stitch can be altered.

Sewing machines are capable of producing decorative linear stitches that can be used to embellish quilt tops.

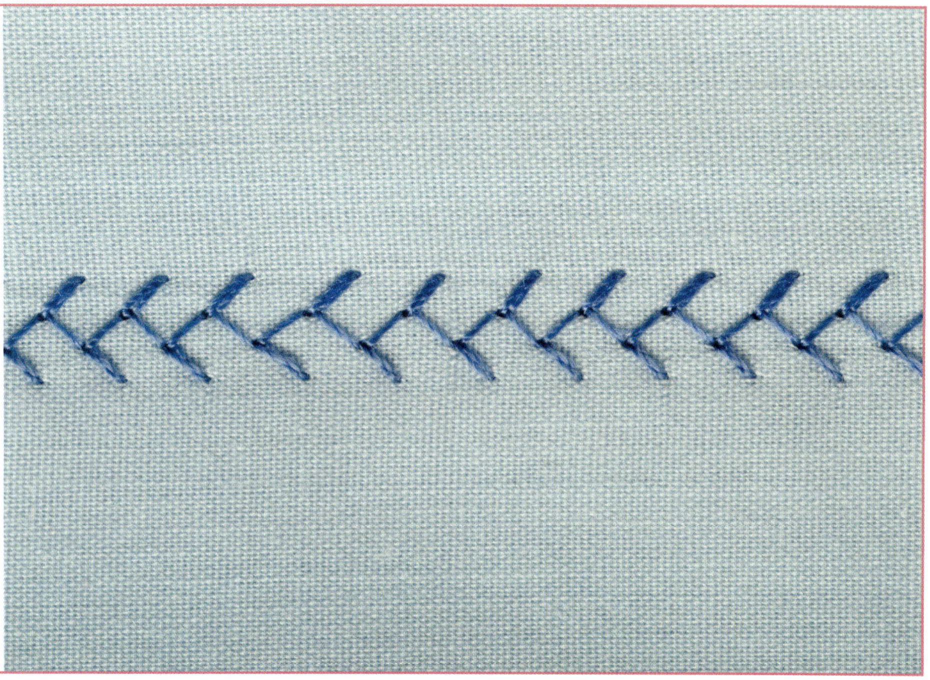

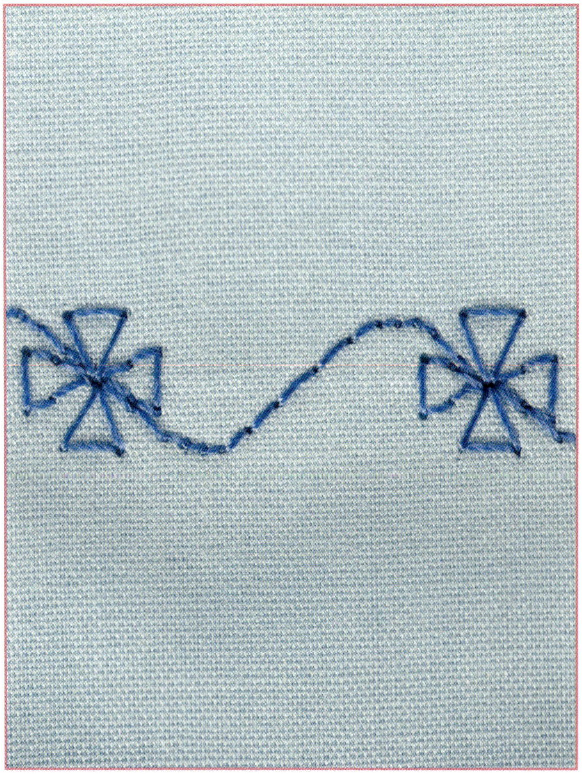

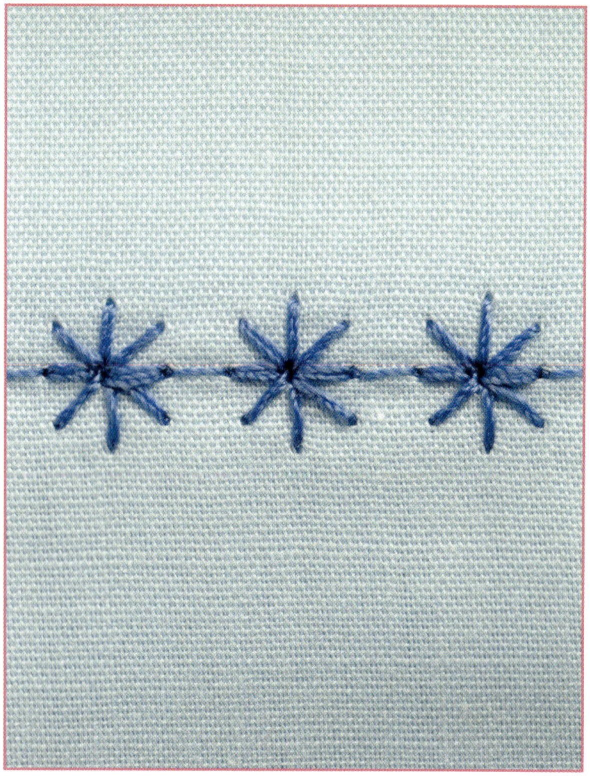

Stitching corners and curves

Not all sewing consists of straight lines. The work will have curves and corners that require manipulation, to produce sharp clean angles and curves on the right side. The technique for stitching a corner shown below applies to corners of all angles. On a thick fabric, the technique is slightly different, with a stitch taken across the corner, and on a fabric that frays badly the corner is reinforced with a second row of stitches.

STITCHING A CORNER

1 Pin the fabric together, right side to right side.

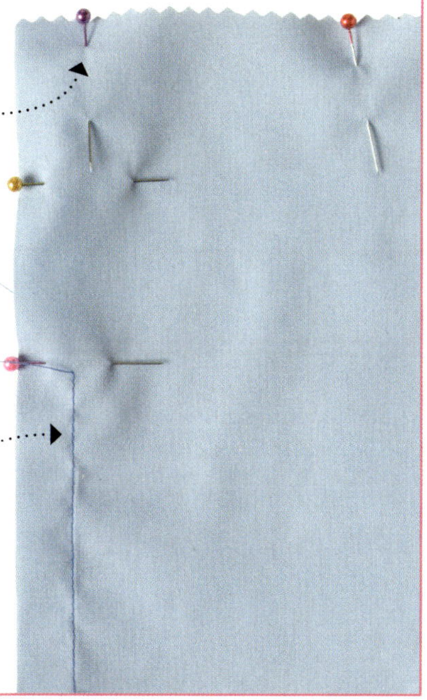

2 Stitch a seam at 1cm (¼in).

3 On reaching the corner, insert the machine needle into the fabric.

4 Raise the presser foot and turn the fabric through 90 degrees (this is pivoting at the corner).

5 Lower the presser foot and continue stitching in the new direction.

6 The stitching lines are at right angles to each other, which means the finished corner will have a sharp point when turned through to the right side.

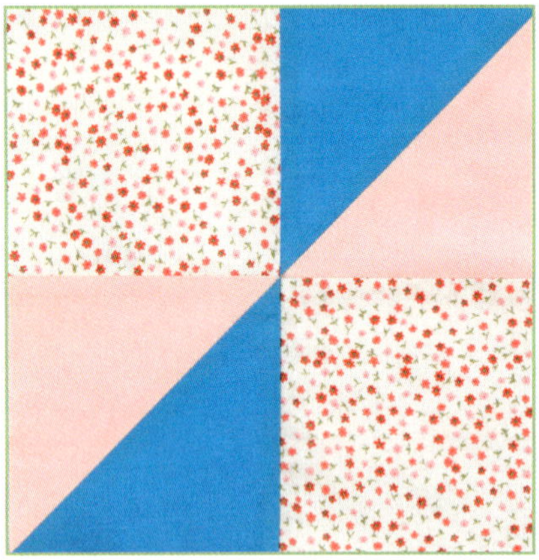

PATCHWORK

STARS AND STRIPES

Ohio star blocks (page 87) have been bordered with small Friendship stars (page 86) and strips of the central star fabric to create a patchwork table mat.

Patchwork

The majority of quilt tops, traditional and contemporary, are patchwork. While many of the basic techniques are the same or overlap, each method has its own issues and solutions. While making a patchwork quilt by machine is quicker, sewing by hand offers a satisfying pastime for many quiltmakers.

Hand piecing

Mark all seamlines on the wrong side of the fabric as guides to accuracy. Take care when sewing seams on bias-cut edges (on diamond, triangle, or hexagon shapes) or around curves, as the raw edge is prone to stretching. Secure the seam with a small backstitch each time you bring the needle through and use a double backstitched loop (see page 44) at the end of a bias seam; do not sew into the seam allowance.

SEWING STRAIGHT SEAMS

1 Place the two units to be joined right sides together. Mark the start and end points with pins, inserting the pins on the marked seamline. Add pins along the seamline, making sure that the line aligns on both sides.

2 At one end, remove the pin and take the needle through the matching points on both pieces of fabric. Secure the thread with a knot or take a couple of tiny back stitches into the seam allowance.

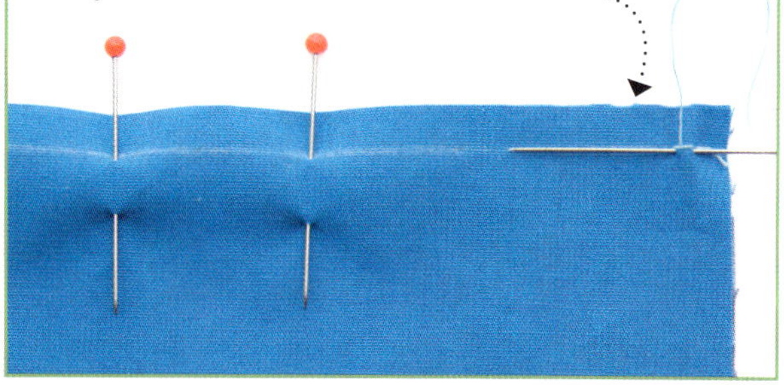

3 Take several short running stitches along the seamline, then pull the needle through. Repeat along the length of the seam, removing pins as you work.

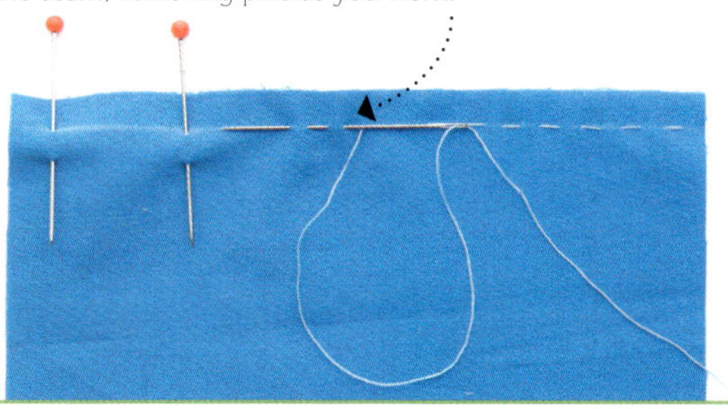

4 Check the back of the fabric to make sure that your stitching is on the line on both sides. Stop at the end matching point. Do not sew into the seam allowance except to take a couple of backstitches to secure the thread.

SEWING CURVED SEAMS

1 Mark the seamlines and any registration marks, especially the centre point, on the wrong side of each piece. If the centre isn't marked on the pattern, fold each piece in half, fingerpress it at the centre seamline, and use the crease as the centre mark.

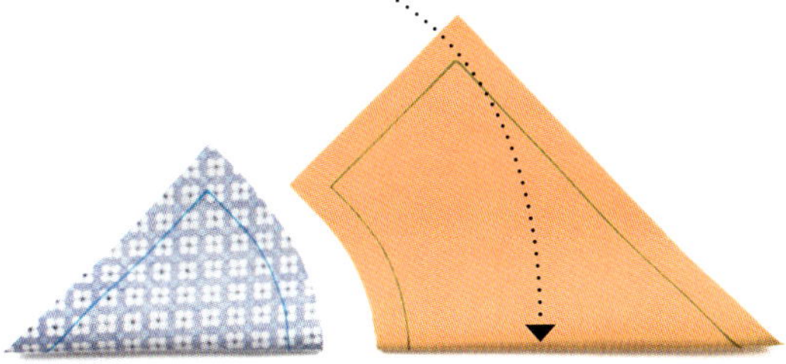

2 Place the smaller convex piece right sides together on the concave one, aligning the centre points. Pin the centre point through both pieces.

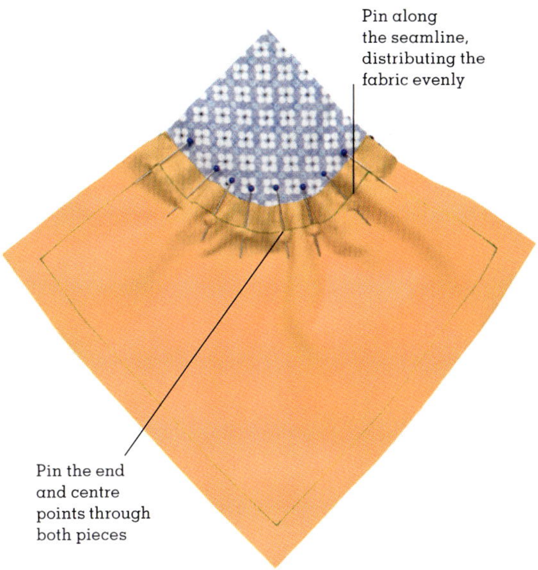

3 Pin the end points of the marked seamline. Then pin along the seamline every 8mm ($\frac{3}{8}$in) or so, manipulating the fabric to eliminate creases.

4 Take out the pin at one end and take the needle through the matching points. If you don't wish to use a knot, use a double backstitched loop in the seamline to secure the thread. (Do not sew into the seam allowance as you would for machine-piecing curved seams.)

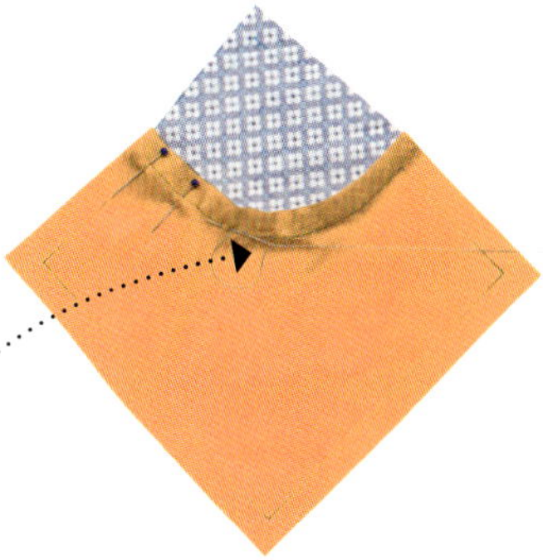

5 Take several short running stitches along the seamline, then pull the needle through. Repeat along the length of the seam, removing pins as you work. The seam will be more secure if you take a small backstitch each time you bring the needle through.

6 Check the back to make sure your stitching is on the line on both sides and stop at the matching point at the end. Do not sew into the seam allowance, but use a double backstitched loop to secure the thread. Do not clip the seam allowance.

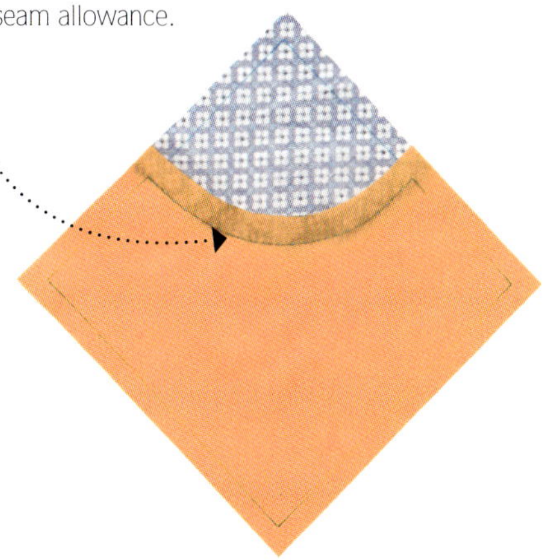

7 Press the seam towards the convex piece. If your stitching is accurate, the piece will lie flat.

SETTING-IN BY HAND

1 Diamonds and triangles sometimes meet at oblique angles. To set a piece into the resulting space needs careful pinning and sewing. Here, a square is to be set in the space between two diamond shapes. Cut the square to size and mark the seamlines. Match one corner of the square to the inner point on the first diamond and pin, right sides together. Then match the outer point and pin. Pin the edges together along the marked seamline.

2 Sew along the marked seamline from the outer point to the inner, removing pins as you work. Take a few small backstitches into the seam at the inner corner, avoiding the seam allowance. Do not cut the thread.

3 Match the adjacent side of the square to the corresponding side of the diamond. Pin. Sew as in Step 2.

4 Press the seam allowances on the square towards the diamonds.

JOINING ROWS BY HAND

Because hand-pieced seams stop at the seam allowance, you need to match corners in a different way from machine piecing when joining rows.

1 Match the seamlines of the rows to be joined right sides together. Pin through both layers at the matching point at every corner of the row. Align the seamlines and pin at various points to make sure the seams are accurate on both sides.

2 Start sewing at one end of the row, working as for straight seams (see page 54), until you reach the first join.

3 Sew through the matching points on both layers, avoiding all the seam allowances.

4 Take a stitch in the second pair of units, then back stitch next to the seam allowance.

5 Continue in this way to the end of the row and tie off with a back-stitched loop.

6 Press the seams on each row to opposite sides and press the just-completed seam to the other side.

7 Finished piece, right side

Machine piecing

Stitching patchwork pieces by machine is a quick way of assembling a piece. As for hand piecing, always ensure that your fabrics are aligned with right sides facing and with raw edges matching. Take a 5mm (¼in) seam allowance and use a standard straight stitch.

PIECED STRIPS

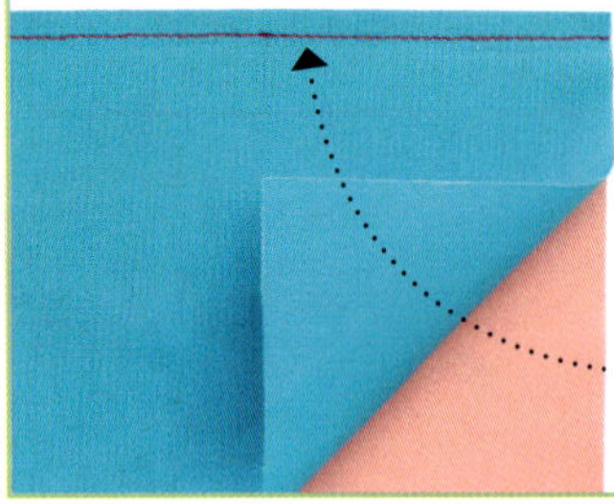

1 Place two contrasting strips of fabric right sides together, raw edges aligned. Sew a straight 5mm (¼in) seam along the strip.

2 Press the seam towards the darker fabric.

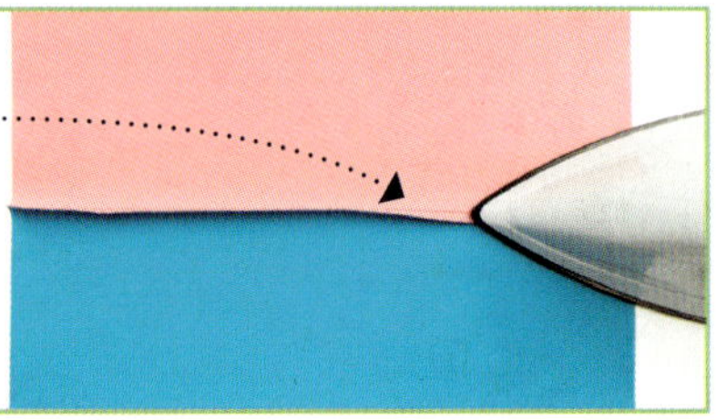

3 When piecing several strips together, reverse the direction each time you add a strip; this helps to eliminate bowing and keeps the strips straight. The seams should all be pressed in the same direction. Then the strip can be cut into pieced units and combined into new patterns.

CHAIN PIECING

1 Feed the units through the machine in sequence without lifting the presser foot or breaking the thread, so that they form a chain, leaving a short length of thread between each.

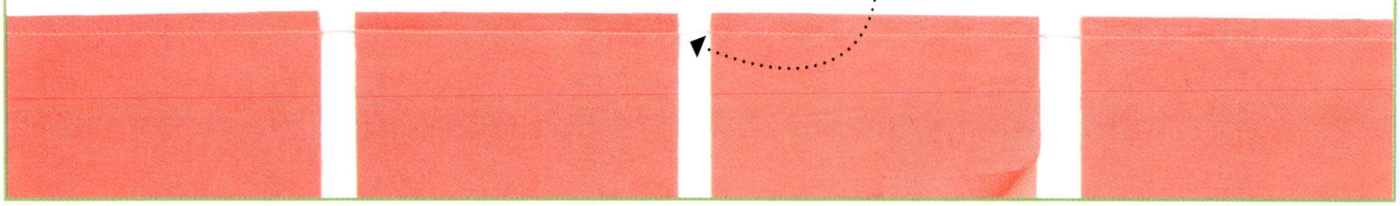

2 Cut the units in the chain apart, using a small, sharp pair of scissors.

TRIANGLE SQUARES

1 To make a unit made of two right-angle triangles, cut two squares of contrasting fabric and place them right sides together, with the lighter colour on top.

2 Using a pencil, mark a diagonal line in one direction across the wrong side of the lighter-coloured square.

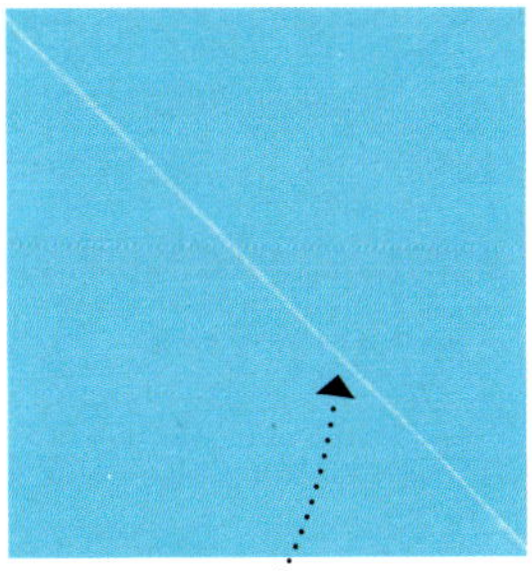

3 Machines stitch on each side of the marked line, stitching 5mm (¼in) from the line. Pivot without breaking the thread.

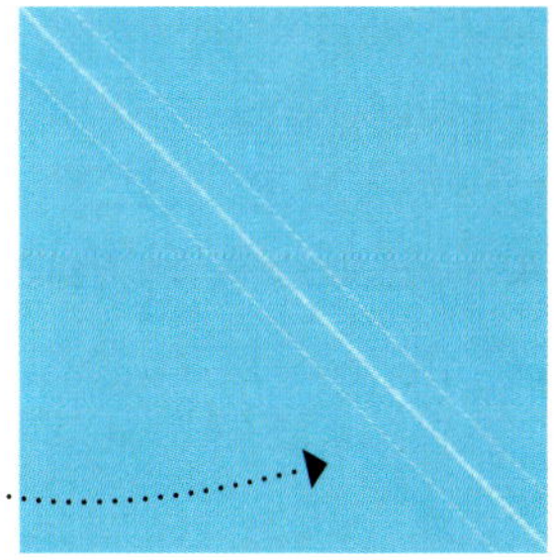

4 Using a rotary cutter or scissors, cut along the central pencil line. Open out the pieces of fabric and press the seams towards the darker fabric to make two identical triangle squares.

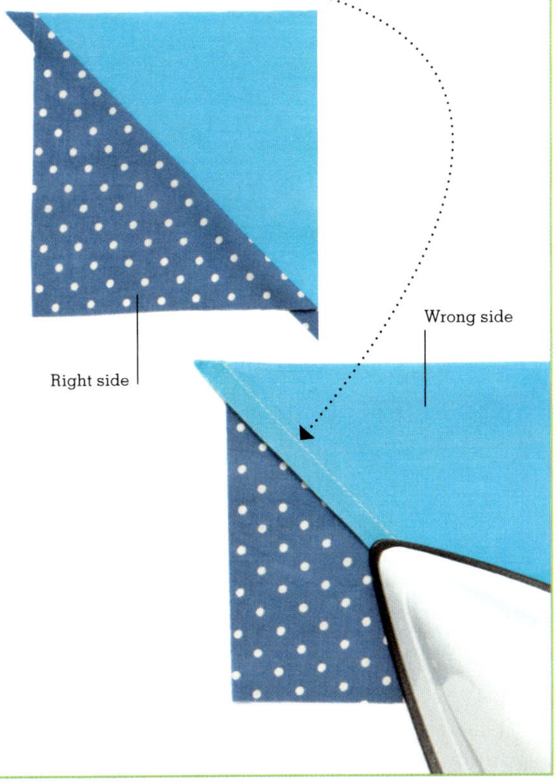

5 Trim the "dog-ear" points at each end of the seam.

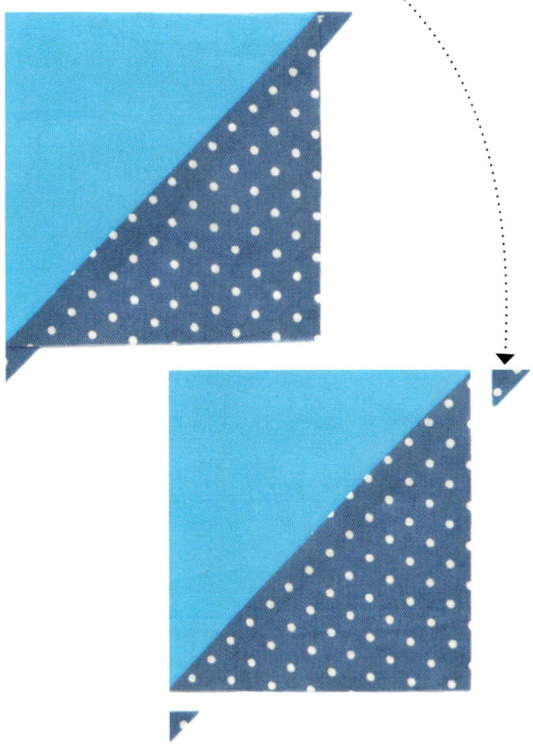

MULTIPLE TRIANGLE STRIPS

1 Multiple units of triangle squares can be made by cutting strips that are the width you want the finished squares to be plus 15mm (7/8in). Place them right sides together and mark squares on the wrong side of the lighter-coloured strip.

2 Draw a diagonal line across each square, alternating the direction of the line.

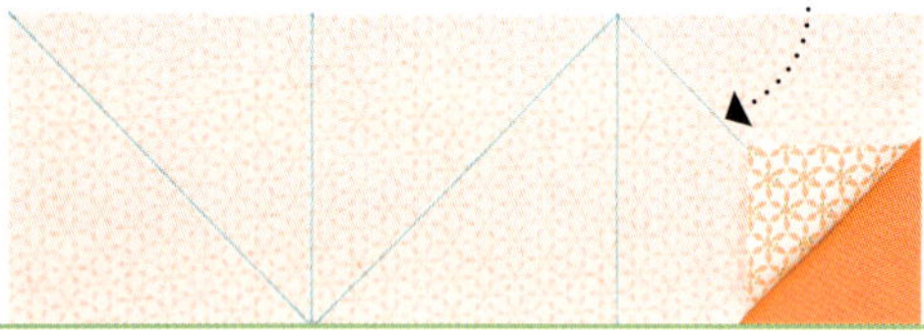

3 Place the strips right sides together with the lighter-coloured strip on top. Sew a 5mm (1/4in) seam on each side of the marked diagonal lines, as described above.

4 Cut along the marked lines to separate triangles and press, as above.

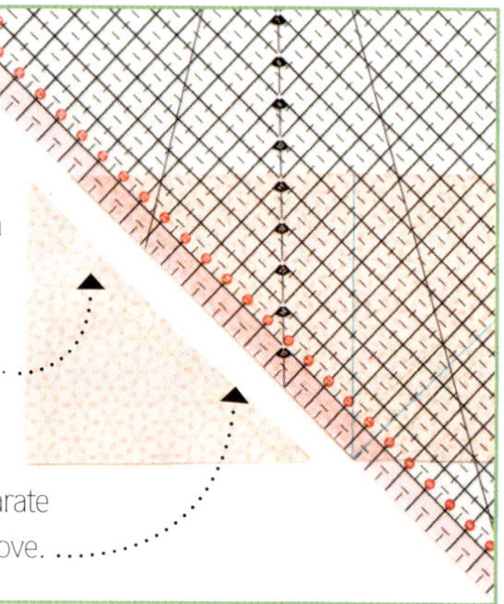

IDENTICAL MULTIPLE STRIPS

1 You can also make identical multiple triangle units by placing two large pieces of fabric together and marking a grid.

2 Mark diagonals in one direction. Remember that each square makes two units, so you will need half as many squares as finished units.

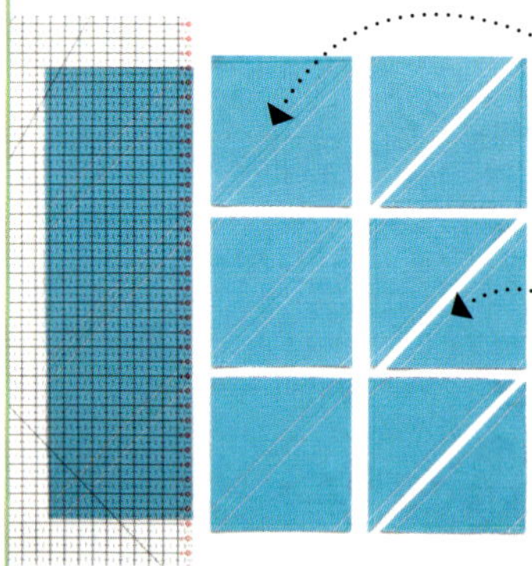

3 Machine stitch on either side of each marked diagonal line, stitching 5mm (1/4in) from the lines.

4 Using a rotary cutter, cut the fabric into squares along the marked lines and then into triangles. Press.

QUARTER-SQUARE TRIANGLES

1 Place the two triangle squares right sides together, with the seams aligned and the contrasting fabrics facing each other.

2 Using a pencil, mark a diagonal line at right angles to the seamline.

3 Sew a 5mm (1/4in) seam on each side of the marked line.

4 Cut the units apart along the marked lines and press.

Wrong side

Right side

JOINING PIECED AND PLAIN UNITS

1 Place one pieced and one plain unit right sides together and sew a 5mm (¼in) seam. The corner of the triangle square will be caught in the seam with the visible corner 5mm (¼in) from the raw edge.

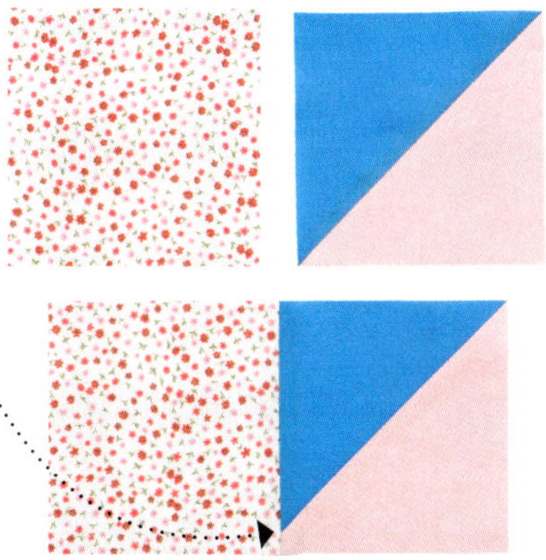

2 Combining two of these units takes up the seam allowance and means that the corners meet in the centre.

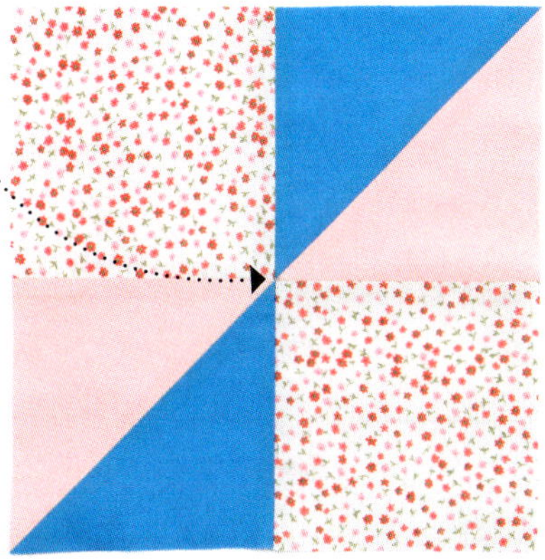

CURVED SEAMS

1 Make templates and mark the centre of the curve on each one. Cut out the fabric pieces, adding a 5mm (¼in) seam allowance.

2 Centre the templates on the wrong side of your fabric pieces, draw around them to mark the seam allowances, then mark the centre point of the curve on the fabric pieces.

3 Pin the two fabric pieces together at the centre point on the seam allowance, then pin at each end.

4 Pin along the edge to stabilize the curve.

5 Stitch along the marked curve without stretching or pulling. Remove the pins as you sew.

6 Press the seam towards the larger piece. It should lie flat without being clipped.

SET-IN SEAMS

1 Using a pencil or fabric marker, make a dot 5mm (¼in) in from each end of the two pieces that are to be joined first. This marks the point where you start and finish stitching: do not go to the very end of the seam.

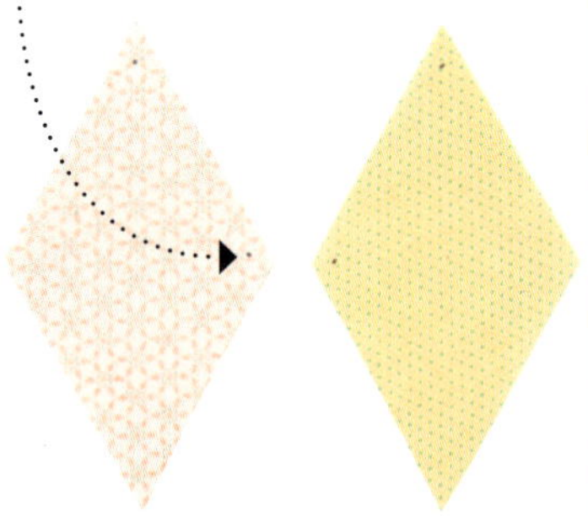

2 Place the shapes right sides together and sew from dot to dot, backstitching at each end. Do not overshoot the dots.

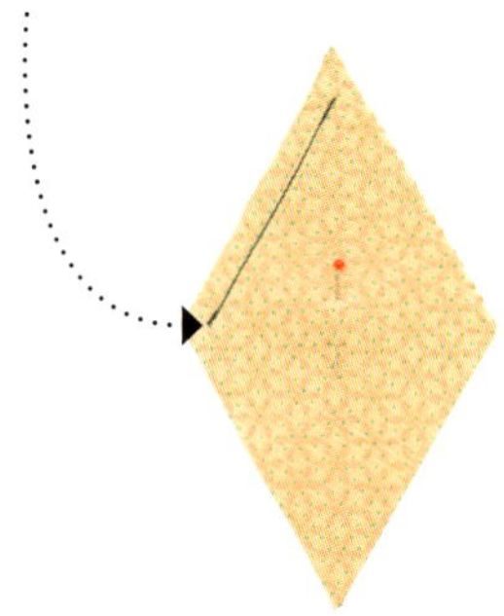

3 Press the seam towards the darker fabric.

4 On the wrong side of the piece that is to be set in, mark a dot 5mm (¼in) in at the three corners of the piece.

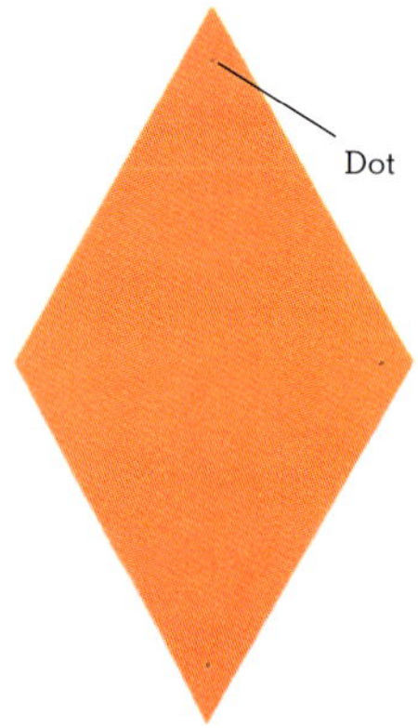

5 Match the middle marked corner of the piece that is to be set in with the corresponding dot on one of the two pieces that have already been joined. Pin the seam at each end and sew from the inside corner to the outer dot.

6 Match the outer dot on the second side of the piece that is to be set in with the outer dot on the other shape. Pin them together at the dot and sew, again stitching from the inside corner to the outer dot.

7 Press the unit flat.

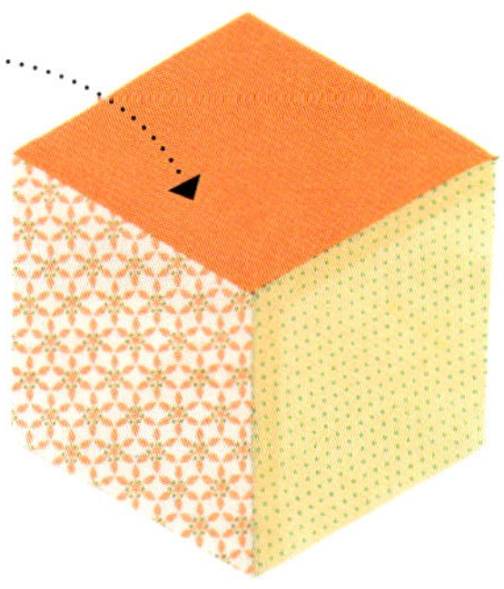

Pressing

Pressing is essential when making accurate patchwork. When pressing, press down in one place, then lift the iron and move it before pressing down on another area. Ironing causes fabric and seams to distort. Set pieces aside to cool after each pressing and always press the seam towards the darker fabric to prevent darker colours from showing through. The temperature of the iron should be appropriate to the fabric.

PRESSING STRAIGHT SEAMS

1 Place the unit or sewn strips with right sides together on the board. Press the iron along the seam. Keep the darker fabric on top and lift the iron at regular intervals. This is called setting the seam, and helps ensure accuracy by locking the threads and smoothing the fibres.

2 Open the pieces and press from one end to the other. If you keep the lighter piece nearest you and press with the tip of the iron, you can press the seam to the darker side at the same time as you open the unit.

PRESSING BIAS SEAMS

Work along the straight grain to keep from pulling the seam out of shape.

WORKING IN ROWS

Press the seams in adjoining rows in opposite directions to eliminate bulkiness at the joins.

PRESSING A PIECED BLOCK

Place the block wrong side up on the ironing board. Do not press hard, but make sure the seams lie as flat as possible.

PRESSING SEAMS OPEN

Where several seams meet, you may need to press seams open to reduce bulk. After setting the seam as in Step 1 of pressing straight seams (see page 65), open the seam and press along the length with the tip of the iron.

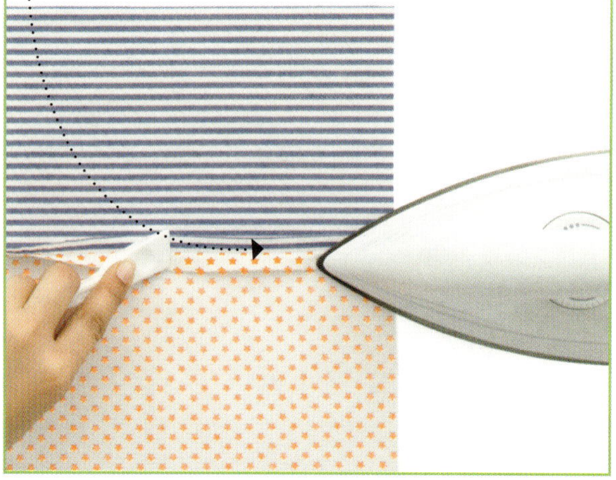

THUMBNAIL

Work on a hard surface. Open the unit out and press first on the wrong side, then on the right, running your thumbnail gently but firmly along the seamline so that the fabric is pressed towards the darker fabric.

LITTLE WOODEN IRON

Place the flat, chisel-shaped edge of the tool on the seamline and run it gently along the seam.

HERA

A hera is a plastic, blade-like device. It is used in certain embroidery techniques but is also useful for fingerpressing.

Four-patch blocks

A simple four-patch block consists of four equal square units joined two by two. It relies on a strong contrast of value to be most effective. Individual units can be pieced to provide variety and secondary patterns. A double four-patch consists of sixteen units made up of four four-patch units.

STRIP-PIECED FOUR-PATCH BLOCK

1 Using a rotary cutter, cut two contrasting strips across the width of the fabric. Here, the finished block will be 15cm (6in) square, so each unit will be 7.5cm (3in) wide, plus a 1cm (½in) seam allowance – so we cut 8.5cm (3½in) wide strips.

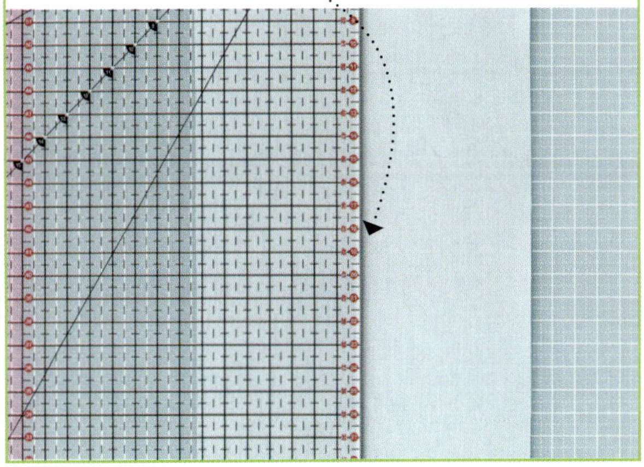

2 Taking a 5mm (¼in) seam allowance, join the strips lengthways, right sides together. Press the seam towards the darker colour.

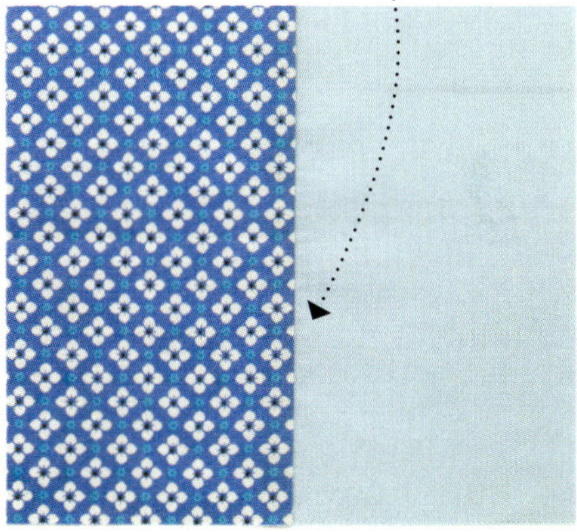

3 Cut the pieced strip across the seam into units 8.5cm (3½in) wide, the same width as the original strips.

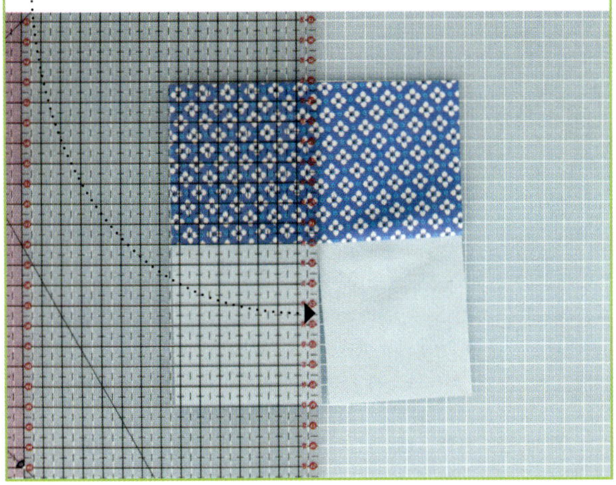

4 Join two units, matching the seams in the centre and alternating the colours. Blocks can be chain-pieced (see page 60). Press.

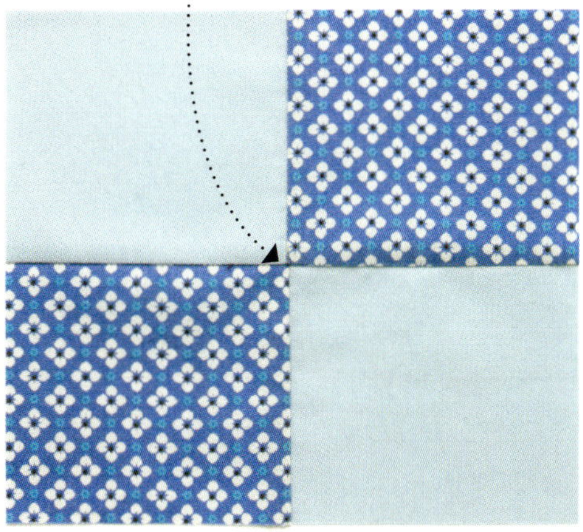

MAKING INDIVIDUAL BLOCKS

1 Cut four squares the same size, two from each fabric. Join them in pairs, taking a 5mm (¼in) seam allowance.

2 Join two pairs right sides together, matching the centre seams and alternating the colours. Press.

COMBINING PIECED AND PLAIN UNITS

1 Make two four-patch blocks. Cut two squares the same size as the pieced blocks from a third fabric.

2 Join the blocks in pairs, taking a 5mm (¼in) seam allowance, and press.

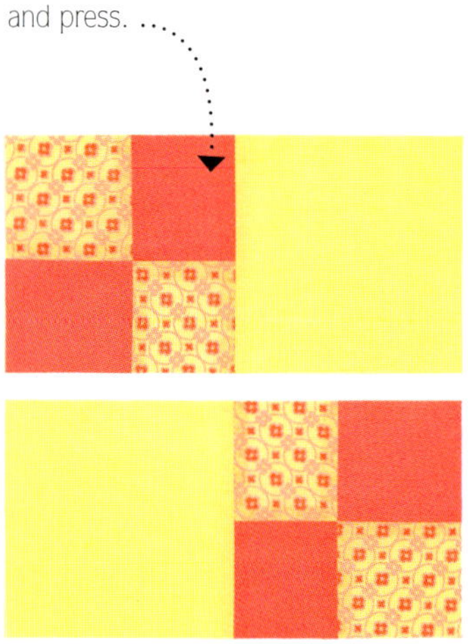

3 Join the two pairs right sides together, matching the centre seams and alternating the colours. Press.

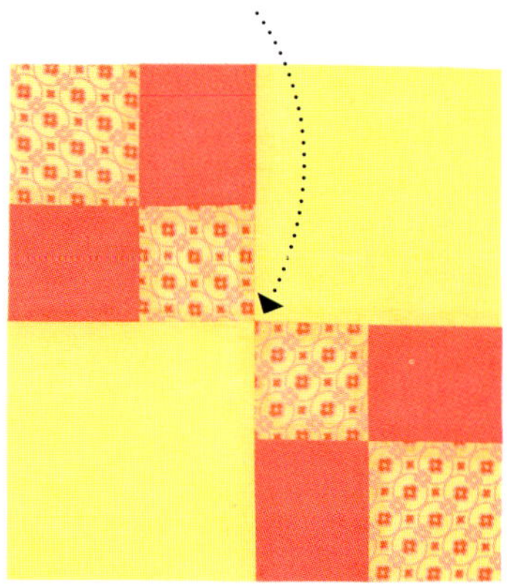

PIECED FOUR-PATCH BLOCK

1 Make four identical half-square triangle units (see page 61).

2 Join them in pairs and press.

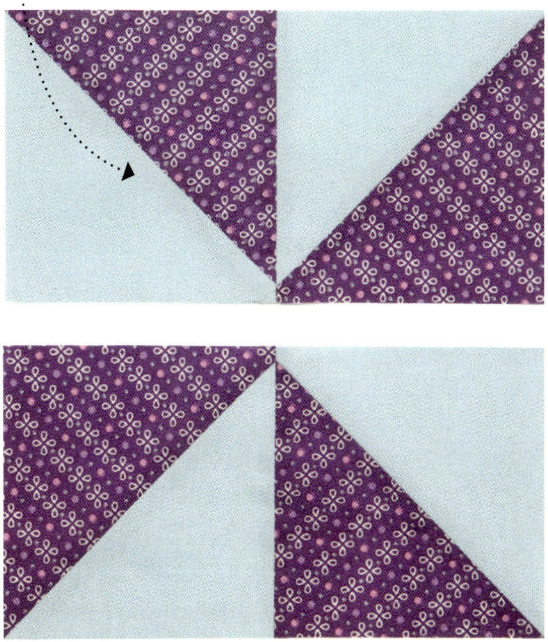

3 Join the two pairs together to complete the block. The block shown here is a traditional pattern known as Pinwheel.

Nine-patch blocks

Nine-patch blocks, based on three rows of three squares each, are among the most versatile and widely used patchwork patterns. Each unit in the grid can either be a plain colour or pieced, resulting in a huge variety of patterns. In double nine-patch, small nine-patch units are combined in a larger nine-patch grid. As with four-patch blocks, units can be subdivided to form complex patterns.

INDIVIDUAL NINE-PATCH BLOCKS

1 Cut nine squares the same size, five from fabric A and four from fabric B.

2 Arrange the squares in a grid, A–B–A, B–A–B, A–B–A. Join them in three rows of three, matching the seams and taking a 5mm (¼in) seam allowance.

3 Join the three rows to complete the block.

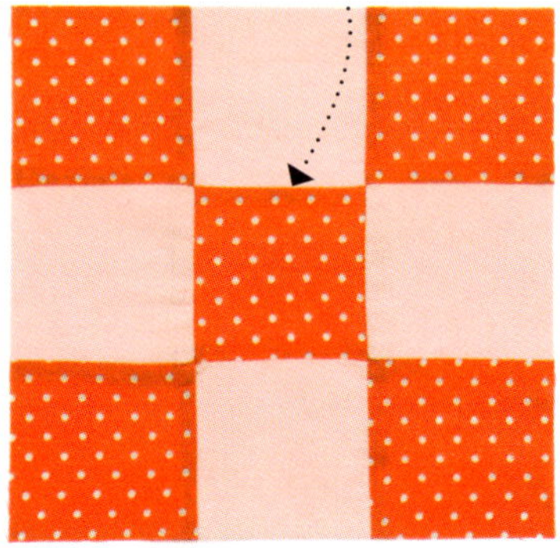

STRIP-PIECED NINE-PATCH BLOCK

1 Using a rotary cutter, cut strips across the width of the fabric from two contrasting fabrics. Here, the finished block will be 15cm (6in) square, so each strip will be 5cm (2in) deep plus a 10mm (½in) seam allowance. Arrange the strips to alternate fabrics, A–B–A and B–A–B, and join them taking a 5mm (¼in) seam. Press towards the darker fabric.

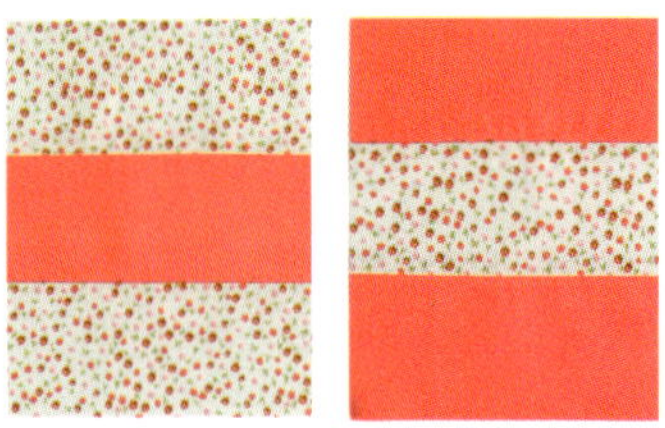

2 Cut both pieced strips across the seams into units 5cm + 1cm (2in + ½in) wide. Note that the cut strips are the same width as the original strips.

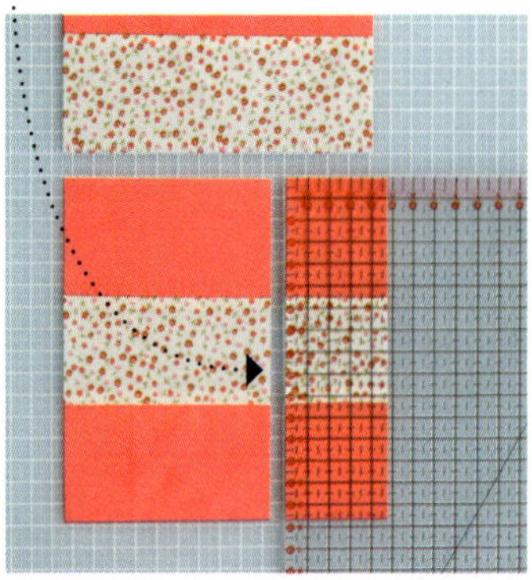

3 Arrange the cut strips in rows of three, alternating the A and B fabrics, and join them, matching the seams. Blocks can be chain-pieced (see page 60). Press.

PIECED NINE-PATCH BLOCK: JACOB'S LADDER

1 Make five four-patch blocks using fabrics A and B (see page 67).

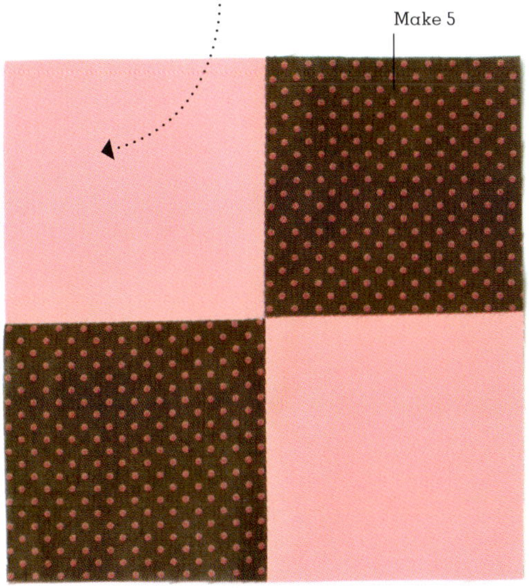

2 Make four triangle squares the same size, using fabrics A and C (see page 61).

3 Arrange the units in rows, as shown, and join them, taking a 5mm (¼in) seam allowance. Press the seams in opposite directions in each row.

4 Join the three rows, matching the seams and taking a 5mm (¼in) seam allowance. Press.

Five- and seven-patch blocks

Five-patch consists of a grid of five units in each direction, or 25 units in total. Seven-patch blocks have seven units each way, for a total of 49. Because these numbers don't divide easily, the size of the finished block should be carefully considered when planning a quilt to make cutting easier. They lend themselves to larger finished blocks – 35, 37.5, 50, or 52.5cm (14, 15, 20, or 21in) – so you need fewer to make a quilt.

FIVE-PATCH: LADY OF THE LAKE

1 Divide the size of the finished block by five to determine the size of each unit. Add a 10mm (½in) seam allowance.

2 Cut three squares from fabric A and three from fabric B. Make 19 triangle squares the same size from fabrics A and B (see page 61).

3 Following the layout carefully, combine the units into five rows of five units each, taking 5mm (¼in) seam allowances. Make sure the triangle squares face in the correct direction.

4 Join the five rows together, matching the seams and taking 5mm (¼in) seam allowances. Press.

SEVEN-PATCH: BEAR'S PAW

1 Divide the size of the finished block by seven to determine the size of each unit. Add a 10mm (½in) seam allowance to this measurement and cut one centre square from fabric A. Cut four squares the same size from fabric B for the corner squares. The arms of the centre cross are one unit wide and three units long. Add the seam allowance and cut four strips from fabric B. The large squares are two units by two. Add the seam allowance and cut four large squares from fabric C.

2 Make 16 triangle squares from fabrics A and B (see page 61). Join them in pairs, taking a 5mm (¼in) seam allowance.

3 Following the layout carefully, add a corner square to four pairs of triangle squares, taking a 5mm (¼in) seam allowance. Note that two of the strips face in the opposite direction to the other two.

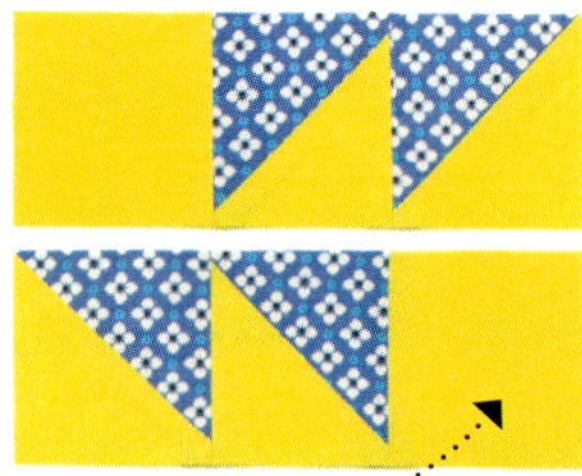

4 Join one of the remaining pairs of triangle squares to one side of each large fabric C square, taking a 5mm (¼in) seam allowance. Note that two of the strips face in one direction and two the opposite way.

5 Following the layout and matching seams carefully, join one strip from Step 3 to one side of each unit made in Step 4. Note that two sets will face in one direction and two will face the opposite way.

6 Join one large unit to each long side of two centre strips.

7 Join one short side of the two remaining centre strips to opposite sides of the centre square.

8 Join the three rows to finish the block.

String piecing

String piecing is similar to strip piecing, but the lengths of fabric are referred to as "strings" and are not necessarily straight strips. This is a good way of using up leftover pieces of uneven widths. String-pieced blocks can be combined to make larger units.

METHOD 1

1 Select a number of "strings" of fabric with plenty of contrast in colour and pattern. Join them lengthways, taking a 5mm (¼in) seam allowance. Alternate the angle in each piece and the direction of stitching to keep the finished piece even.

2 Press the seams to one side. Trim the piece to the desired size and shape.

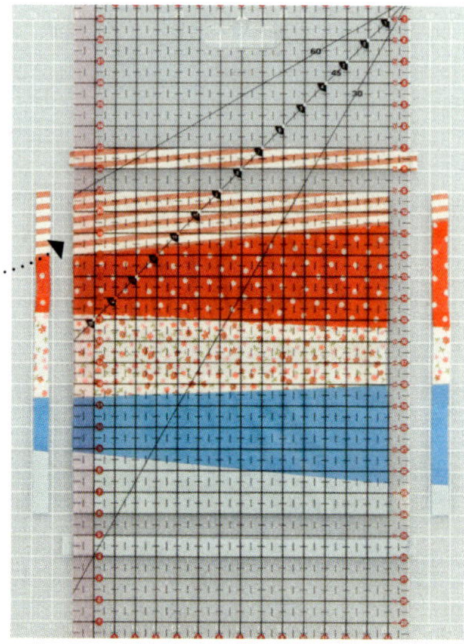

METHOD 2

1 Cut a muslin or paper foundation block, plus seam allowances. Place the first string right side up in the centre of the foundation and lay the second piece right-side down on top. Make sure both pieces are longer than the widest point on the foundation.

2 Machine stitch along one edge of the strips through all layers. Flip the pieces open and press.

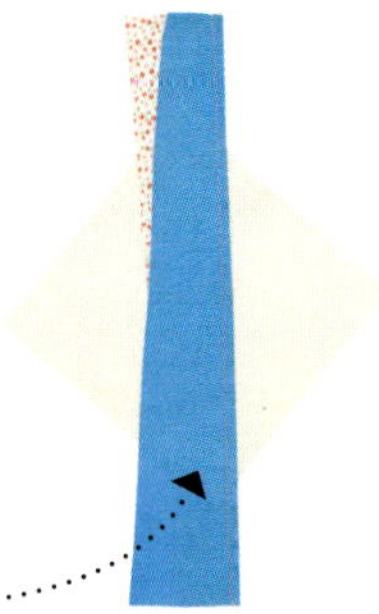

3 Turn the foundation and add a new string, right side down, to the opposite edge of the first piece. Flip it open and press.

4 Continue to add strings, flip, press, and stitch, until the foundation is covered. Trim the edges level with the foundation. Leave a 5mm (¼in) allowance if the foundation is to be removed. Carefully tear away paper foundations. Press.

Finished piece

Strip piecing

Strip piecing is a good way to build blocks quickly. In principle, several long strips are joined and then cut apart before being stitched together again in a different sequence. It is the method by which many blocks are made, including Log cabin (see pages 78–81) and Seminole patchwork (see pages 82–85).

STRIP-PIECED BLOCKS: RAIL FENCE

1 From three contrasting fabrics, cut three strips of equal width. Join them lengthways taking a 5mm (¼in) seam allowance. To prevent the pieced strip from bowing, sew to the end of strips 1 and 2, then reverse the direction to add strip 3. Press the seams to one side away from the centre.

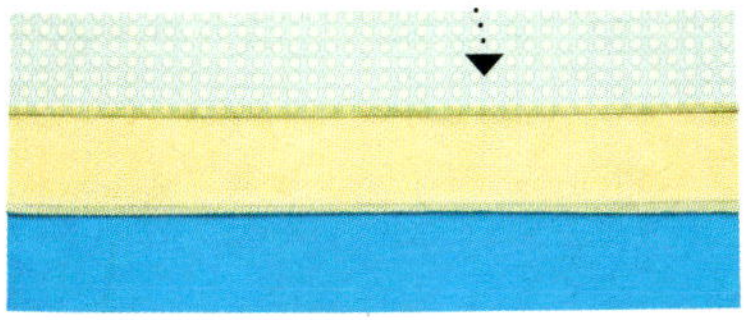

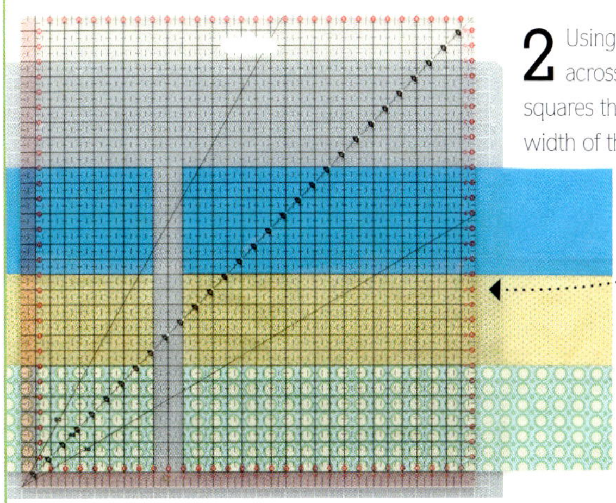

2 Using a rotary cutter, cut across the seams to make squares the same size as the width of the pieced strip set.

3 Following the layout, arrange the squares in rows.

4 Join the squares to make three horizontal rows, taking a 5mm (¼in) seam allowance. Press, alternating the direction in each row.

5 Join the rows, matching the seams and taking a 5mm (¼in) seam allowance.

Log cabin

Log cabin is perhaps the most versatile block of all. Blocks can be made individually or chain-pieced. Log cabin lends itself to scrap quilting if the values have a strong contrast, and is stunning in simple two-colour versions. The crucial centre piece can be virtually any shape, and the order of piecing can vary. Blocks can be set (see page 154) in many ways to create secondary patterns. Always use a 5mm (¼in) seam allowance.

METHOD 1: INDIVIDUAL BLOCKS

1 Cut a centre square of the desired size, plus seam allowances. Cut a second square the same size from fabric A and join them right sides together along one edge. Press open.

2 Cut strip 3 from fabric A the width of the centre square and the same length as the pressed unit and join it right sides together along the long side. Start at the corner of the second square and finish at the bottom of the centre square. Press open.

3 Now add two strips from fabric B in the same way, working in a clockwise direction to help the centre stay square.

4 Continue adding strips, two from A and two from B, always working in a clockwise direction, until the block reaches the desired size.

METHOD 2: COURTHOUSE STEPS

1 Cut a centre square.

2 From fabric A, cut two squares the same size as the centre and join them to opposite sides of the centre square. Press the seams away from the centre.

3 Cut strips the same width as the centre square from fabric B, and add one strip to each long side of the pieced unit. Trim to the same length as the three-piece unit. Press away from the centre.

4 Continue adding strips – first two strips of fabric A, then two of fabric B – to opposite sides of the block until it reaches the desired size. Press each strip away from the centre.

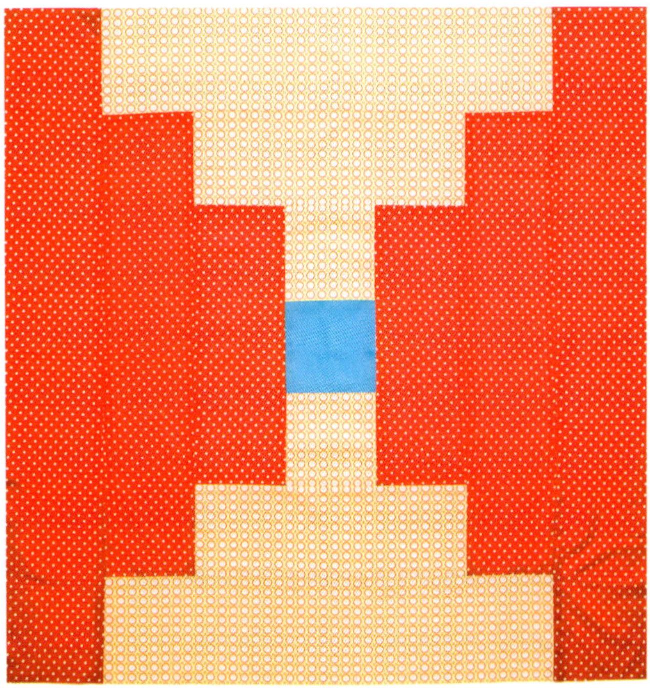

METHOD 3: CHAIN PIECING

1 Cut the required number of centre squares from fabric A. Cut strips the same width as the centre and place one centre square right sides together at one end of a strip of fabric B. Stitch, taking a 5mm (¼in) seam allowance.

2 Leave a small space and add a second square in the same way without raising the needle or breaking the thread. Continue to add squares until you reach the end of the strip.

3 Cut the units apart, making sure the two sides are the same size, and press.

4 Place the pieced units on a second light-coloured strip right sides together with the centre square at the bottom. Stitch and press, then trim, making sure the unit is square.

5 Place the units on a fabric C strip right sides together, again with the centre square at the bottom. Stitch, press, and trim, as before.

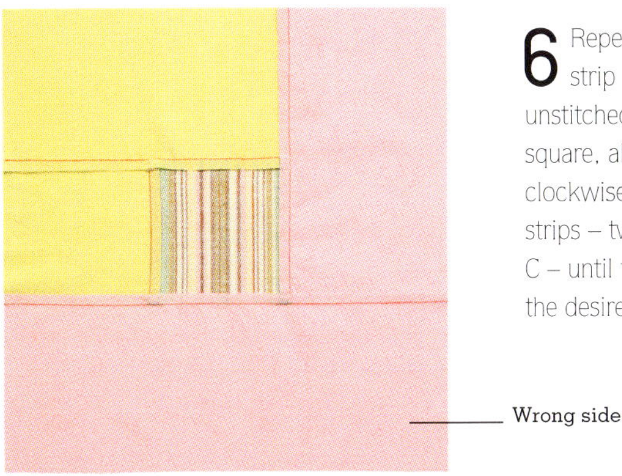

6 Repeat to add the fourth strip (fabric C) along the unstitched edge of the centre square, always working clockwise. Continue adding strips – two B, and then two C – until the block reaches the desired size.

Seminole patchwork

Used by the Seminole tribe of Native Americans in Florida, this type of strip-pieced patchwork is useful for borders or blocks. The method often involves cutting pieced strips at an angle and re-joining them.

METHOD 1: STRAIGHT BAND

1 Cut strips from three contrasting fabrics. The width ratio here is 2:1:3, which gives an even offset.

2 Join them right sides together, with the narrow strip in the centre, taking a 5mm (¼in) seam allowance. Press towards the darker colour.

3 Using a rotary cutter and ruler, cut across the seams to the desired width.

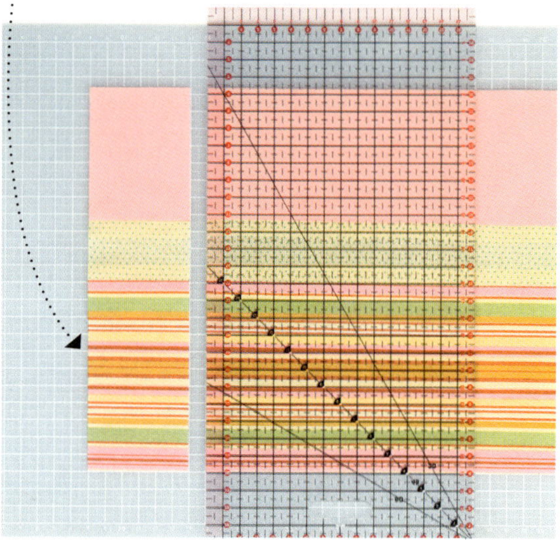

4 Alternating the top and bottom of each adjacent strip, sew them back together, taking a 5mm (¼in) seam allowance. Press the seams in the same direction.

METHOD 2: ANGLED BAND

1 Cut strips from three contrasting fabrics; the widths can vary.

2 Join them right sides together, with wider strips on the outside. Press the seams in the same direction.

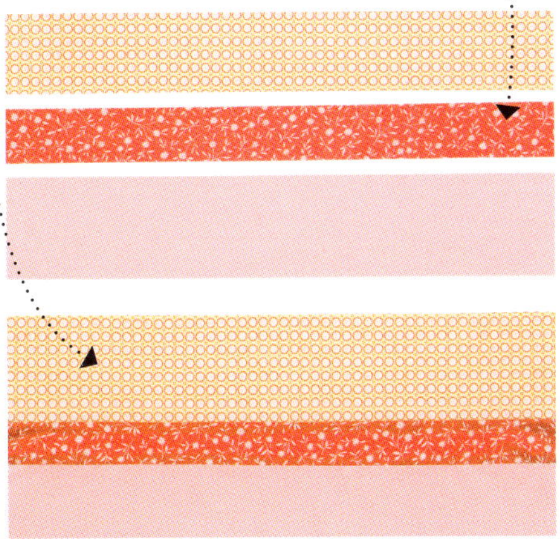

3 Cut across the seams to create pieced strips of the desired width.

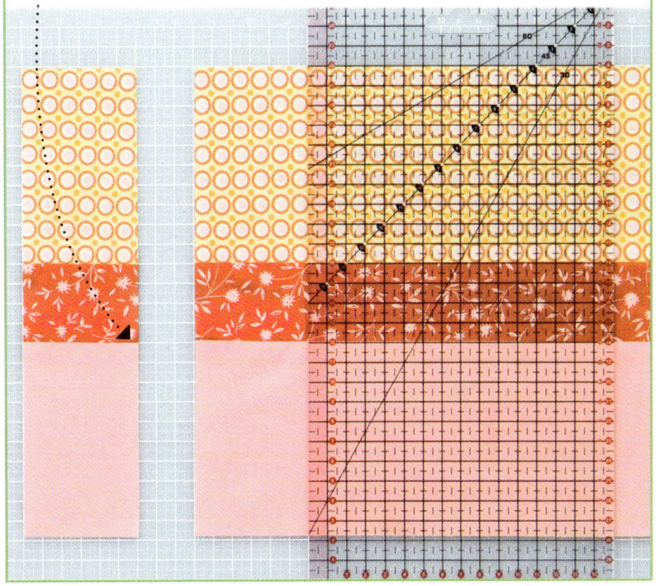

4 Sew the strips back together, taking a 5mm (¼in) seam allowance and offsetting the centre squares each time. Press the seams in the same direction.

5 Trim the points at both edges of the pieced strip.

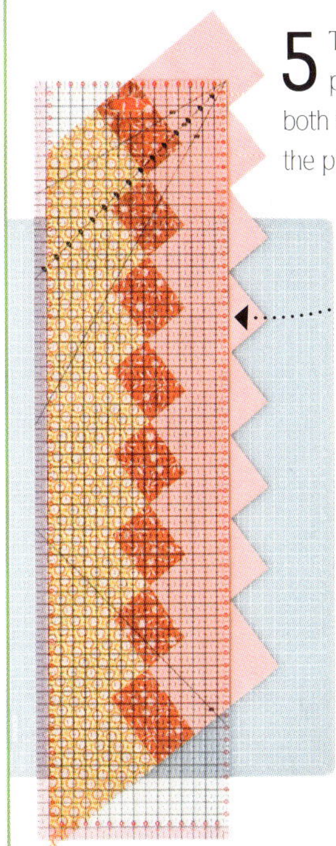

6 Square up both ends.

METHOD 3: CHEVRON BAND

1 Cut strips the same width from three contrasting fabrics. Join them right sides together. Press the seams in the same direction. Make a second identical pieced strip.

2 Cut across the seams at an angle in one direction on the first pieced strip.

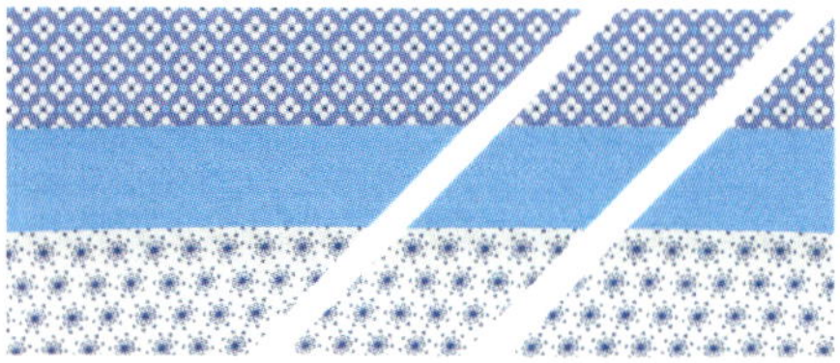

3 Repeat on the second strip, using the same angle but reversing the direction of the cut.

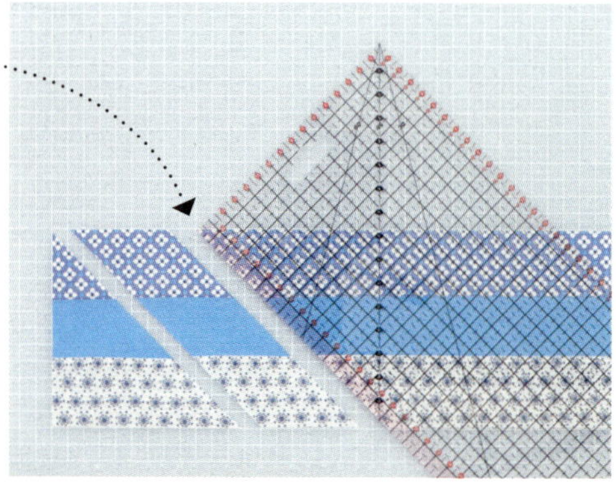

4 Match the seams of a cut strip from strip 1 to the seams of a cut strip from strip 2 and join, taking a 5mm (¼in) seam allowance. Repeat to join in pairs.

5 Join the pairs to create a chevron band. Press the seams in the same direction. Trim the points at both edges.

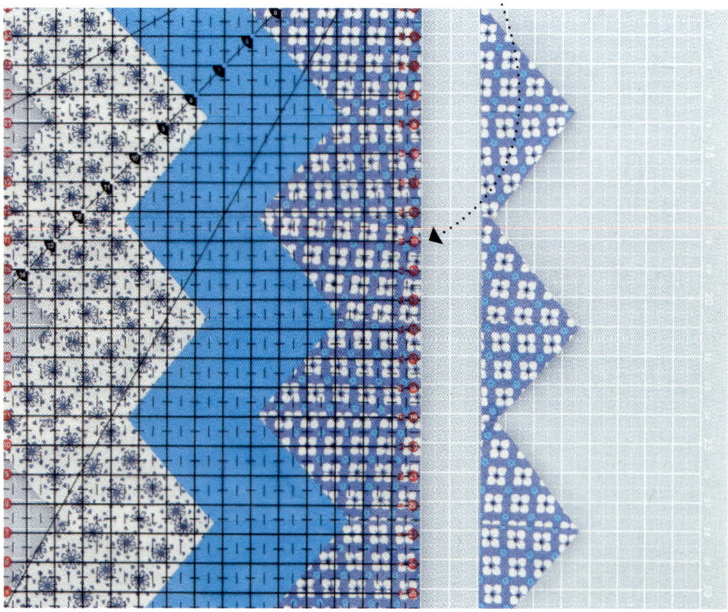

6 The central fabric creates a chevron pattern.

Star blocks

Star designs make up the largest group of patchwork patterns, ranging from simple four-patch examples to highly elaborate ones with multiple points. They combine many techniques and the following patterns are the starting point for numerous variations.

SINGLE STAR: DOUBLE FOUR-PATCH

1 Divide the size of the finished block by four. Add seam allowances. Cut four squares each of fabric A and fabric B. Make eight triangle squares from fabrics A and B (see page 61).

2 Following the layout, join the squares and triangle squares in rows of four units each, taking a 5mm (¼in) seam allowance.

3 Join the rows, matching the seams and taking a 5mm (¼in) seam allowance.

FRIENDSHIP STAR: NINE-PATCH

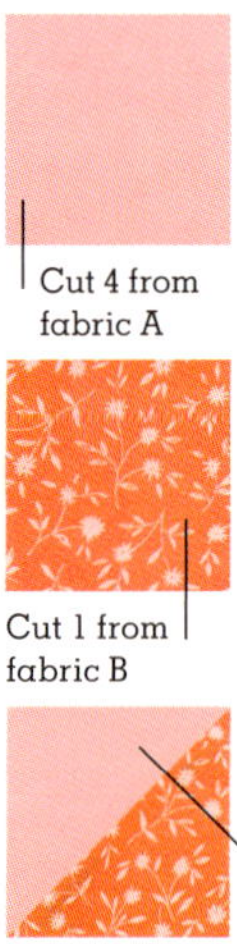

1 Divide the size of the finished block by three. Add seam allowances. Cut four squares from fabric A and one square from fabric B. Make four triangle squares from fabrics A and B (see page 61).

2 Following the layout, join the squares and triangle squares in rows of three units each, taking a 5mm (¼in) seam allowance.

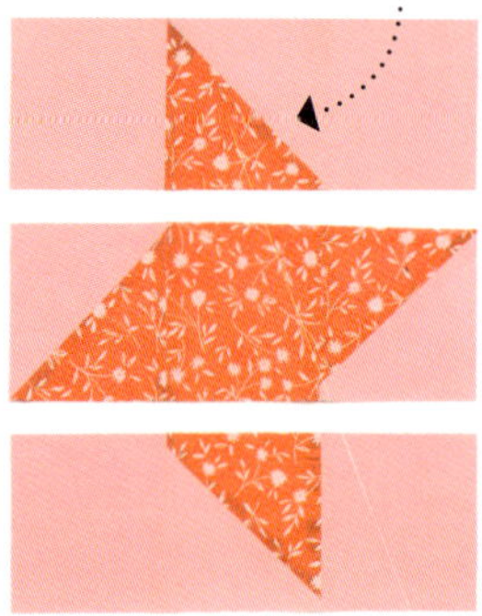

3 Join the rows, matching the seams and taking a 5mm (¼in) seam allowance.

OHIO STAR: NINE-PATCH WITH QUARTER-SQUARE TRIANGLES

1 Divide the size of the finished block by three. Add seam allowances. Cut four squares from fabric A and one square from fabric B. Make four quarter-square units from fabrics A and B (see page 62).

Cut 4 from fabric A

Cut 1 from fabric B

Make 4 from fabrics A and B

2 Following the layout, join the squares and quarter-square units in rows of three, taking a 5mm (¼in) seam allowance.

3 Join the rows, matching the seams and taking a 5mm (¼in) seam allowance.

HEXAGON STAR: 60-DEGREE ANGLES

1 Copy the template to the desired size and cut a pattern. Cut three star points each from fabrics A and B, and six setting diamonds from fabric C, adding a seam allowance all around when you cut out each piece.

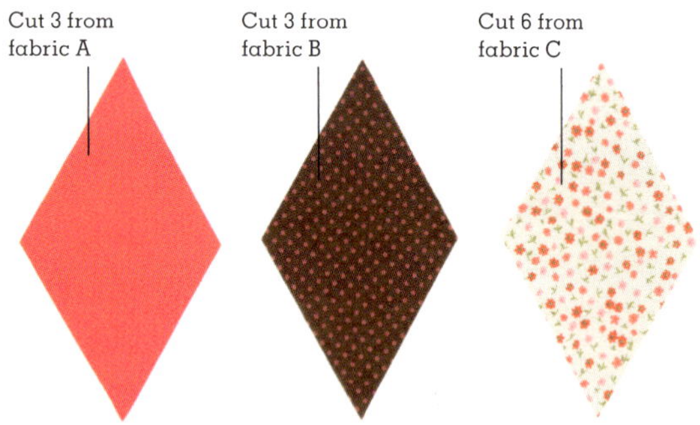

2 Join the three star points in sets, alternating the fabrics.

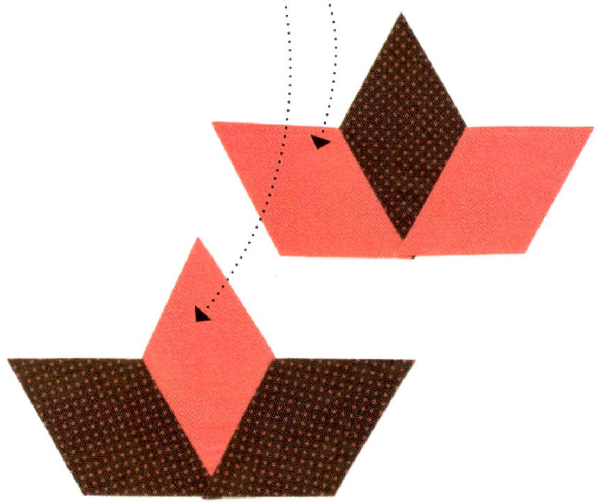

3 Join the units to make the star.

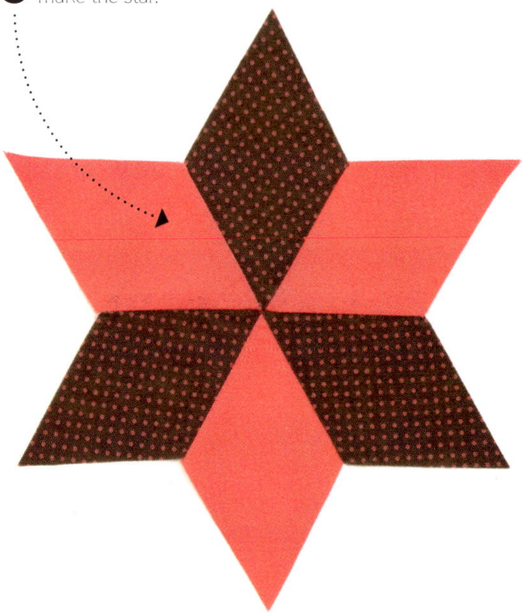

4 Set in the diamond units (see page 56).

EIGHT-POINT STAR: 45-DEGREE ANGLES

1 Make templates to the desired size for the star points, corner squares, and setting triangles. Cut four star points (see page 40) each from fabrics A and B, and four corner squares (see page 37) and four setting triangles (see page 39) from fabric C.

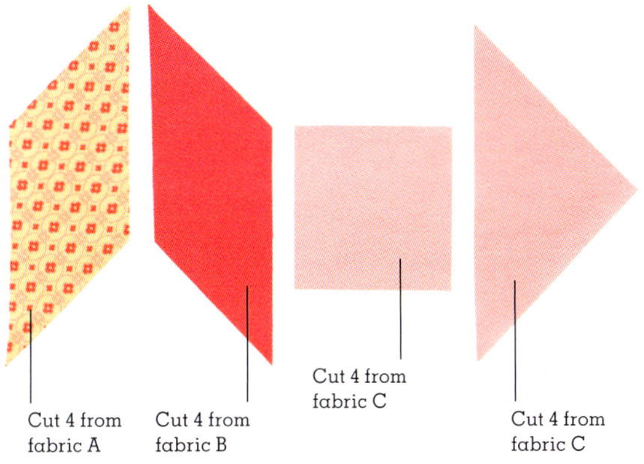

2 Join the star points in four identical pairs, alternating the fabrics.

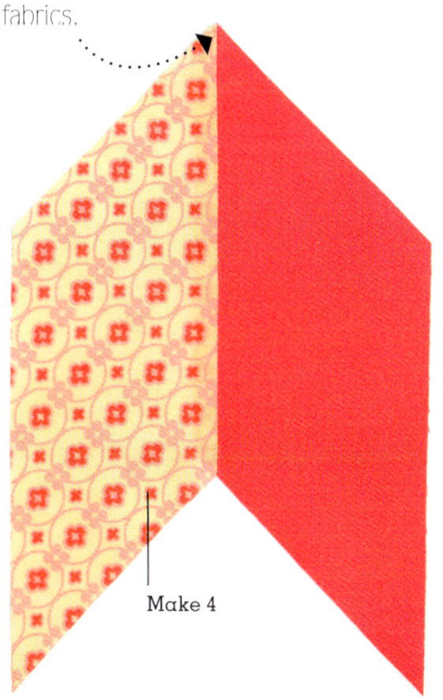

3 Join two pairs together to make half the star, then join the two halves to complete the star.

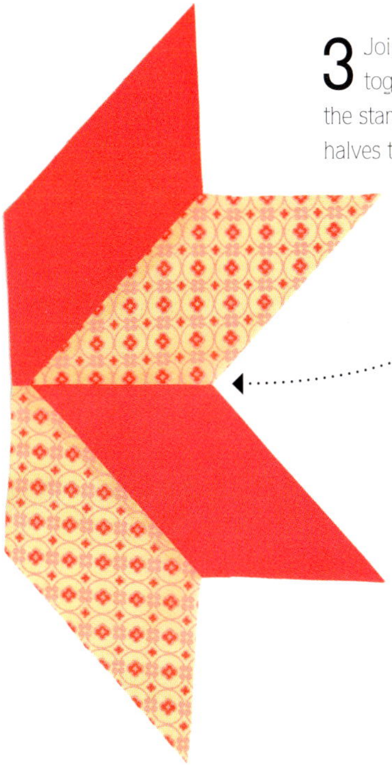

4 Set in the triangle units, then set in the corner squares (see pages 56 and 64).

Pictorial blocks

Most pictorial quilt blocks are appliquéd, but there are a number of representational blocks, traditional and modern, that are pieced. Many of them, such as flowers and leaves, derive from nature, and most look best if they are spaced out on a quilt, not set together edge to edge. Sashing (see page 156) can be used to separate blocks to show them off, or they can be alternated with plain spacer blocks.

LILY: EIGHT-POINT STAR

1 Cut six "petal" points (see page 40) from fabric A, two petal points from fabric B, and four corner squares and eight right-angled triangles (see page 39) from fabric C. From fabric D, cut a strip 2.5cm (1in) wide and long enough to fit across the diagonal of one square for the "stem".

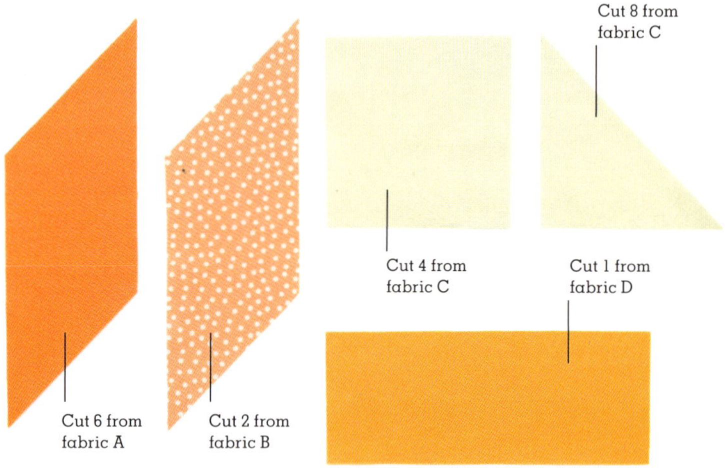

2 Apply the strip diagonally across one of the fabric C squares. Turn the raw edges under on the long edges and level both short ends even with the corners of the square (see Maple leaf, page 92).

3 Matching the colours, join the "petals" in pairs.

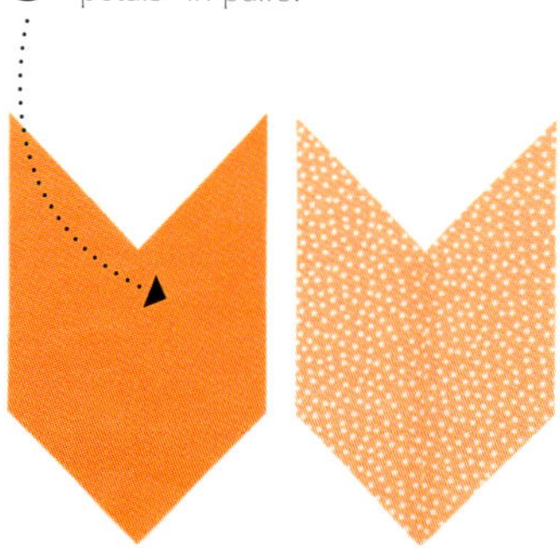

4 Add a right-angled triangle to both long sides of each pair of "petals".

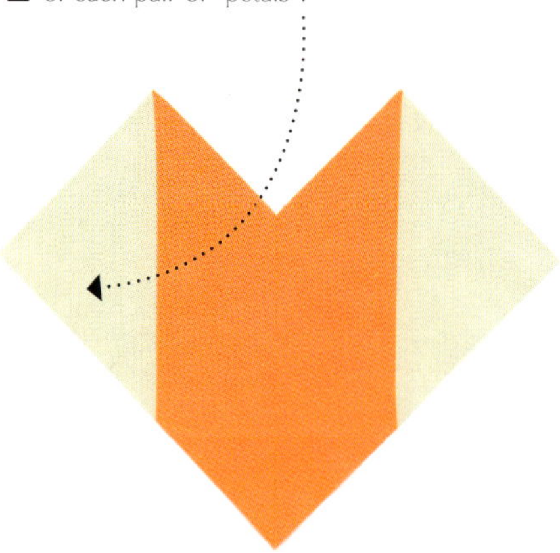

5 Set in the corner squares to make four units. Make sure you catch the raw edges of the "stem" square in the seams.

6 Join the units in pairs, then join the pairs, manipulating the seams in the centre to help them lie flat.

MAPLE LEAF: NINE-PATCH

1 Divide the size of the finished block by three. Add seam allowances. Cut two squares that size from fabric A and three from fabric B. From fabric B cut a strip 4cm (1½in) wide and long enough to fit across the diagonal of one square for the "stem". Make four triangle squares (see page 61) from fabrics A and B.

Cut 2 from fabric A

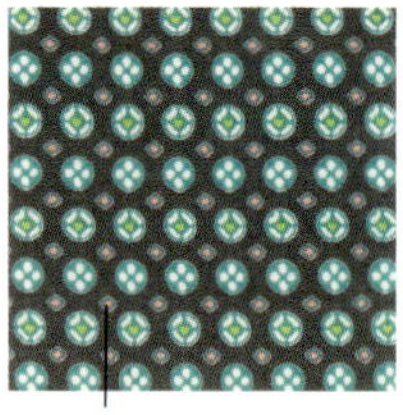

Cut 3 from fabric B

Cut 1 from fabric B

Make 4 from fabrics A and B

2 Apply the stem strip diagonally across one of the fabric A squares. Turn under the raw edges on the long edges and one short edge. Trim the other corner level with the corner of the square.

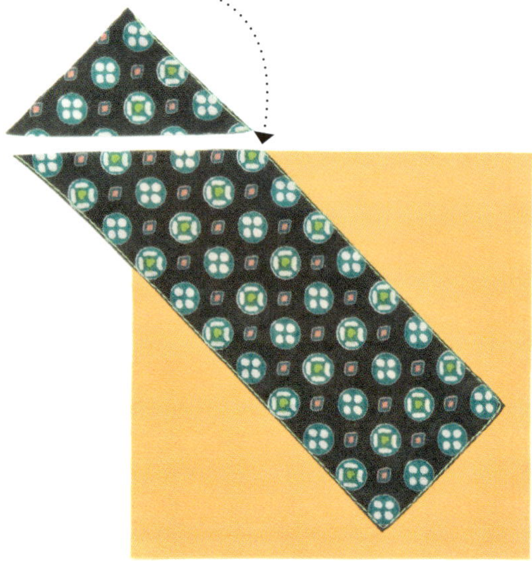

3 Following the layout, join the units in three rows of three.

4 Join the rows, making sure you catch the raw edge of the "stem" strip in the seams.

CAKE STAND BASKET: FIVE-PATCH

1 Divide the size of the finished block by five. Add seam allowances. Cut eight squares this size from fabric A. Make eight triangle squares (see page 61) from fabrics A and B.

Cut 8 from fabric A

Make 8 from fabrics A and B

2 The finished centre triangle square is three times the size of the outside squares. Cut one triangle from fabric A and one from fabric B to this size and join them on the diagonal.

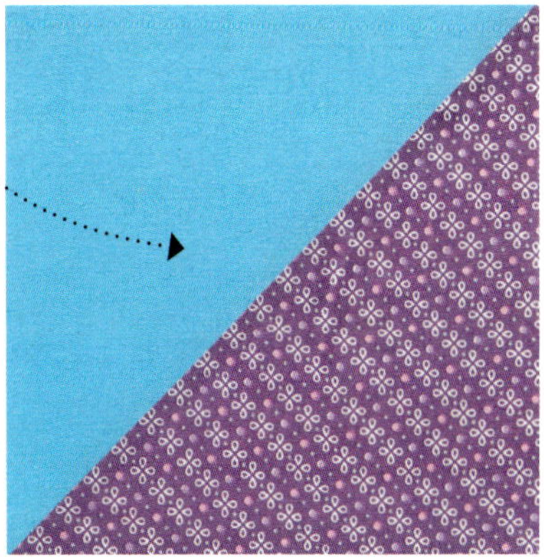

3 Join three small triangle squares.

4 Join one small triangle square to two small plain squares. Following the layout, add the strips to opposite sides of the large triangle square.

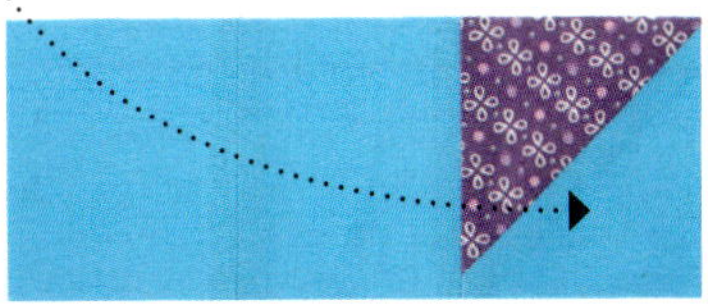

5 Following the layout, join the remaining small squares into two strips and add one strip to opposite sides of the large unit. Match all seams carefully.

SHIP

1 Divide the size of the finished block by four. Add seam allowances. Cut four squares this size from fabric A and two from fabric B. Divide this by three and add 10mm (½in) to determine the size of the strips that make up the "sea". Cut four strips in each of three colours to that measurement times the width of the square units. Make two triangle squares from fabrics A and B and four from fabrics A and C (see page 61).

2 Join the sea strips to make four units the same size as the plain squares. You can make the "sea" from three long strips if you prefer. They should be the width determined in Step 1. The length of each strip is the same as the finished measurement of the block plus seam allowances.

3 Following the layout, join the units in four rows.

4 Join the rows to complete the block.

HOUSE

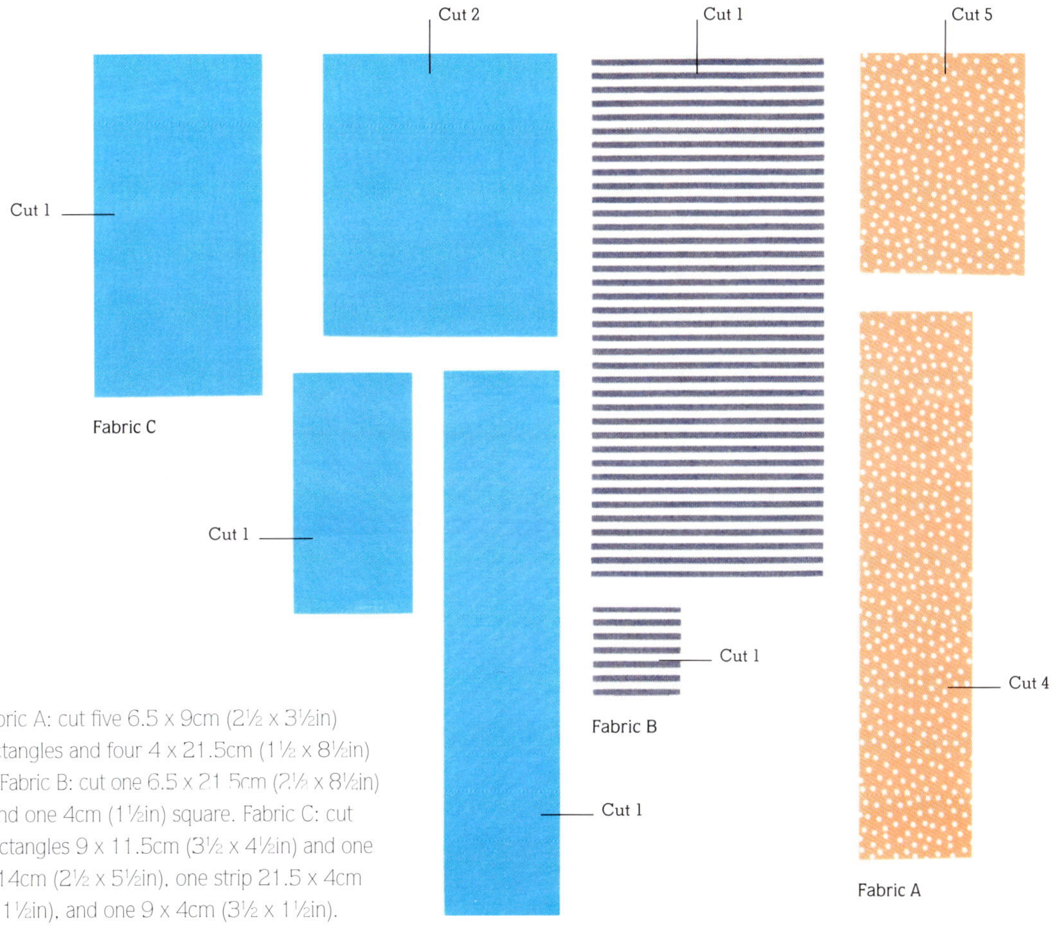

1 Fabric A: cut five 6.5 x 9cm (2½ x 3½in) rectangles and four 4 x 21.5cm (1½ x 8½in) strips. Fabric B: cut one 6.5 x 21.5cm (2½ x 8½in) strip and one 4cm (1½in) square. Fabric C: cut two rectangles 9 x 11.5cm (3½ x 4½in) and one 6.5 x 14cm (2½ x 5½in), one strip 21.5 x 4cm (8½ x 1½in), and one 9 x 4cm (3½ x 1½in).

2 Cut one 6.5 x 11.5cm (2½ x 4½in) rectangle from fabric B and one from fabric C. Cut them in half diagonally to make two irregular triangles (see page 40) and join these to create two triangle rectangles. Join one triangle rectangle to each end of the 4 x 21.5cm (2½ x 8½in) fabric B strip to make the "roof".

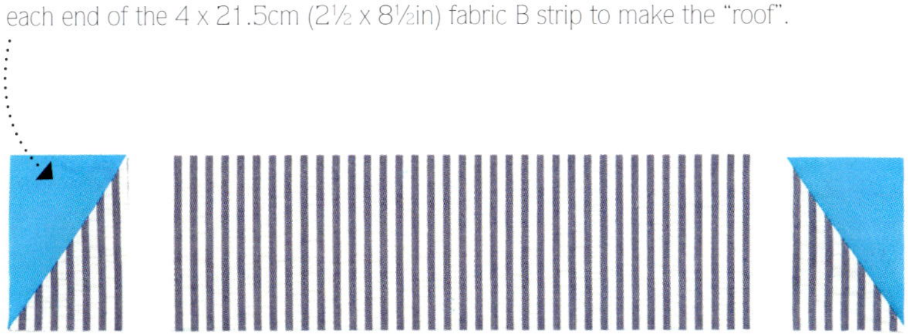

3 Make the chimney strip from the smallest square (fabric B) and the two narrow fabric C strips.

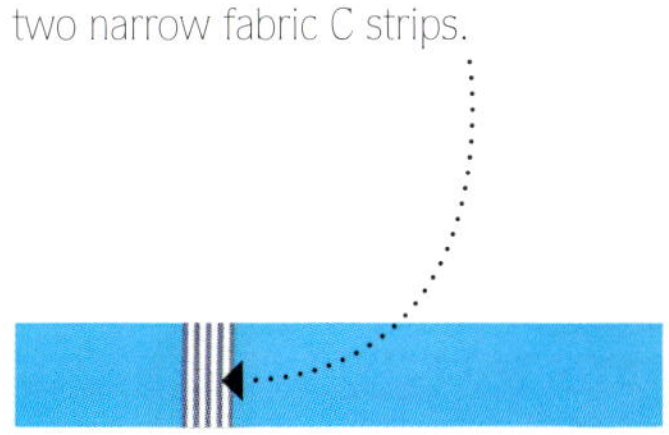

4 Make two window units by adding a 6.5 x 9cm (2½ x 3½in) fabric A rectangle to the short ends of each 9 x 11.5cm (3½ x 4½in) fabric C rectangle.

5 Make the door unit by joining the remaining fabric A rectangle to the 6.5 x 14cm (2½ x 5½in) fabric C rectangle.

6 Join the window and door units by adding the remaining four fabric A strips to the long edges.

7 Join the chimney and roof elements together.

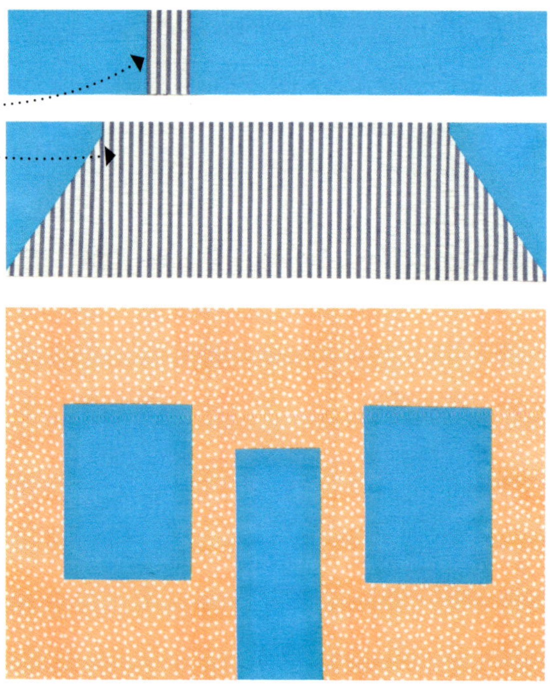

8 Join the roof and house to complete the block.

Curves

Patchwork patterns based on curves are less common than those with straight seams, which are easy to cut and stitch. But although curves can be fiddly, they give more options and, with careful preparation at every stage from template making to cutting and pinning, they are straightforward to sew. Many people find curves easier to work by hand, but it is not difficult to machine stitch them (see page 63).

FANS

1 Transfer the outlines to card or template plastic and cut out the shapes. Make two sets of templates – set 1 for the cutting lines, and set 2 with the seam allowances trimmed off the curved edges for the stitching line.

2 For a six-blade fan, cut three blades each from fabrics A and B. Cut a small corner piece from fabric C and a background from fabric D.

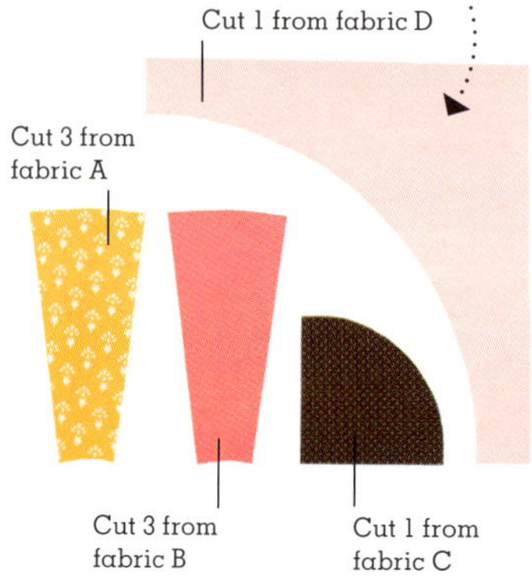

3 Join the fan blade pieces, alternating the colours and taking a 5mm (¼in) seam allowance. Press the seams in the same direction.

4 Mark the seam allowances on the top and bottom edges of the fan unit.

5 Mark the seam allowance on the small corner piece and pin it to the lower edge of the fan unit. Join them as in Steps 5 and 6 of Drunkard's Path (see pages 99–101). Press towards the fan.

6 Mark the seam allowance on the background piece and pin it to the upper edge of the fan unit. Join them as before. Press the seam towards the background.

DRUNKARD'S PATH

1 Make two sets of templates from card or plastic – set 1 for the cutting lines, and set 2 with the seam allowances trimmed off the curved edges for the stitching line. Place the registration marks precisely on both sets.

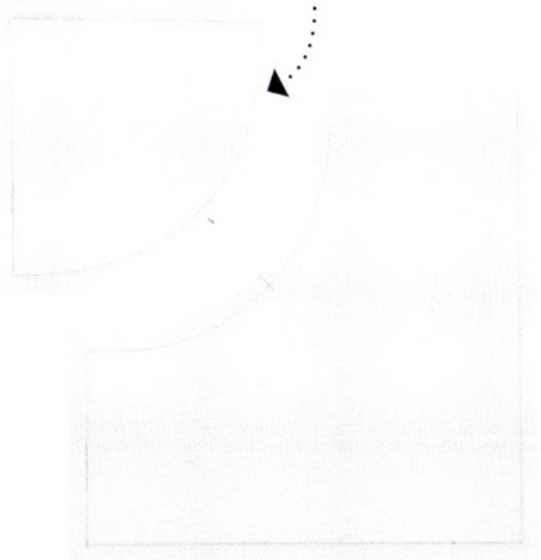

2 Transfer the larger outlines to the wrong side of the chosen fabrics. Make sure the registration marks are transferred accurately.

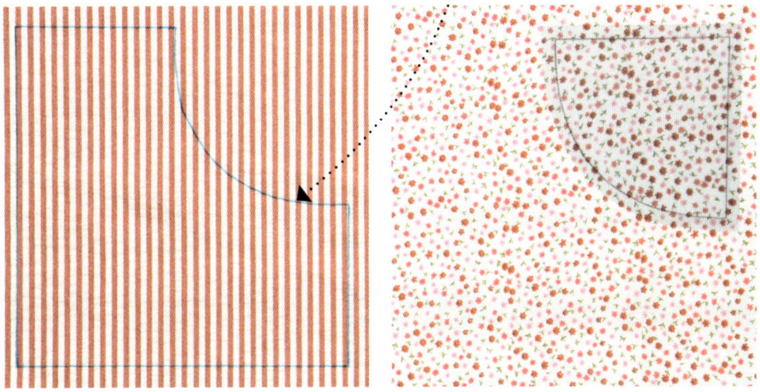

3 Cut out the shapes. If you are using scissors, cut around the curve, not into it. If you prefer to cut with rotary equipment, use the smallest size blade and a perfectly smooth cutting mat for best results.

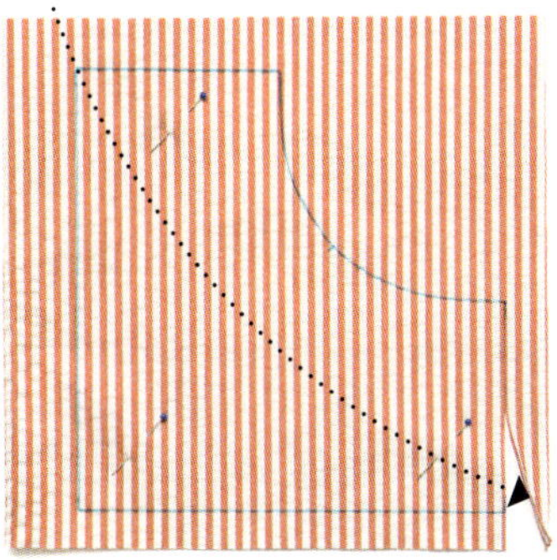

4 Separate the cut-out shapes and, using the set 2 templates, transfer the seamlines and registration marks to the wrong side of each fabric piece.

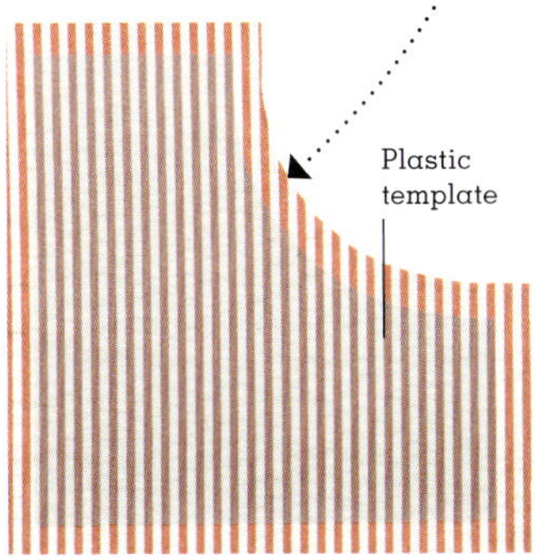

5 Pin one of each shape and fabric right sides together, with the convex piece on top of the concave one. Match and pin the centre marks first, then pin the corners.

6 Place pins in between, every 8mm (⅜in) or so, matching the seamlines on both pieces as necessary and using your fingers and thumbs to manipulate the fabric to eliminate uneven distribution.

7 Stitch along the seamlines marked on the curved seam of each piece, removing pins as you sew. If you pin in advance, you can chain-piece these units.

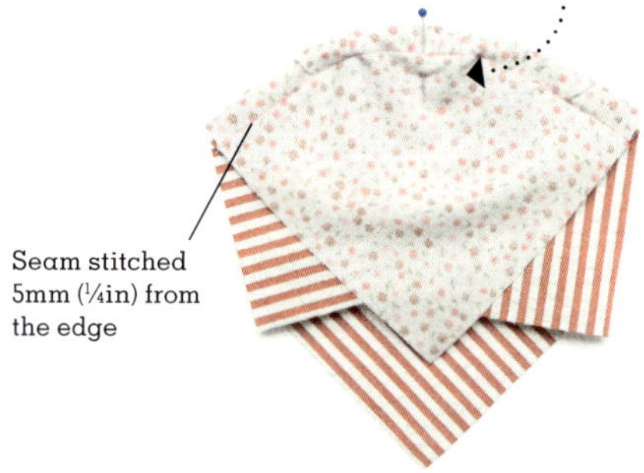

8 Press the seams. There should be no need to clip the curves.

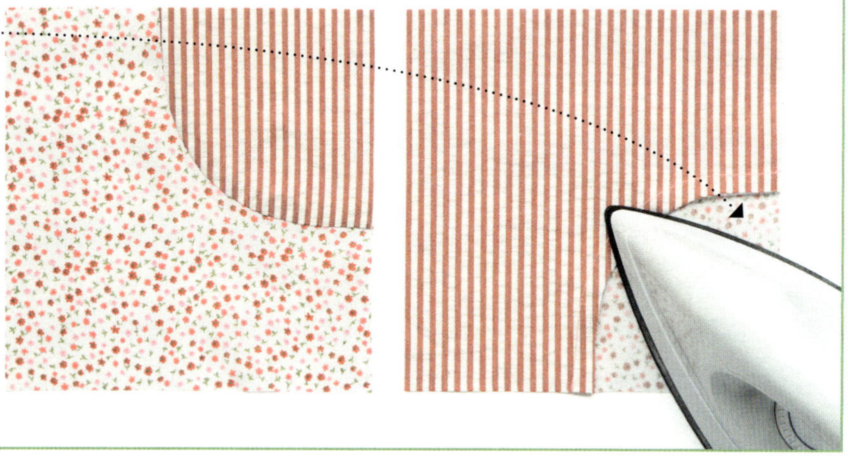

9 Following the layout and alternating colours, combine the units in four rows of four. Press the seams in opposite directions on alternate rows.

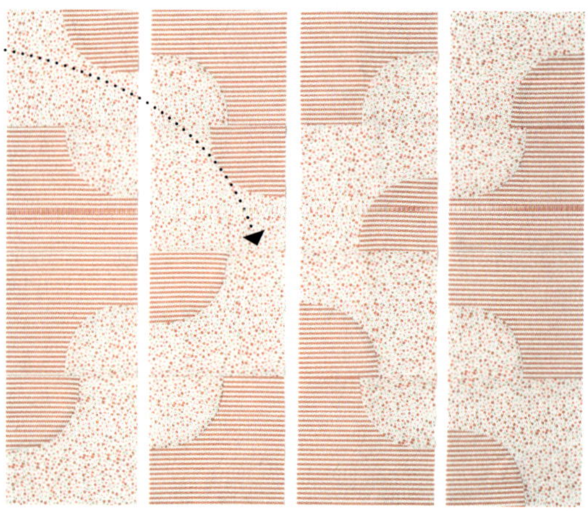

10 Join the rows, matching the seams carefully. Press.

English paper piecing

This is a traditional method for making a quilt of mosaic shapes. The fabric pieces – hexagons, honeycombs, diamonds, and triangles, all of which have at least two bias edges – are tacked to pre-cut paper templates the size of the finished element. The technique is usually done by hand. The backing papers can be cut from virtually any heavy paper but freezer paper can be ironed on quickly and is easy to remove.

BASIC PAPER-PIECING TECHNIQUE

1 Unless you are using pre-cut paper shapes, make a template. Draw around it to make the necessary number of shapes. Using paper scissors, carefully cut out the backing papers.

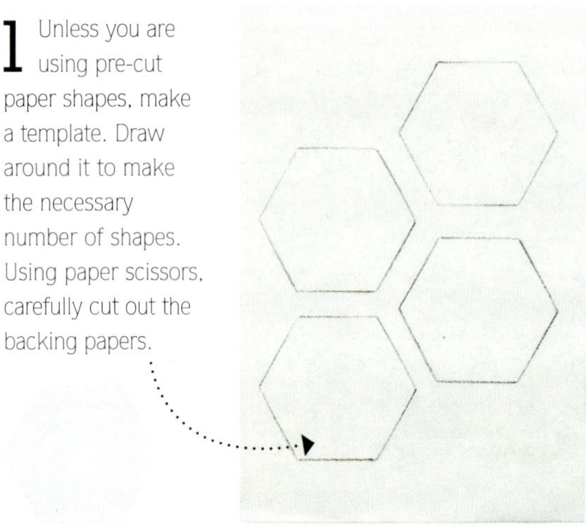

2 Pin a plain-paper shape or iron a freezer-paper shape (paper side up) to the wrong side of the fabric. Leave enough space for seam allowances.

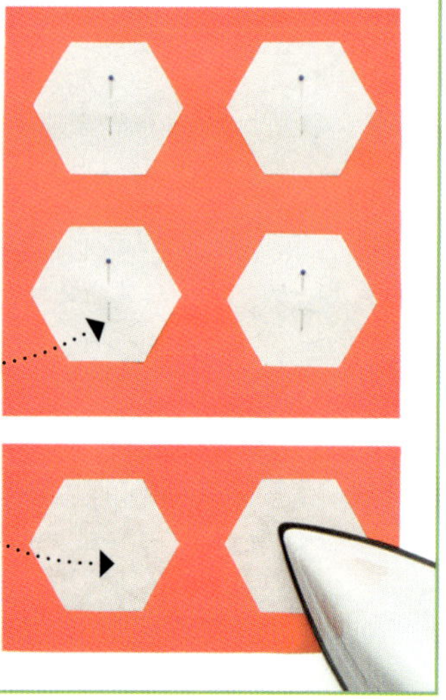

3 Cut out each shape from fabric, leaving a 5mm (¼in) seam allowance all around. You can use scissors or a rotary cutter, but take care to keep at least one side of the shape along the straight grain of the fabric.

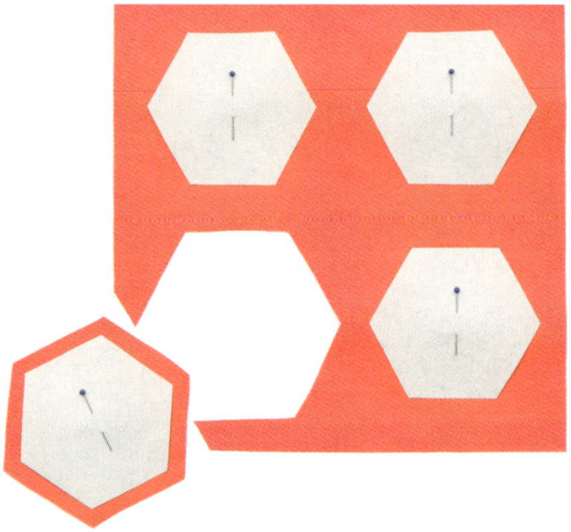

4 Turn the seam allowance to the wrong side over the edge of the paper shape. Tack along each side in turn, folding each corner neatly and stitching through the fold to hold it securely.

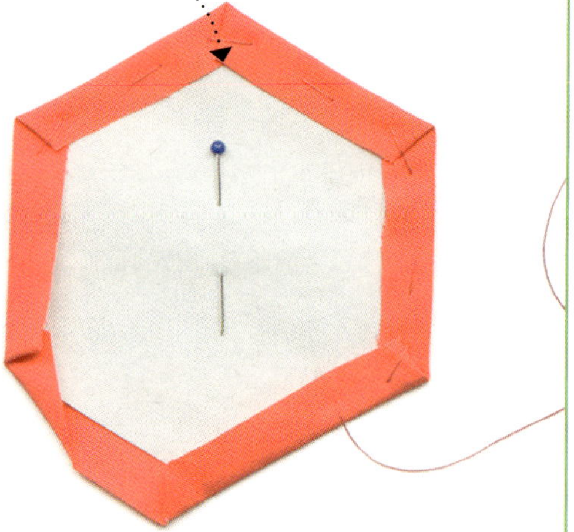

5 To join patches into units, place two shapes right sides together. Make a back-stitched loop (see page 44), and oversew to the corner. Do not sew through the backing papers.

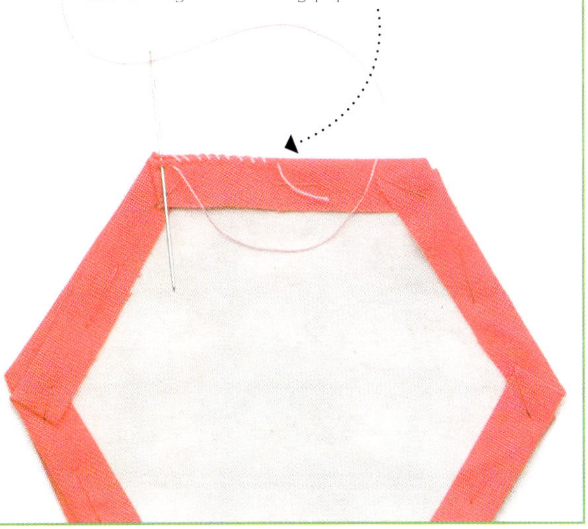

6 Oversew along the same edge to the opposite corner, again taking small stitches. When you reach the corner, backstitch in the opposite direction for 5mm (¼in).

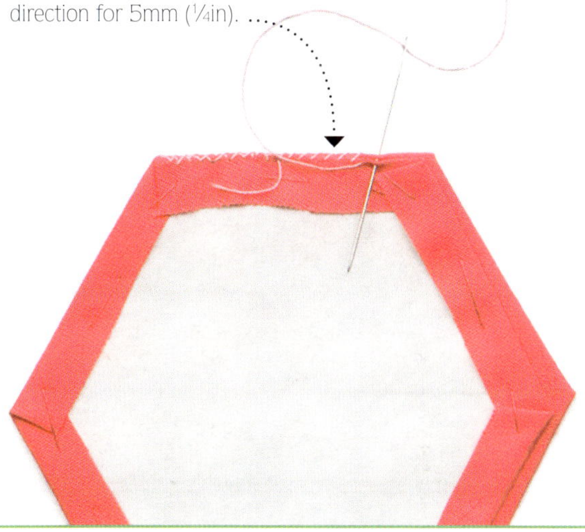

7 Continue adding shapes until complete.

8 If you wish to re-use papers, you can remove them once all the shapes adjoining a particular piece have been added.

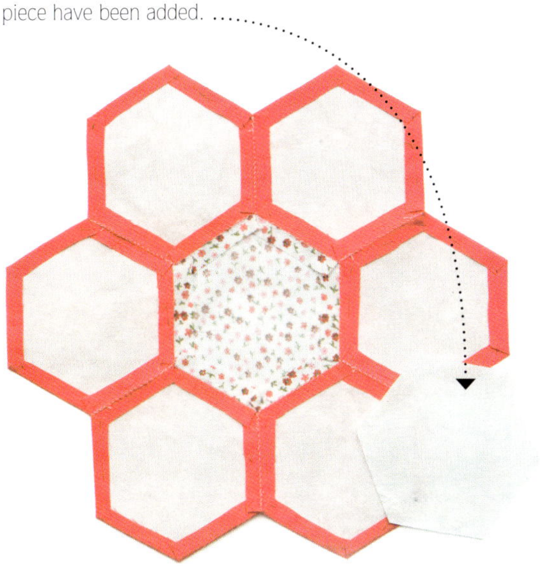

9 Remove the tacking stitches.

SETTING IN HEXAGONS

1 To set in a third hexagon, oversew one side of the seam, starting at the centre point.

2 Align the second sides to be joined at their outer points, folding back the pieces as necessary, and stitch as before.

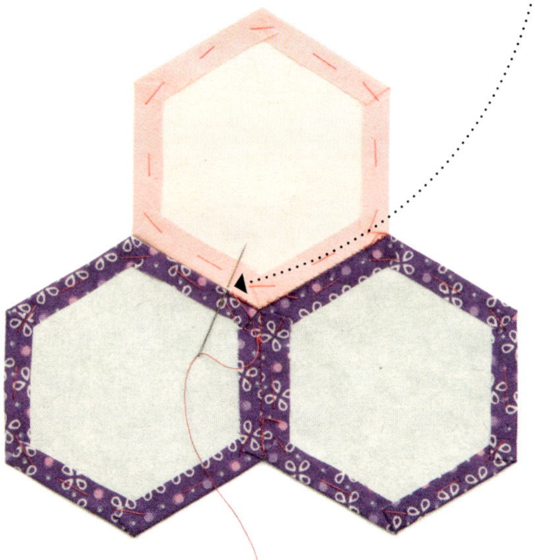

NEAT FOLDS

1 To make a neat fold at the sharp points when tacking diamonds and triangles, start sewing in the middle of one side. When you reach the point, fingerpress the extended seam allowance.

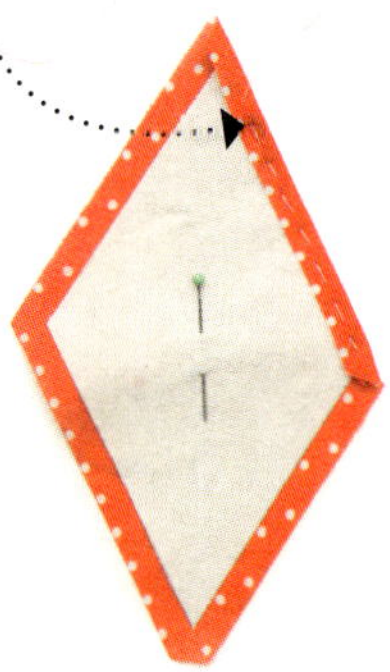

2 Fold over the allowance from the next side neatly. Take a stitch through the fold and continue. Do not trim off the fabric extensions.

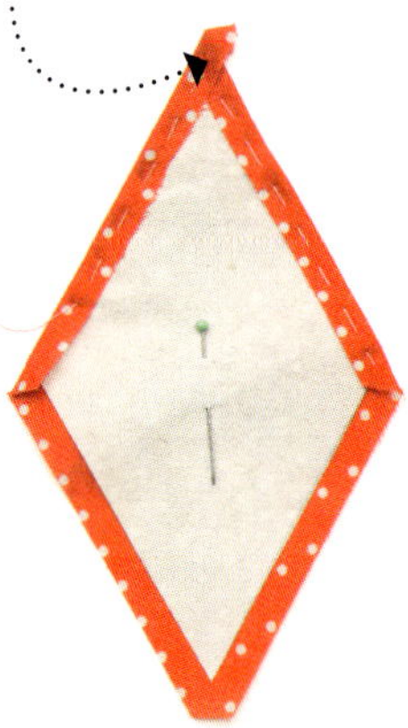

NEAT JOINS

To make a neat join when you sew pieces together, fold the extension to the side so that you don't stitch through it. Where several come together, the unstitched extensions will form a spiral around their meeting point and lie flat.

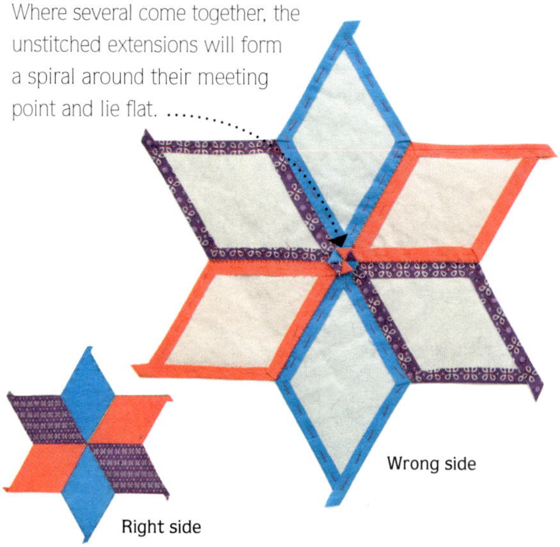

Working on a foundation

Several patchwork techniques are worked on a foundation, also known as stitch-and-flip. Crazy patchwork uses random shapes and is a great way to use up scraps. It is best made on a lightweight foundation fabric, such as calico. Reverse-pieced foundation piecing (see page 106) ensures accuracy and is a quick way to make blocks. You can make patterns for each segment, or cut the shapes with generous seam allowances.

FOUNDATION PIECING: TOP PIECED

1 Cut a foundation of lightweight calico the size you want the finished block to be plus a 2.5cm (1in) seam allowance all around.

2 Gather a selection of straight-sided pieces of various shapes and colours. Starting in the centre, place two pieces right sides together and sew along one side. Take a 5mm (¼in) seam allowance, whether you are working by hand or machine.

3 Press or fingerpress the pieces open.

4 Add piece 3 along one edge of the combined shape made in Step 1. Open and press. If necessary, trim the seam allowance level before you add the next piece. Snip off thread ends if machining.

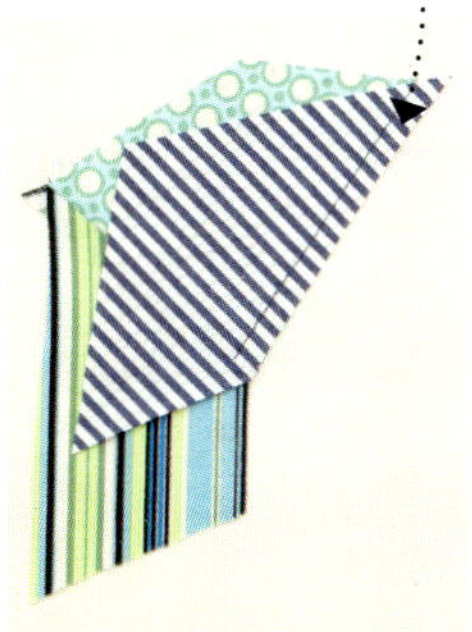

5 Continue clockwise around the centre piece until the foundation is completely filled. Keep the arrangement random and avoid parallel lines. Run the seams in different directions and vary the angles. Press each piece open as you work.

6 Trim the edges level with the edges of the foundation fabric. Embellish the finished piece if you wish.

1 Cut the chosen foundation (you can use paper, calico, wadding, or non-woven interfacing) to size, with a generous amount added all around.

2 Trace or transfer the design to the foundation. Number the piecing order clearly on the foundation. You will be sewing from the back of the foundation, so the block will be the reverse of the foundation itself.

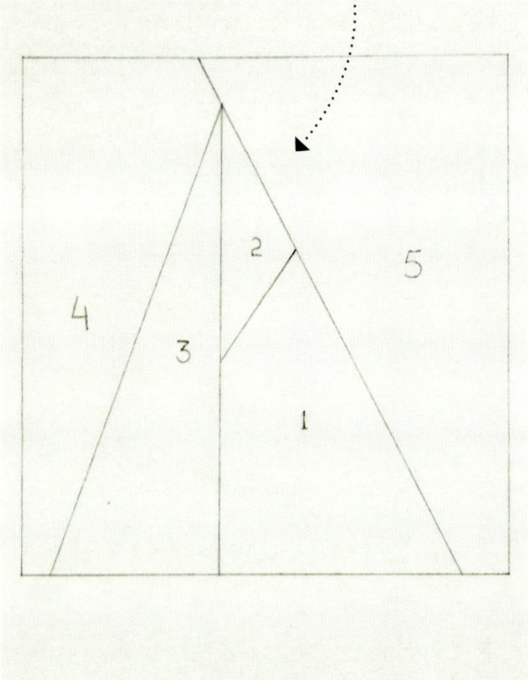

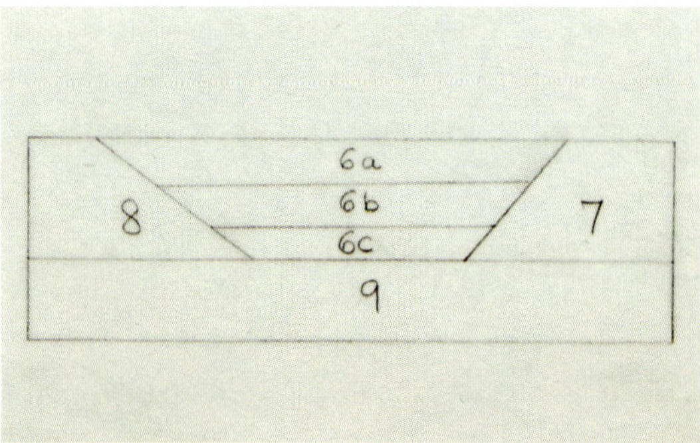

3 Cut out piece 1 and pin it right side up on the reverse side of the foundation. Make sure that it extends beyond the stitching lines; you can check this by holding it up to the light.

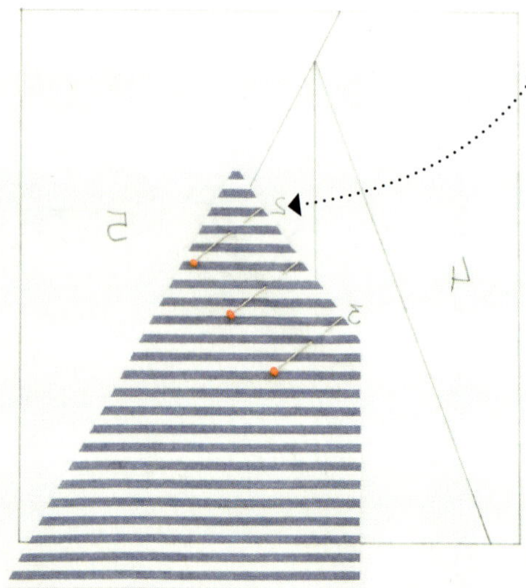

4 Cut out piece 2 and place it right sides together on piece 1, along the seam to be sewn. Pin through all layers.

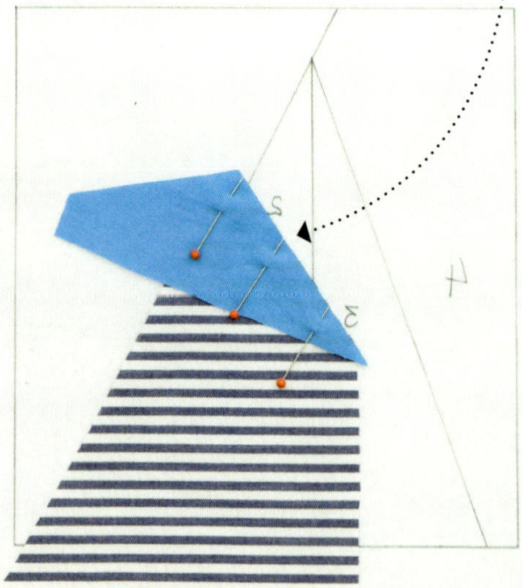

5 Turn the foundation right side up and re-pin carefully to avoid catching any pins in the feed dogs of your sewing machine.

6 Stitch the seam, joining pieces 1 and 2. If your foundation is paper, use a short stitch to make it easier to remove. If necessary, trim the seam allowance to 5mm (¼in).

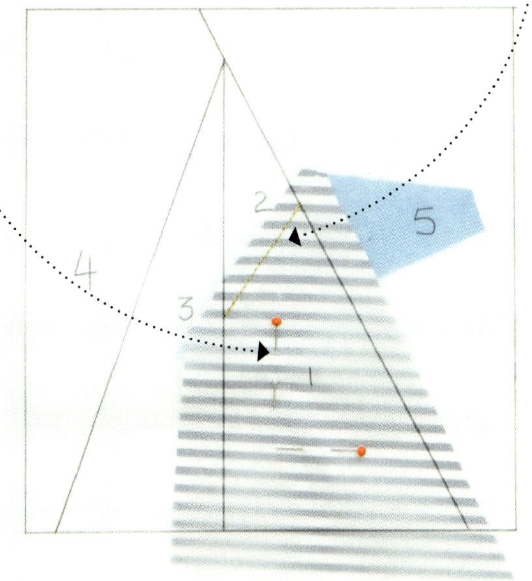

7 Turn the foundation fabric right side up, remove the pins, open the pieces and press.

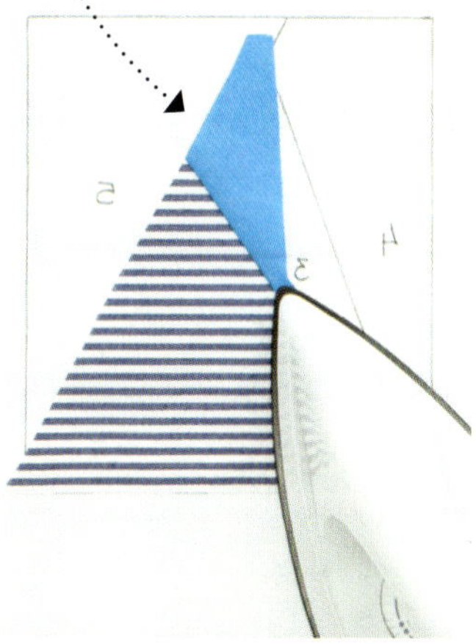

8 Cut piece 3 as before and align it next to piece 2. Pin it on top, then turn the foundation over and stitch as in Steps 3–7.

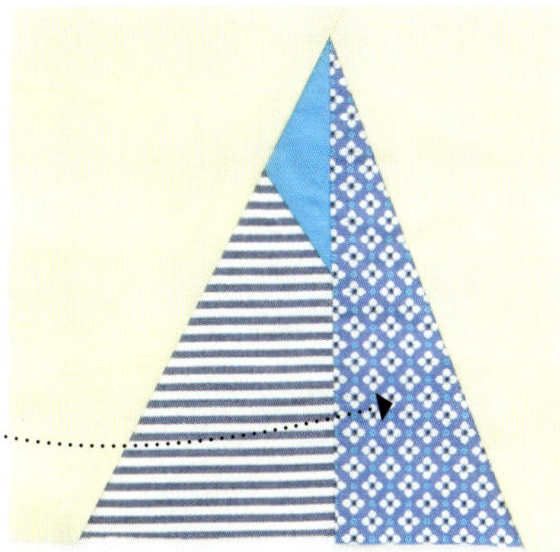

9 When the top section is complete, make the bottom section the same way.

10 Join the sections. Then trim the foundation level with the edges of the patchwork design. If the foundation is removable, carefully tear it away.

Folded patchwork

There are a number of specialized patchwork techniques that involve manipulating fabric by folding it in specific ways before joining pieces together. They can all be used to make quilts, but because they are, by definition, made from more than one layer, they are also good for making household items, such as placemats.

CATHEDRAL WINDOW

1 Decide the size of the finished square (10cm/4in) and multiply the measurement by two (20cm/8in). Add 10mm (½in) seam allowance and cut four squares this size from the background, fabric A.

2 Fold each square diagonally one way and press, then fold along the other diagonal and press firmly to mark the exact centre. Open out. Turn the seam allowance to the wrong side on all sides of all squares. Press firmly.

3 Fold each corner of each square to the centre and press the folds firmly. Make sure that the new corners are sharply defined.

4 Take a small cross stitch across the centre into each point, through all the layers to hold the points in place.

5 Fold each corner to the centre again and press firmly. Take a small cross stitch as before through all the layers to hold the points in place. The square is now half the size of that cut in Step 1.

6 With folded edges together, join the four squares in pairs, oversewing with tiny stitches along the edge. Then join the two pairs to make a square. If you are making a large piece, you can also work in rows that are joined before the windows are added.

7 Cut four contrasting window squares from fabric B. (Each window square should just fit inside a quarter segment of the background square; to work out the size, measure the distance from the centre of one folded square to the outside corner.)

8 Place the first window square over a seam, on the diagonal. Pin in place. If necessary, trim the edges slightly to make it fit.

9 Roll one folded edge in the background square over the raw edge of the first window square.

10 Matching the thread to the background fabric, sew the rolled, slightly curved overlap in place with tiny stitches, catching in the raw edge completely. Do not stitch through the background fabric. Repeat to catch in the other three edges of the window.

11 Repeat Steps 7–9 to fill the other spaces in the square. If you work in rows, add windows after you join rows together.

FOLDED STAR

1 Cut a foundation from calico the finished size plus 5cm (2in) on all sides. Our star has four rounds, or layers, each one in a contrasting fabric. For round 1, the central star, cut four 10cm (4in) squares. For rounds 2, 3 and 4, cut eight 10cm (4in) squares.

2 With wrong sides together, press each square in half. Fold the top corner of the resulting rectangle to the centre of the raw edges and press, then repeat to make a right-angled triangle with the raw edges along the long side.

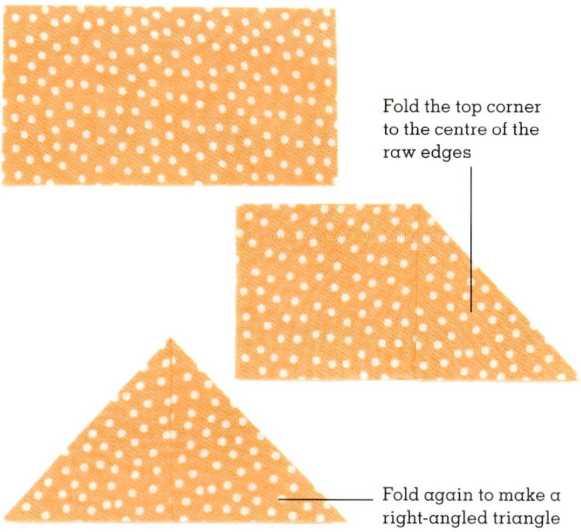

3 For a square foundation, fold the foundation fabric in half horizontally and vertically and press to create guidelines. Fold in half again along the diagonals and press. For a circle, fold the foundation in quarters and press.

4 Place the four folded squares (the right-angled triangles) along the pressed guidelines, so the points meet in the centre, with folded edges on top. Pin or tack in place along the raw edges. Secure each point with a small hidden stitch.

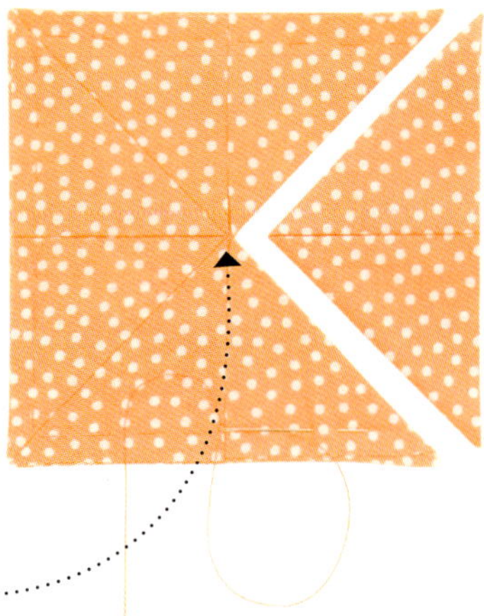

5 Add the next round by placing four triangles in fabric B, made as in Step 2, with the points 10mm (½in) from the centre, with the raw bottom edges aligned with the four sides of the square. Secure as in Step 4.

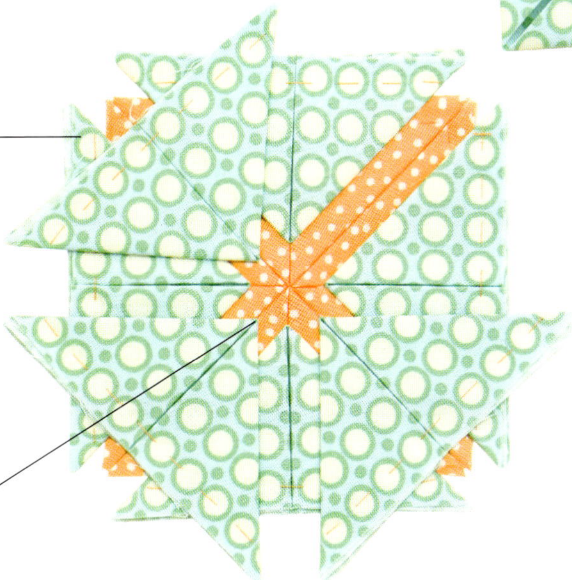

The raw edges of the first 4 triangles are parallel to the sides of the square

The centres of the second 4 triangles align with the diagonal crease line and also point towards the centre of the star

6 Add four more fabric B triangles in the gaps made in Step 5, aligning their raw edges with the diagonal crease lines on the foundation. Secure as before. Measure 10mm (½in) from the points and mark.

7 Add subsequent rounds in the same way. Trim the edges to match the foundation shape. Remove the tacking and trim and finish the edges as desired.

SECRET GARDEN

1 Make a folded square as for Steps 1–3 of Cathedral Window (see pages 108–109). Fold and press the corners, as in Step 4, but do not stitch in place. Cut a window square the size of the finished square.

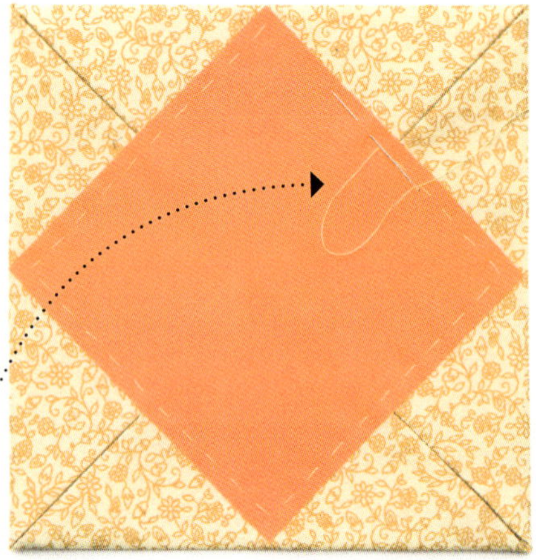

2 Open the pressed corners and place the window square on point within the lines. If necessary, trim the raw edges to fit and anchor with small tacking stitches.

3 Fold the four corners of the background square in to the centre. Press. Anchor each corner in the centre with a small cross, stitching through all layers.

4 Pin 5mm (¼in) in from each corner through all layers to stabilize the square.

5 Turn under one edge of the background square to form a curving "petal" shape. Sew in place, working outwards from the centre and using thread to match the background fabric.

6 Repeat on all eight folded edges of the background square, removing the pins and securing each corner with a double tacking stitch.

Gathered patchwork

Yo-yos, also called Suffolk puffs, are fabric circles that have been gathered to make two layers. They are widely used as decorations in appliqué and can be further embellished. Joined edge to edge, they can be made into tablecloths, cushion covers, or openwork bedcovers. Yo-yo projects are a great way to use up small scraps of fabric.

YO-YOS

1 Cut circles of fabric twice the desired finished size. You can use almost anything circular as a template, from cotton reels to bottles or cups.

2 Knot a length of strong thread, doubled if necessary, and secure it close to the edge on the wrong side of the circle. Turn the raw edge 5mm (¼in) to the wrong side and take small gathering stitches through both layers all around the edge, to make a single hem.

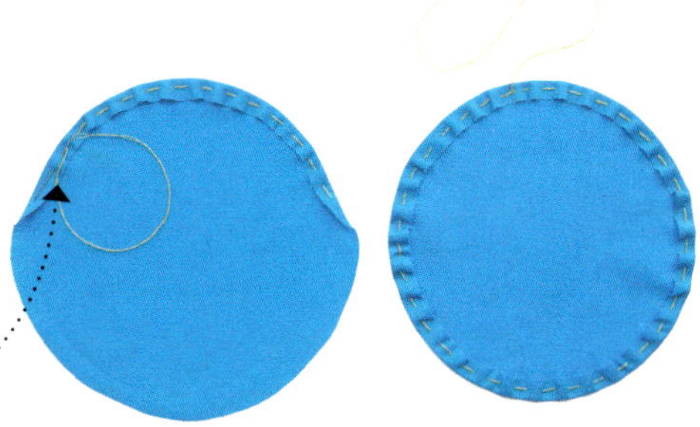

3 Finish next to where you started. Do not remove the needle or cut the thread, but pull the thread gently to gather the circle into a smaller one, with pleats around the centre. The raw edge will disappear inside the circle. Secure the thread with a couple of tacks or backstitches, then knot it. Cut the thread.

4 Flatten the circle by gently fingerpressing the edges. The gathered side is normally the front, but sometimes the back is used instead.

5 To join yo-yos, place them gathered sides facing and oversew the flattened edges for a short distance, taking small, tight stitches. Join yo-yos together until you have a row that is the desired length; join rows together in the same way.

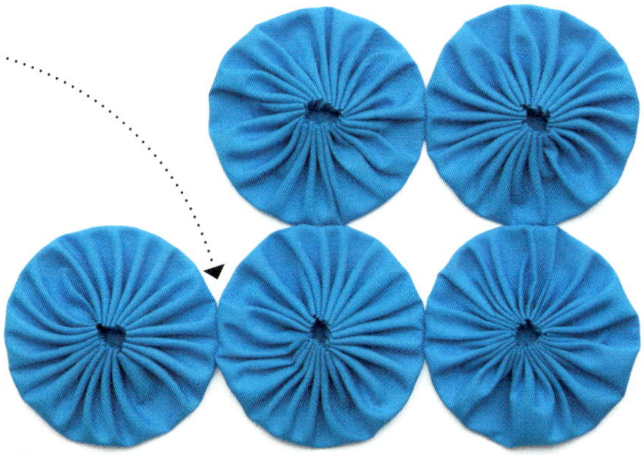

PATCHWORK BLOCK GALLERY

Patchwork block gallery

There are literally hundreds of traditional patchwork patterns and we have space to show only a few – but once you've mastered the basic construction techniques shown in the preceding pages, you will be able to look at a block pattern and work out both the constituent elements and how to piece it together.

Four-patch blocks

The simplest four-patch blocks are made up of just four squares (patches), but those four squares can also be created by piecing together two half-square triangles, or four quarter-square triangles, or various combinations thereof.

Yankee puzzle

Chevron, or Streak of lightning

Broken pinwheel

Flyfoot

Nine-patch blocks

Nine-patch blocks are made of nine units in three rows of three. By adding a third colour to a simple nine-patch of two colours, you can create myriad variations.

Red cross – Three-colour nine-patch

Three-colour Double nine-patch

Rocky road to California

Building blocks

Five- and seven-patch blocks

Five-patch blocks consist of a grid of five units in each direction, or 25 units in total, while seven-patch blocks have no fewer than 49 units (seven in each direction). With so many elements, each one of which can be sub-divided in several ways, there is almost infinite scope for creating different patterns.

Star and cross

Duck and ducklings

Hens and chickens

Dove in a window

Pictorial blocks

Patchwork pictorial blocks tend to be highly stylized, with the individual elements of the design being made up of square and triangle units in varying combinations.

Grape basket

Colonial basket

Basket of scraps

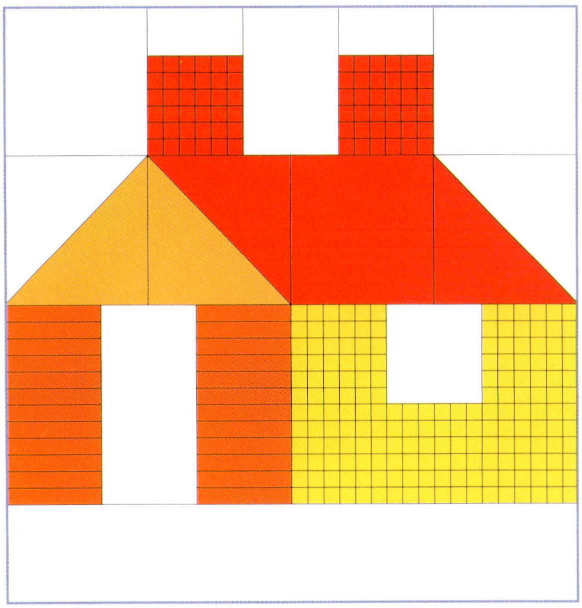

House with fence

Strip-pieced blocks

Strip-pieced patterns can be put together in random colour and fabric combinations or in repeating patterns. If two fabrics are pieced A–B–A and B–A–B, the resulting squares can be alternated to create a Basketweave block. Use more fabrics for a more complex effect. Seminole bands can be angled or set square and are wonderful for creating pieced border strips.

Basketweave

String-pieced divided square

Double-chevron Seminole

Log cabin blocks

There are many variations in Log cabin blocks and settings. Strips of light and dark fabrics can be alternated, placed on adjacent or opposite sides, made of varying widths, or pieced from a combination of smaller squares and rectangles. The centre square can be pieced, turned "on point", or made from a rectangle, triangle, or diamond.

Cabin in the cotton

Thick and thin

Chimneys and cornerstones

Pineapple

Star blocks

There are probably more kinds of star blocks than any other patchwork motif; the construction ranges from simple four-patch stars to extremely complex designs created by cutting 60-degree diamonds in half lengthways or crossways. The basic eight-point star alone, with its 45-degree angles, is the starting point for numerous variations, including the intricate Lone star (see page 124).

Repeating star

Evening star – Morning star

Constellation block

Nine-patch star

Braced star

Card basket

Eisenhower star

Trailing star

Tennessee star

Lone star

Silver and gold

Ozark diamonds

TIPS

- **When marking,** make sure the marker has a sharp point. If you mark with dashes, not a continuous line, the fabric is less apt to shift or stretch.

- **Remember the rule:** measure twice, cut once. And bear in mind that measurements from one brand of ruler or mat are not always exactly the same as another brand. For accuracy, try to use the same ruler and mat, as well as the same machine foot, throughout the piecing process.

- **If you make a sample block to begin,** you can measure your finished blocks against it to ensure accuracy.

- **Whenever possible,** sew a bias edge to a straight edge to minimize stretching.

- **If you need to trim a block to make it smaller,** trim back an equal amount from all sides to keep the design of the block accurate.

Mosaic Blocks

Though many of these can be machined, most are made by piecing together geometric shapes using the "English" paper-piecing method (see pages 102–103). The most familiar block is Grandmother's flower garden.

Grandmother's flower garden

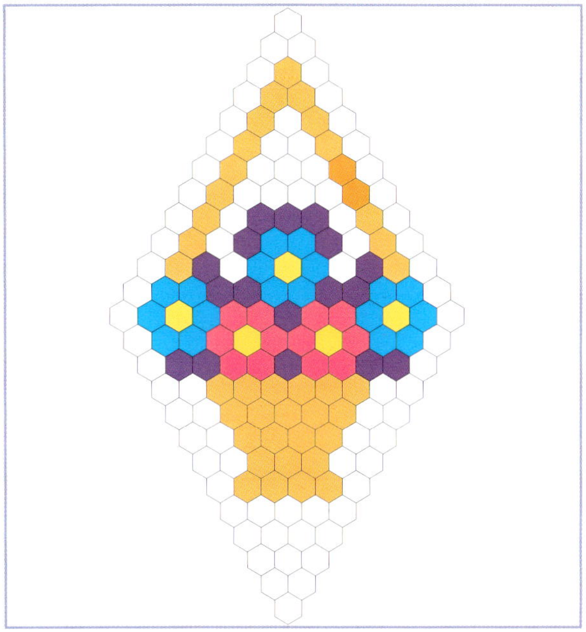

Flower basket

Tumbling hexagons

1000 Pyramids

Curved blocks

Probably the most popular of all traditional curved blocks is the Drunkard's path (see pages 99–101) – a double four-patch. When the orientation or colour values of the four units is altered, a number of complex curving patterns result. Changing the size and shape of the curves also alters the block considerably.

Falling timbers

Wonder of the world

Robbing Peter to pay Paul

Orange peel

Chain links

Drunkard's puzzle

Fan blocks

Fans are based on quarter-circles and can be arranged in a number of different ways. However they are arranged, a curving pattern results. Fan variations such as Dresden plate patterns are full circles and are often appliquéd to a background. The segments can be curved or pointed, or a combination of the two. The centre can be open to allow the background to show through or applied separately for contrast.

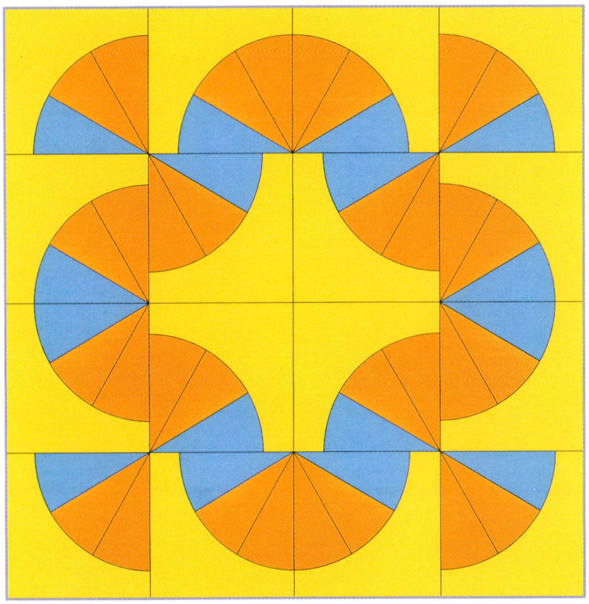

Mohawk trail

Dresden plate

APPLIQUÉ

HAWAIIAN FLOWERS

Squares of simple Hawaiian appliqué blocks (pages 138–139) alternate with plain squares of the same size.

Appliqué

Appliqué is a decorative technique in which shapes are cut from one fabric and applied to a background fabric. It has been used in quiltmaking for centuries and is found on many other items, from clothing to cushions. Hand appliqué is the traditional method but working by machine can be effective.

TIPS FOR APPLIQUÉ

- **Blanket stitch** (opposite) is the most popular decorative stitch for hand appliqué, but many basic embroidery stitches can be used as decoration, including cross stitch, herringbone, chain stitch, and feather stitch.

- **Make sure that** decorative stitches sit tight against the turned-under edge and are in proportion with the size of the applied pieces.

- **In most appliqué** techniques, a seam allowance has to be added to the shapes. The secret is to make an allowance that is wide enough to keep fraying at bay and narrow enough to be undetectable once it has been stitched.

- **Most seam allowances** for appliqué can be cut by eye, following the outline of the shape. Remember that you can trim away any excess as you work, but you can't add it once it has been removed. The ideal seam allowance is around 3mm (⅛in).

- **If you need** only one piece of a particular shape, draw it on tracing paper and cut it out. Pin the tracing-paper shape to the fabric and cut it out, in the same way as a dressmaking pattern.

- **Appliqué designs** usually have a right and a wrong side. When transferring a design, make sure that the right side of the fabric will be the right way around when the shape is cut out and applied.

- **Some methods call** for the outline of a design to be marked on the background fabric. In this case, make sure that the outline will be covered or can be removed when the stitching is completed. Draw the design lightly on the right side of the fabric or tack around the outlines.

- **When tacking**, make sure that any knots are on the wrong side of the background fabric, as this will make it easier to remove the thread later.

- **If the fabric is light** or you have access to a lightbox, you may be able to trace from an original pattern directly onto fabric.

- **When working machine appliqué**, work a practice row or two using the same fabrics as the design to make sure your settings are correct.

Needle-turned Hawaiian appliqué

Stitches for appliqué

Appliquéd shapes can be attached to the background in two ways, either hidden (using blind stitch) or calling attention to themselves as part of the design. Machine appliqué is almost always worked with decorative stitches such as zigzag or satin stitch, or with one of the many stitches programmed into modern sewing machines.

BLIND STITCH OR SLIP STITCH

Bring the needle up on the right side of the background fabric, next to the turned-under edge of the shape being applied. Insert it a few threads into the folded edge. Go back through the background fabric and continue taking tiny stitches 3mm (⅛in) apart around the entire shape.

BLANKET STITCH

Bring the needle up on the right side of the background fabric, next to the turned-under edge of the shape being applied. Take a stitch into the shape 3–5mm (⅛–¼in) to the right and perpendicular to the edge. Bring the needle out at the edge and loop the thread under the point. Pull tight and repeat.

Dealing with peaks and valleys

Both "peaks" (shapes that come to a sharp point) and "valleys" (sharp points between two sides of a shape) can be pointed or curved, and both can be difficult to work neatly. The points of peaks should, of course, be pointed, and you risk creating a lump under the point where you turn the edges under. The seam allowance in valleys needs to be clipped to make the edge neat.

PEAKS

1 Trim the tip of the point a few threads shy of the seam allowance.

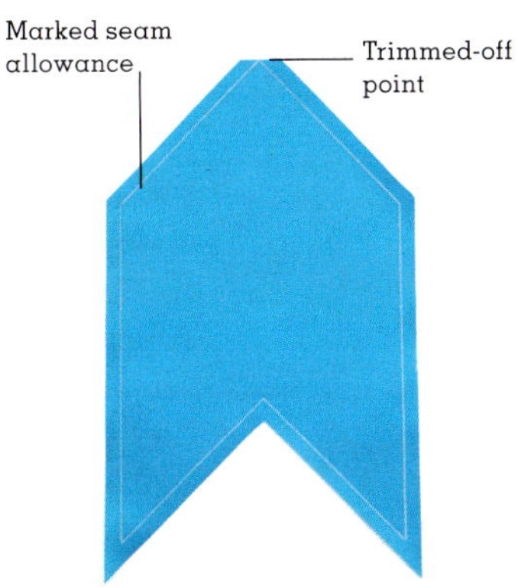

2 Fold the sides of the point along the seam allowance. Ensure that the raw edge at the point is hidden. Press the edges.

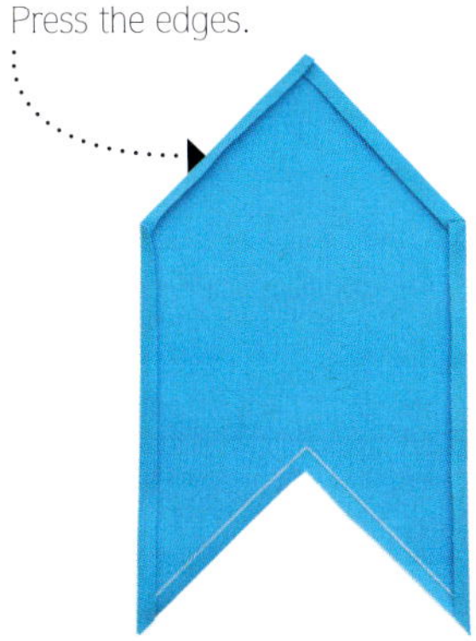

VALLEYS

At the bottom of the valley, clip to within a few threads of the marked seam allowance. Fold the edges to the wrong side. When applying the piece, take several tiny stitches in the valley to secure the cut threads.

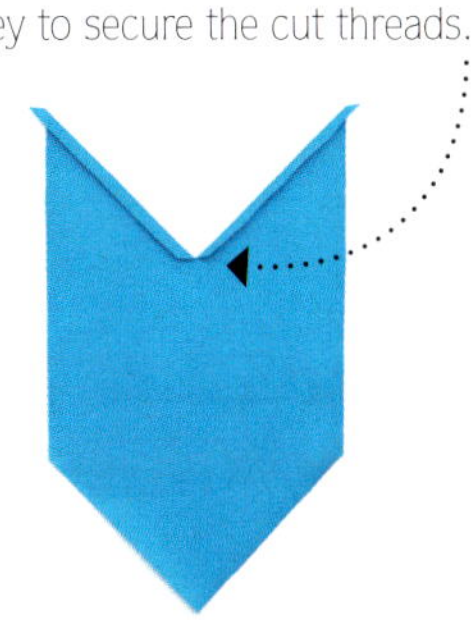

Dealing with curves

Curves can be difficult to keep smooth. The raw edge of an outward (convex) curve is slightly longer than the folded-under edge and can cause bunching under the fold unless the seam allowance is clipped. Inward (concave) curves will sometimes stretch smoothly, but shallow curves may need to be clipped before being stitched.

CONVEX CURVES

1 Cut tiny V-shaped notches into the seam allowance to remove excess fabric.

2 When it is turned under, the curved edge will lie flat.

CONCAVE CURVES

Clip straight cuts into the seam allowance as you work, one section at a time. The clips will form notches that will spread open and allow the edge to lie flat.

Needle-turned appliqué and bias stems

Needle-turned or turned-edge appliqué is the traditional method for applying shapes to a background. This motif also incorporates narrow bias strips that must be applied first.

1 Wash and press the background fabric.

2 Make templates for the appliqué shapes. Transfer the shapes to the right side of the appliqué fabric and cut them out, adding a scant 5mm (¼in) seam allowance all around.

3 Cut the bias stems three times the finished width. Here they are 15mm (¾in) wide and cut on the true bias. With wrong sides together, fold each strip in half and machine stitch a seam 5mm (¼in) from the folded edge. Do not press. Trim the raw edge close to the seam.

4 Lay the stitched strip folded edge down and press flat, pressing the seam open. This makes a strip with the seam running down the centre of the back.

5 Lay the stems in position on the background fabric and pin in place. Blind stitch along first one edge, then the other, with the seam hidden under the stitched strip.

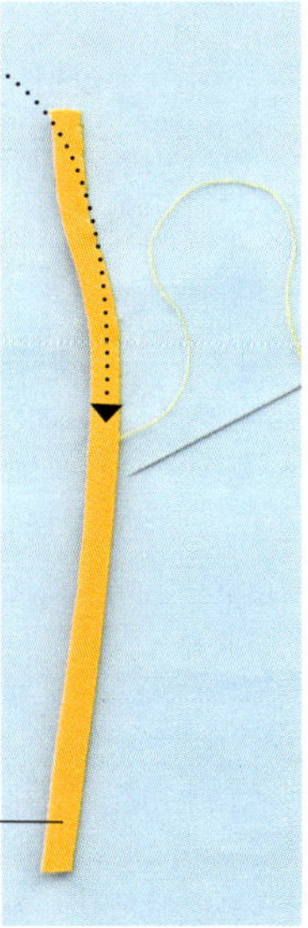

6 Position the shapes on the background fabric, covering the raw end of the stem. Tack in place, working 5mm (¼in) inside the marked line.

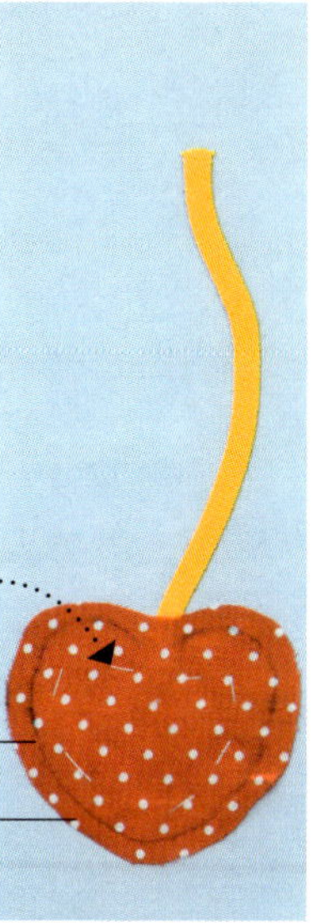

7 With the needle point, turn under a small section of the seam allowance until the raw edge touches the tacked line. Blind stitch in place.

8 Repeat, taking small stitches along the edge until the piece is stitched. Fasten off on the back. Add any remaining pieces. Remove the tacking and press the piece from the wrong side.

Freezer-paper appliqué

Freezer paper is a stiff, white paper coated on one side with a film that can be ironed on fabric and easily removed without leaving a residue. The paper side is ideal for drawing on patterns. It can be found in craft shops, at supermarkets, and online. Seam allowances can be pressed over the edge to the wrong side to give a hard crease that makes it easy to sew shapes in place accurately.

1 Trace the templates in reverse on the paper side of the freezer paper and cut out. Iron the paper pieces to the wrong side of the fabric.

2 Cut out the fabric shapes, leaving a 5mm (¼in) seam allowance all around. Clip or notch any corners and difficult curves up to the paper. Press the seam allowance to the wrong side, using the edge of the freezer paper as a guide.

3 Remove the paper shapes by peeling them off gently. Make sure that the raw edges lie flat on the wrong side.

4 Decide on the order in which to work, making sure that any underlapping pieces are covered. Pin or tack the first piece in place, then blind stitch it to the background.

5 Add the remaining pieces in order, one at a time. If you pin the pieces in place, remove the pins as you work. If you tack them in place, remove all the tacking stitches when the work is complete.

Hawaiian appliqué

Hawaiian appliqué originated in Hawaii when women native to the islands were taught to sew by early missionaries. The patterns are usually square and cut as eight-sided motifs from a single piece of folded fabric. The designs are traditionally based on flora indigenous to the Pacific outpost, but six-sided snowflake motifs can also be used. Finished pieces are usually echo quilted (see page 172).

1 Cut a piece of paper to the size of the finished block. Fold the paper in half twice, then along the diagonal once to make a triangle. Draw on the triangle or cut freestyle through all the layers, with the main part of the design on the folded edge.

2 Cut out one triangular section and transfer it to card to use as a template in Step 3.

3 Cut a square of freezer paper the same size as the original paper pattern. Fold it in half twice, paper side out, then fold it once along the diagonal to make a triangle. This matches the template. Transfer the template outline to the paper, making sure that the fold of the paper matches the fold on the template.

4 Staple the layers together inside the design lines. Cut out along the marked line.

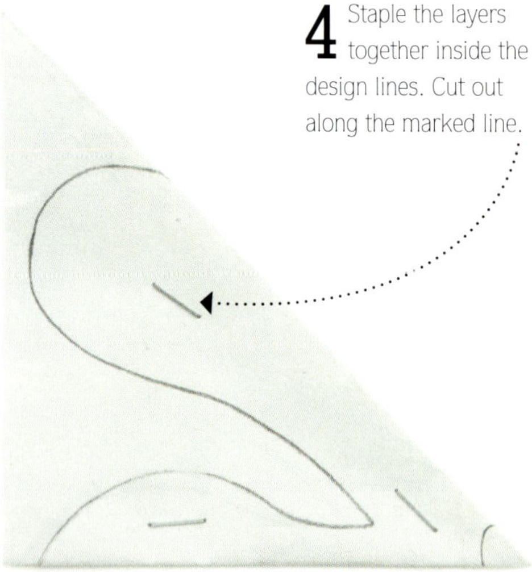

5 Remove the staples carefully and open out the paper pattern.

6 Cut a square of the appliqué fabric and one of the background fabric, both 5cm (2in) larger than the pattern square. Fold both in half twice to find the centre and position them, wrong side of the appliqué fabric to right side of the background.

7 Centre the freezer-paper pattern on the right side of the appliqué fabric, sticky side down, and iron it in position.

8 Tack the layers together 5mm (¼in) from the inside edge of the paper pattern.

9 Work a small section at a time by cutting away the appliqué (top) fabric along the edge of the pattern, leaving a 5mm (¼in) seam allowance outside the pattern. Turn the seam allowance under so that it's level with the edge of the pattern and blind stitch the fabric to the background.

10 Continue cutting and stitching until the entire pattern has been applied to the background (see page 134 for dealing with curves). Remove the tacking and peel the pattern away.

Raw-edge appliqué

Non-woven fabrics, such as felt and felted wool, that won't fray can be used effectively in decorative appliqué, but remember that they cannot be laundered. No seam allowances are needed.

1 Trace your entire pattern onto the background fabric. Then trace the pattern pieces separately on tracing paper. Cut out each paper pattern and pin to the fabrics.

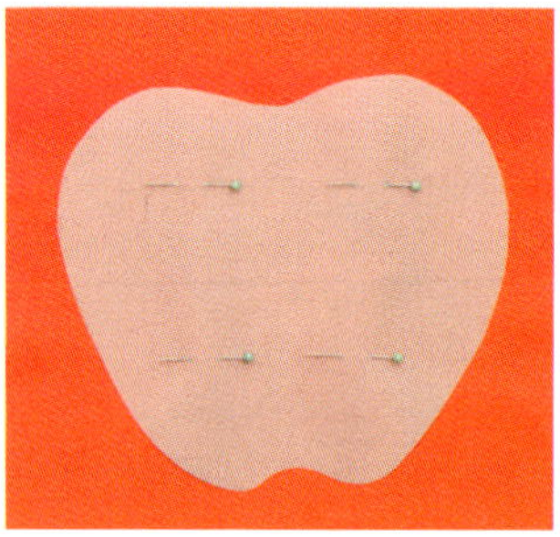

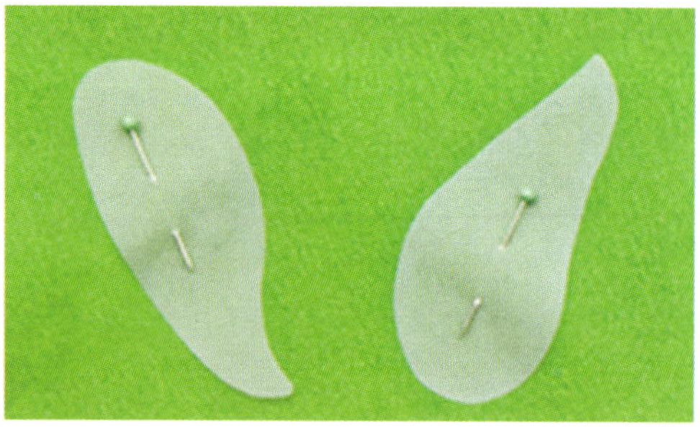

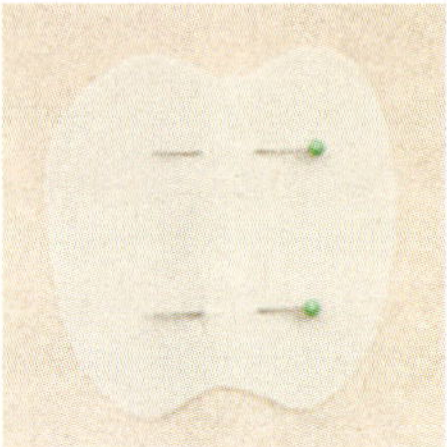

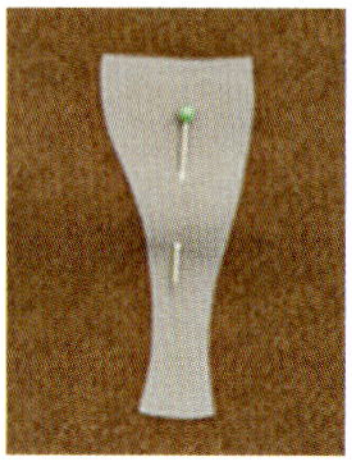

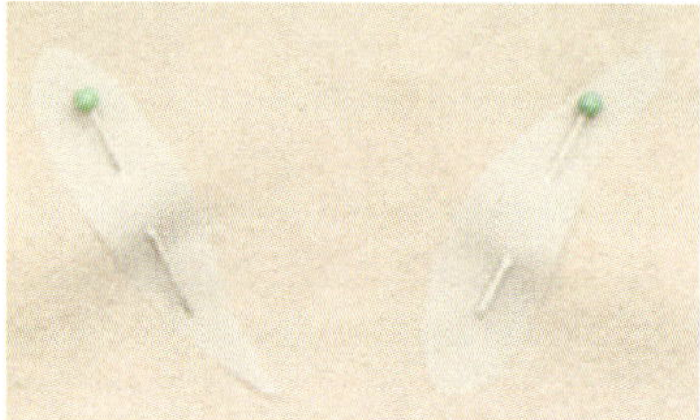

2 Cut out the appliqué pieces (without a seam allowance). Pin the first piece to the background and stitch in place, using a decorative stitch (see page 132).

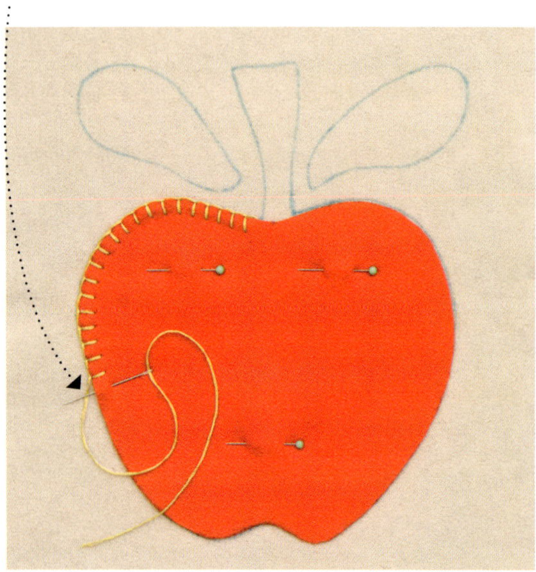

3 Add pieces in order. Remove all the pins and press from the wrong side.

Reverse hand appliqué

This technique uses two or more layers of fabric, cutting away the top layers to reveal the fabric beneath. The raw edges are turned under to finish the shape. Floral, pictorial, and geometric designs work well.

1 Choose two or three fabrics and tack them together, right-sides up, around the outside edge.

2 Trace the motif onto the non-shiny side of freezer paper and cut it out. Iron it to the centre of the fabric sandwich.

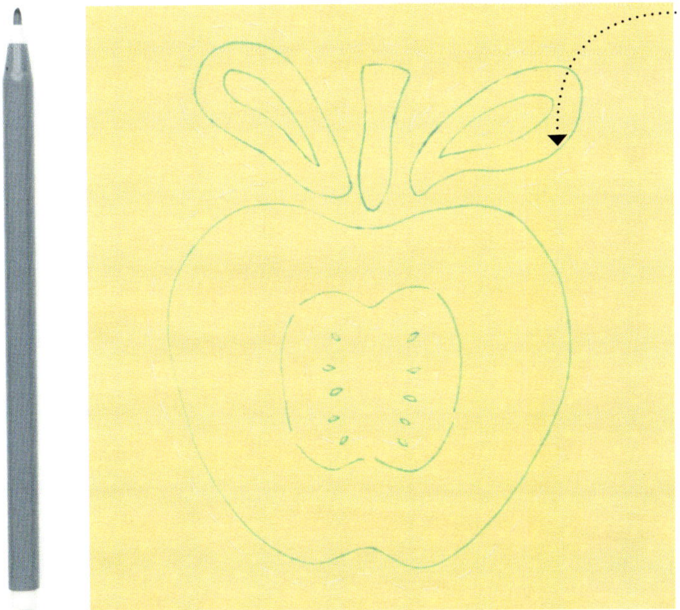

3 Using a removable marker, draw around the freezer-paper shape on the top fabric. Remove the template. Tack around the outline 10mm (½in) from the outside edge.

4 Using small sharp scissors, begin cutting away the shape 5mm (¼in) inside the marked line, being careful to cut only the top layer of fabric. Cut one section at a time, clipping or cutting small notches into any curves.

5 Turn under the seam allowance along the marked line. Using thread to match the top fabric, slip stitch the edge in place.

6 Mark the areas to be cut out from the second layer. Tack as in Step 3. Cut away the second layer, which will be smaller than the top layer. Always cut inside the marked line.

7 Using thread to match the second layer of fabric, slip stitch as in Step 5.

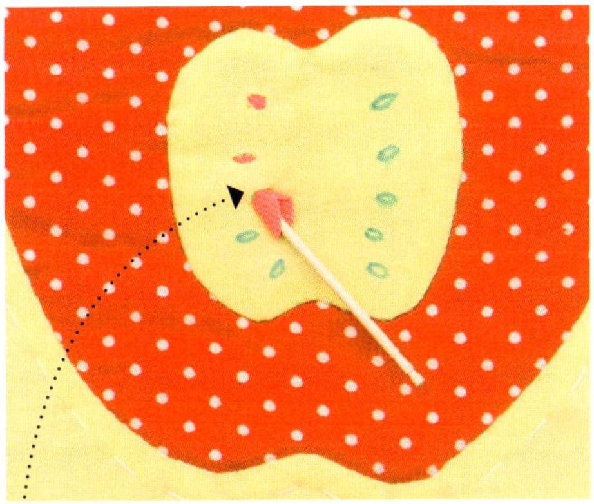

8 To add small areas of different colours under the second layer, cut a piece of fabric slightly larger than the area to be filled. Insert it into the cut-out area, using a toothpick or the tip of your needle. Turn under the edge on the second fabric and slip stitch. Remove all tacking stitches.

Finished piece

Broderie perse

Persian embroidery, or broderie perse, is a technique in which motifs are cut from one printed fabric and applied to a different background. Several motifs, not necessarily from the same fabric, can be layered and rearranged to create a new design.

1 Cut out the motif with a generous 5mm (¼in) seam allowance. Clip any curves inside the seam allowance. If there are areas that are too small to cut away, leave the background fabric in place.

2 Pin the motif in position on the background and tack it 10mm (½in) inside the outline. For narrow areas such as stems, tack along the centre. Trim outside seam allowances to reduce bulk wherever possible.

3 Using the needle tip, turn the seam allowance under and blind stitch the motif to the background, using thread to match the motif, or use a decorative stitch and contrasting thread as shown.

4 This appliqué technique allows you to make a small piece of expensive printed fabric go a long way, as individual motifs can be applied over a larger and less costly background fabric.

Machine appliqué general techniques

Machine appliqué is quick and will stand many washes, especially if you use a tightly woven fabric and finish the edges with zigzag or satin stitch. Before you begin, it's a good idea to practise on scraps of your material. Try out different stitch widths and lengths to see what works best.

OUTER CORNERS

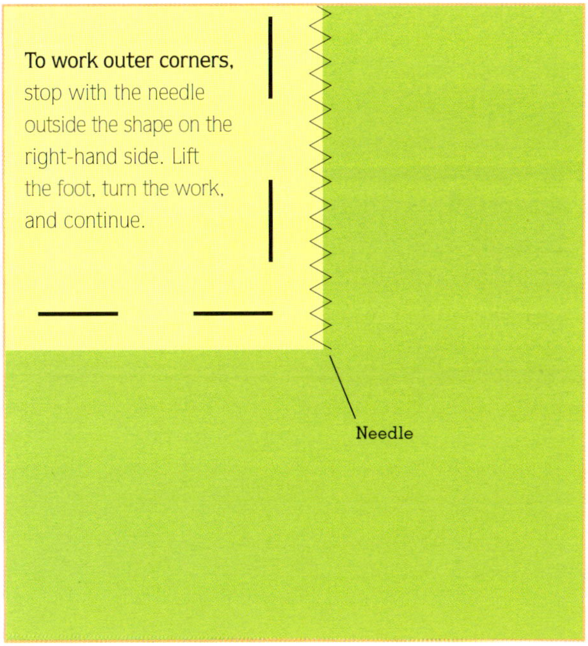

To work outer corners, stop with the needle outside the shape on the right-hand side. Lift the foot, turn the work, and continue.

INNER CORNERS

To work inner corners, stop with the needle inside the shape on the left-hand side. Lift the foot, turn the work, and continue.

CONVEX CURVES

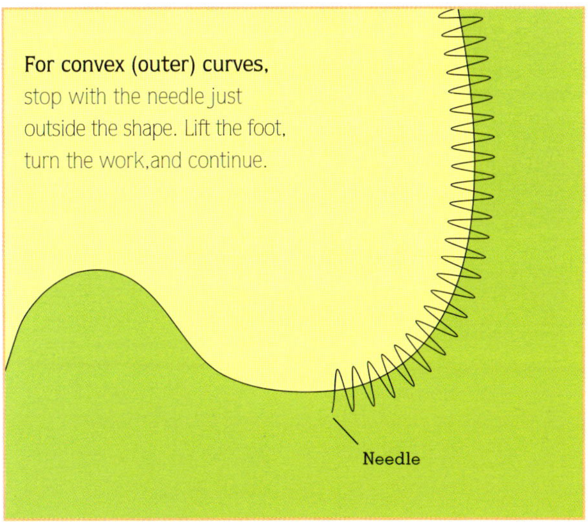

For convex (outer) curves, stop with the needle just outside the shape. Lift the foot, turn the work,and continue.

CONCAVE CURVES

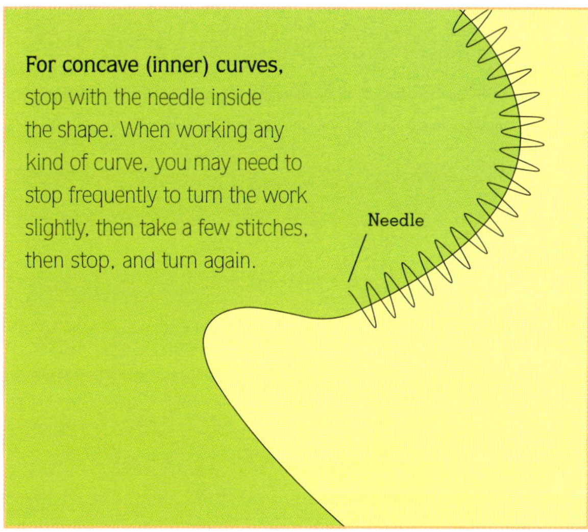

For concave (inner) curves, stop with the needle inside the shape. When working any kind of curve, you may need to stop frequently to turn the work slightly, then take a few stitches, then stop, and turn again.

Stitch-and-cut appliqué

In this quick machine method, the motif is marked on the appliqué fabric and then sewn along the marked line before being cut out along the stitching line. The edges can then be finished by machine or by hand.

1 Make templates for the shapes. Draw around each shape on the right side of the fabric and add a 10mm (½in) seam allowance all around. Cut out the fabric shapes.

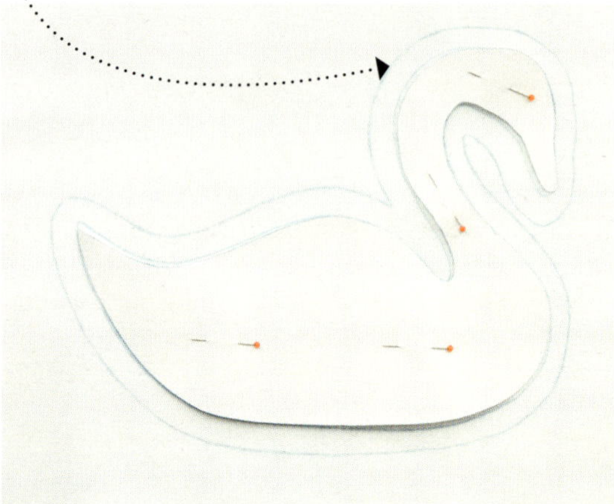

2 Pin the shapes to the background fabric, making sure that the pins will not get caught in the machine foot, and use a straight stitch to sew along the marked line. (Here, we've used a contrasting colour of thread for clarity.)

3 Using small, sharp scissors, trim away the seam allowance, cutting as close to the stitching line as possible without cutting the stitched thread.

4 Zigzag or satin stitch along the trimmed edge to finish the raw edge and hide the straight stitching.

Fused appliqué

Fusible bonding web is a non-woven fabric impregnated with glue that is activated by heat. One side is anchored to paper on which shapes can be drawn. When ironed to the wrong side of a shape and then to the background fabric, it forms a firm bond that is almost impossible to remove. It is most suitable for machine appliqué, because it creates a stiffness that is difficult to sew by hand.

1 Transfer the shapes, in reverse, to the paper side of the web and cut them out roughly. If you group pieces that are to be cut from the same fabric close together, you can cut the whole group in one go, rather than cutting each individual shape separately.

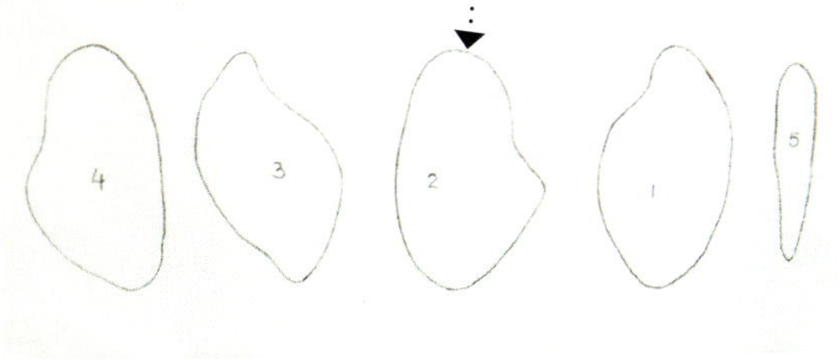

2 Following the manufacturer's instructions, place the rough, non-paper side on the wrong side of the fabric and press in place.

3 Cut out the shapes, cutting carefully along the drawn line, and peel off the backing papers. Position the shapes on the background fabric and iron in place.

4 Finish by stitching around the edges of each appliquéd piece with machine zigzag or satin stitch.

Stained-glass appliqué

Stained-glass appliqué gets its name from the bias strips that separate the elements in the design, which resemble leading in church windows. You can make bias strips yourself (see pages 180–181) or purchase bias strips with fusible bonding web on the back, which can be ironed in place to secure the strip while you stitch it in place. If your design features straight lines, you can use strips cut on the straight grain.

1 Transfer the pattern onto the background fabric. If the design is complicated, number the shapes on the background.

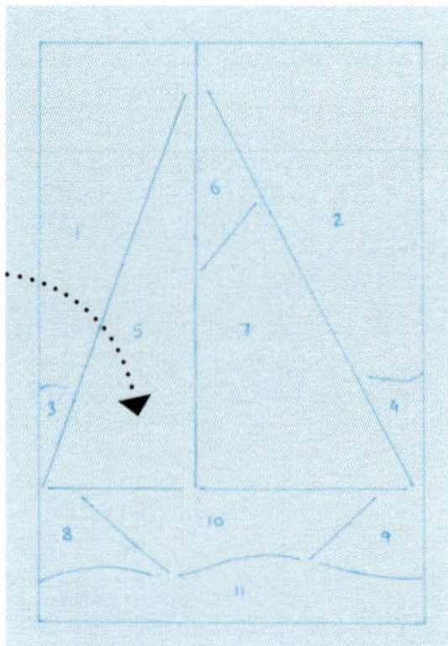

2 Trace the appliqué pieces onto lightweight fusible bonding web, cut them out, and iron them to the wrong side of the appliqué fabrics. If you have numbered the background fabric, do the same with the appliqué pieces.

3 Cut out the appliqué shapes without adding any seam allowances. Iron them in place on the background.

4 Butt each piece up tightly against its neighbour, so that it will be easier to catch the raw edges under the bias strips.

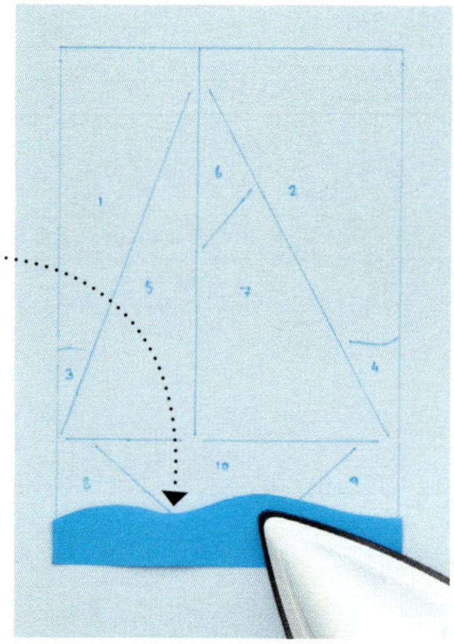

5 Plan the order in which you apply the bias strips so that you can cover any raw ends with another strip. Iron on the strips and stitch them in place, using a machine blindstitch.

6 The bias strips cover the raw edges of the pieces over which they are placed.

SETTING, SASHING, AND BORDERS

BORDER PATROL

A simple design of alternating striped and plain squares has been bordered (pages 158–161) with a plain blue band that is the same width as the individual patches.

Setting

The way quilt blocks are arranged in a finished top is called the set, or setting. The following section can give only an outline of the virtually infinite possibilities for putting blocks together. The way to work out the best setting for a quilt is to lay the blocks out and view them from a distance.

Quilt layouts

Many quilt blocks, even fairly simple ones, can create interesting secondary patterns when they are joined, and rotating or reversing blocks makes a quilt look entirely different.

STRAIGHT SETS

The simplest sets are rows of repeating blocks stitched together edge to edge, referred to as "straight set".

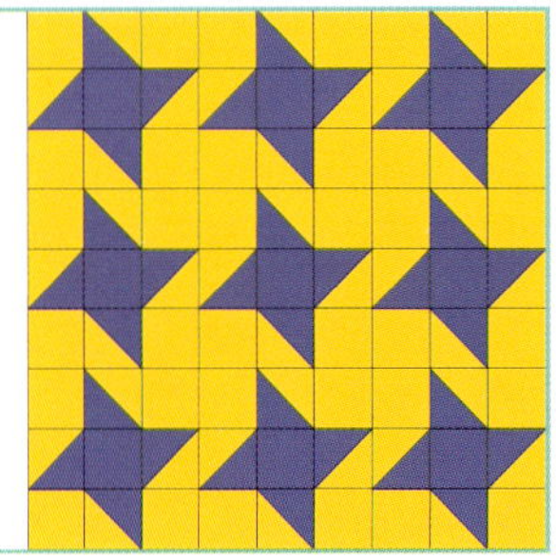

ALTERNATING PIECED AND PLAIN

Alternating a pieced block with a plain one means fewer blocks to put together and allows large, open areas for quilting in the plain squares.

ON POINT: SOLID SET

Blocks can be set "on point" (turned on the diagonal), with setting triangles around the edges.

ON POINT: ALTERNATING PIECED AND PLAIN BLOCKS

This setting needs triangles added to each corner and along each side to fill the edges.

ROTATING BLOCKS

This setting creates new patterns once several blocks are set, particularly with asymmetrical patterns.

LOG CABIN

There are so many possible sets for Log cabin designs that each version has its own name. These examples all have the same number of identical blocks. In each case, the way each row is turned determines the final effect.

Light and dark

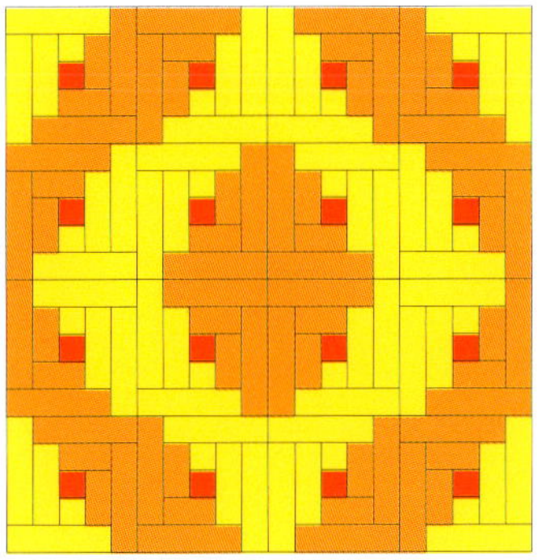

Barn raising

Straight furrow

FRAME SETTINGS

Also known as medallion settings, these have a central block, sometimes an elaborate appliqué, surrounded by several borders of various widths, some pieced, some plain. The centre can be set square or on point as here.

STRIPPY SET

When blocks are arranged vertically, a strippy set results. The first strippy quilts were usually simple strips of fabric joined to make the width of a quilt, but beautiful strippy quilts can be made from pieced blocks.

Sashing

Sashing is comprised of strips of fabric placed between blocks to frame them. Sampler quilts and star blocks are usually sashed to give each block the chance to shine. The space created by the sashing is flexible: try out various widths and colours before you cut the strips. Squares, plain or pieced, can be placed at the corners of each block within sashing strips to delineate the pattern further or continue a chained effect.

Each block in this piece is framed by straight-set simple sashing.

Straight-set simple continuous sashing

Adding a square in each corner between the blocks can create additional pattern. The corner squares can also be pieced; simple pinwheel, four-patch, and nine-patch designs work well.

Straight set with corner square sashing

Blocks can be assembled in vertical or horizontal rows with sashing in only one direction.

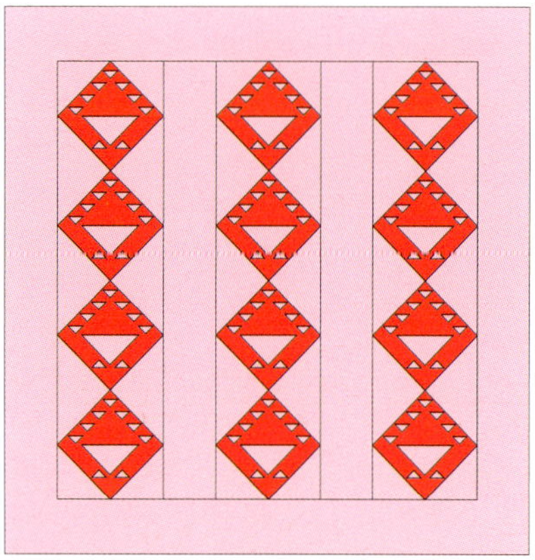

Vertical set with sashing

Blocks set on point can be sashed and assembled in strips with side triangles added to make a chevron sash.

Diagonal set (on point) with sashing

SIMPLE CONTINUOUS SASHING

1 Cut strips to the desired width plus 10mm (½in) seam allowance and the same length as the measurement of one side of the blocks. With right sides together, taking a 5mm (¼in) seam allowance, alternate strips and blocks to make a vertical row. Press seam allowances towards the sashing.

2 Cut strips to the desired width plus 10mm (½in) seam allowance and the same length as the joined row of blocks.

3 With right sides together, taking a 5mm (¼in) seam allowance, sew a strip along the top and bottom of the row of blocks. Press seam allowance towards the sashing.

4 Continue alternating rows of sashing strips and blocks until the quilt top is the required size.

SASHING WITH CORNER SQUARES

1 Repeat Step 1 of Simple continuous sashing (above) to make rows of blocks.

2 Cut strips the same length as the width of the block, and squares the same width as the strips. With right sides together, taking a 5mm (¼in) seam allowance, alternate squares and strips to make a long strip.

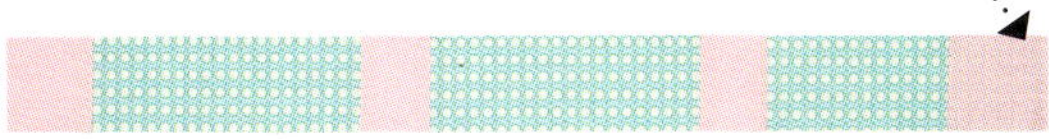

3 With right sides together, taking a 5mm (¼in) seam allowance, machine stitch one long strip along the top and bottom edges of the first row of blocks. Ensure that the corners of the blocks and the corner squares match up. Continue alternating rows of sashing strips and blocks until the quilt is the required size.

Borders

The outside edges of most quilts are finished with strips called the border, which frame the piece and protect the edges. They can be single or multiple, wide or narrow, pieced or plain. To help choose a size, try dividing the block measurement in half or three-quarters. If possible, strips should be cut along the lengthways grain, selvedges removed, in one long piece. Never cut borders on the bias.

Straight borders

Pieced inner border with straight outer border

Mitred borders

Multiple borders with corner squares

JOINING STRIPS TO MAKE A BORDER

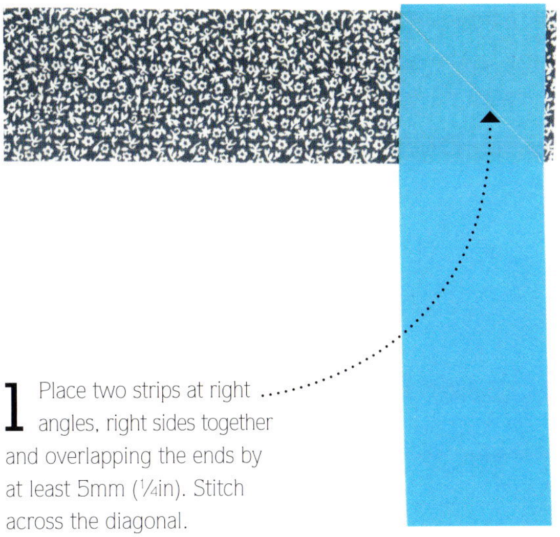

1 Place two strips at right angles, right sides together and overlapping the ends by at least 5mm (¼in). Stitch across the diagonal.

2 Trim the seam to 5mm (¼in) and trim the sides level. Press seam to one side.

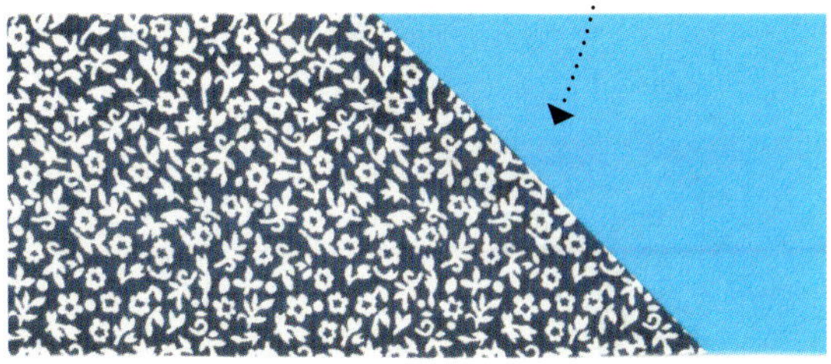

STRAIGHT BORDERS

1 Cut or piece two border strips the same length as the sides of the quilt, plus 10mm (½in) seam allowances. Mark the centre of the strips and the sides of the quilt, and pin right sides together. Join, taking a 5mm (¼in) seam allowance. Press seams towards border strips.

2 Measure the top and bottom of the quilt plus borders and cut two strips to that length. Mark the centre of the strips and top and bottom of the quilt, as in Step 1, and pin right sides together. Join, taking a 5mm (¼in) seam allowance. Press seams towards the border strips. Repeat Steps 1 and 2 to add additional borders.

3 The quilt top is now completed and ready to be quilted (see pages 162–177).

CORNER SQUARES ON A STRAIGHT BORDER

1 Follow Step 1 of straight borders (see page 159) to add the two side borders. Press seams towards the borders.

2 Cut two strips the same length as the top and bottom of the quilt without the side borders, plus a 10mm (½in) seam allowance.

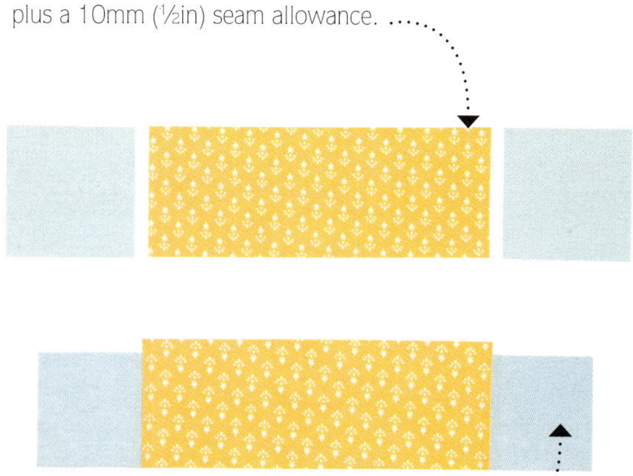

3 Cut four corner squares the same size as the width of the border strips. Add a square to each end of the strips. Press the seams towards the centre.

4 Add the pieced strips to the top and bottom of the quilt. Press the seams towards the border strips.

5 The quilt top is now completed and ready to be quilted (see pages 162–177).

MITRED BORDERS

1 Cut border strips to the desired width, plus 10mm (½in) seam allowance, and 10cm (4in) longer than the sides of the quilt.

2 Place a pin as a marker in the centre of the strips and the top and bottom of the quilt. Pin them right sides together. Place a pin as a marker 5mm (¼in) from each corner.

3 Join the border strips to all sides of the quilt, taking a 5mm (¼in) seam allowance. Do not stitch into adjoining border strips. Press the seams towards the borders.

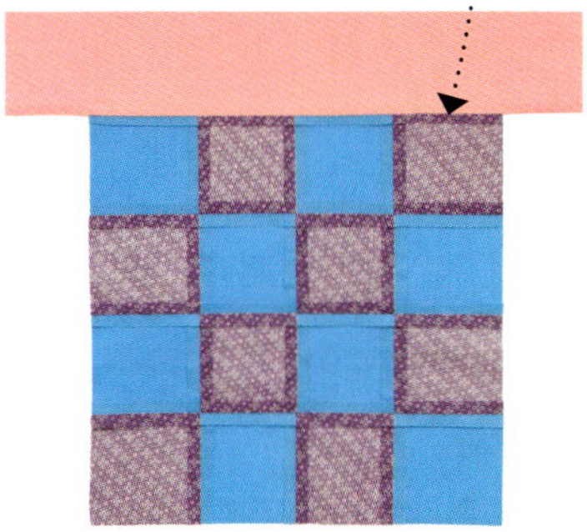

4 Place the quilt right side up on a flat surface and fold under each end of each strip to the wrong side, at a 45-degree angle. Pin the folds in place from the right side and make sure the angle is correct. Remove the pins and press the folds.

5 Working from the wrong side, re-pin the mitre along the pressed fold. Tack if desired. Stitch from the quilt edge to the outside corner. Trim the seam allowance and press it open. Repeat to mitre all corners.

MULTIPLE MITRED BORDERS

If you are using multiple borders, join them together and attach to the quilt top in one go, then mitre as above, making sure you match the seams for each border in the mitre.

QUILTING

QUILTED PLATES

This pattern, called Dresden Plate, has many seams and lends itself to being quilted "in the ditch" (page 177) either by machine or by hand.

Quilting

Quilting holds the layers of a quilt together, gives a quilt its texture, and should add to the overall beauty of the piece. Quilting motifs range from geometric grids and simple heart shapes to elaborate scrolls. Some appliqué motifs look best if they are outlined or echoed by quilting.

Transferring designs

Once the quilt top is finished, you need to transfer the quilting pattern onto it. Use equipment that can be removed, such as water- or air-soluble pens or light pencil marks, to mark the pattern. Tailor's chalk applied lightly can usually be removed. Slivers of soap can make effective and washable marks on dark fabrics. Dressmaker's carbon paper is indelible and not recommended.

MASKING TAPE

1 After the quilt has been layered with wadding and backing, apply 5mm (¼in) masking tape in lines as a guide. This method only works for quilting designs in straight lines.

2 Stitch along the edge of the tape by hand or machine, then remove the tape as soon as possible. When the rows are complete, repeat in the other direction.

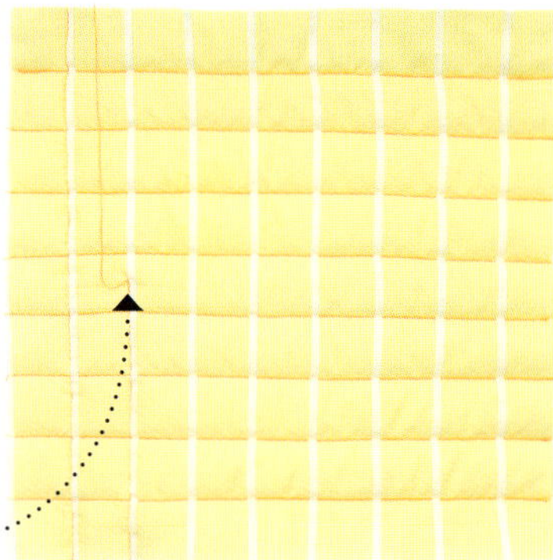

TRACING

If your project is small and light in colour, you can trace the pattern directly on the fabric. Place the quilt top over the pattern on a lightbox or a glass-top table with a table lamp underneath. Alternatively, tape it to a clean window. Trace the design lightly onto the fabric.

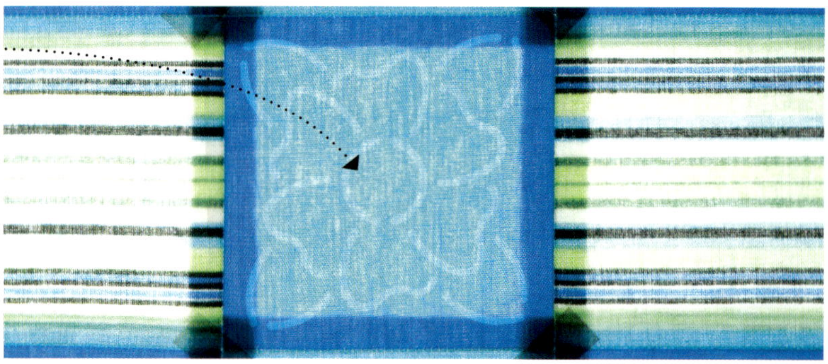

TRACE AND TACK

1 Use on fabrics that are hard to mark. Transfer the pattern to the quilt top before you layer it. Transfer the design to tissue paper and pin in place. With the knot on top, sew along the pattern lines with a small running stitch. Secure with a double backstitch.

2 Pull the paper away gently without disturbing the tacking. If necessary, score the marked lines with a pin to break the paper.

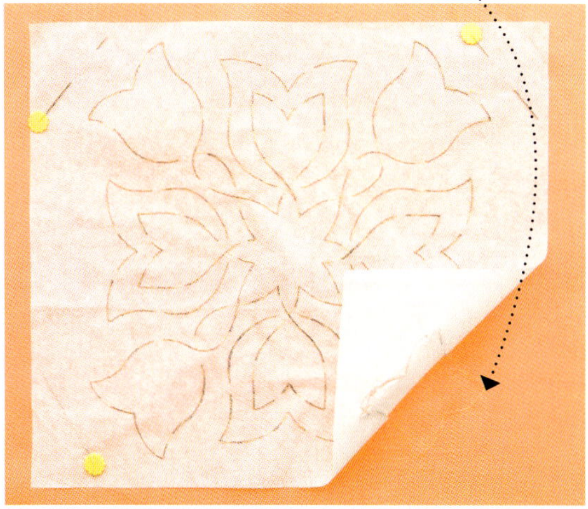

TEMPLATES OR STENCILS

1 Mark the design on the finished top before you layer it. Place the pattern on the quilt top and secure it with masking tape or weights. Draw around a template or in the channels of a stencil with a very sharp pencil. Keep the line as light as possible.

2 Move the pattern as necessary and repeat until the entire top has been marked.

Assembling the quilt layers

Once you have marked the quilting pattern on the quilt top, it is time to assemble the quilt "sandwich", which is the layers of top, wadding, and backing that make up the quilt. If the wadding has been folded, open it out flat and leave it for several hours to relax the wrinkles.

1 Trim the wadding and backing 7.5–10cm (3–4in) larger all around than the finished top. Lay the backing wrong side up on the work surface and smooth it flat. Secure it to the surface with masking tape.

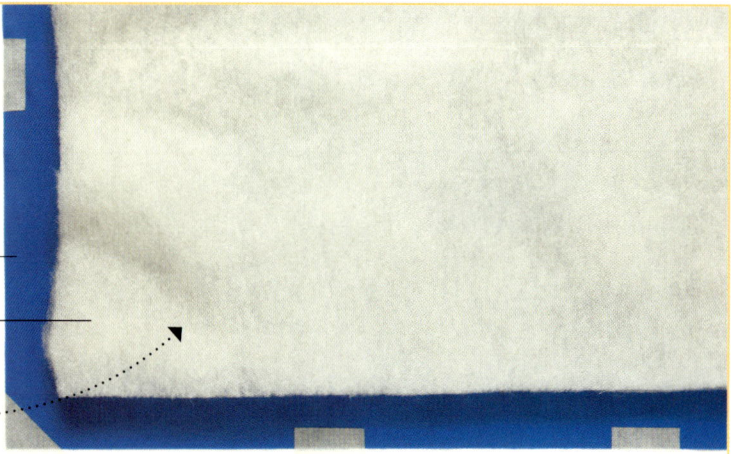

2 Centre the wadding on the backing, and smooth it out.

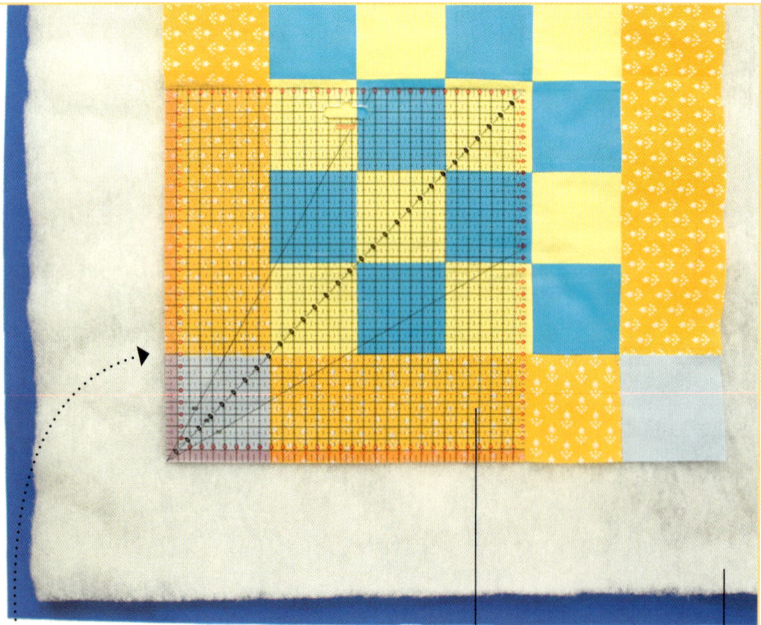

3 Position the quilt top right side up, centring it on the wadding. Use a ruler to check that the top is squared up. Using large quilter's straight pins, temporarily pin along each squared edge as you work.

4 Working from the centre out diagonally, horizontally, and vertically, tack or safety pin the layers together. Remove the pins along the edge as you reach them. Keep smoothing the layers. Take tacking stitches 5cm (2in) long – first vertically and horizontally, then diagonally. If pinning, follow the same pattern and insert the pins at 7.5–10cm (3–4in) intervals.

Bagging out

Sometimes you may want to finish the edges of the quilt before you quilt it. The technique works well on smaller projects, such as baby quilts. Cut the wadding and backing slightly larger than the quilt top.

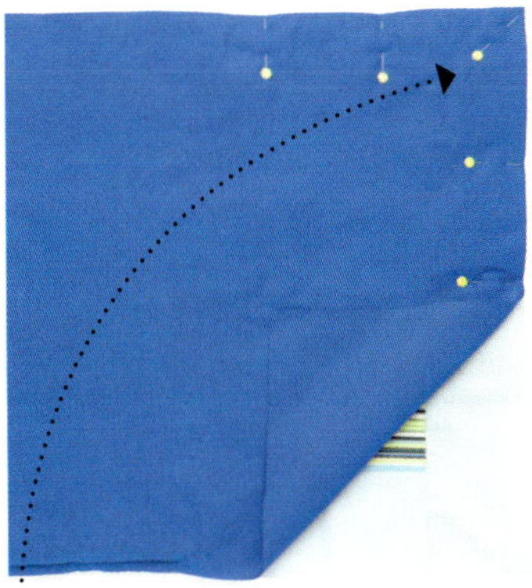

1 Centre the quilt top right-side up on the wadding. Centre the backing on the quilt top, right-side down. Pin or tack the layers together around the edge.

2 Start machine stitching at the bottom edge, several centimetres (about an inch) from the corner, taking a 5mm (¼in) seam. Secure with backstitching.

3 At the corners, stop 5mm (¼in) from the edge with the needle down. Raise the presser foot. Pivot the fabric, lower the presser foot and continue sewing. On the fourth side leave an opening of 12–25cm (5–10in). Secure with backstitching.

4 Clip the corners to reduce bulk. If necessary, trim and grade the seams, then turn right-side out through the opening.

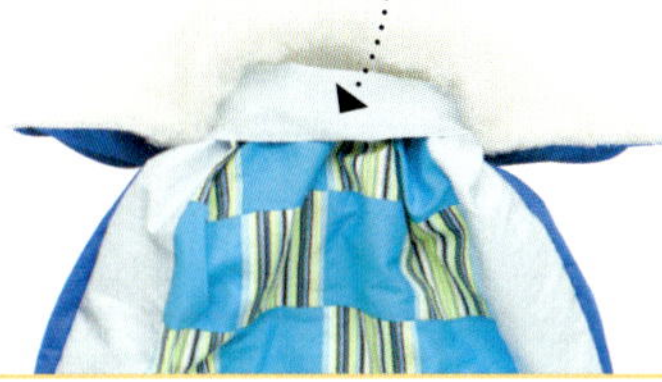

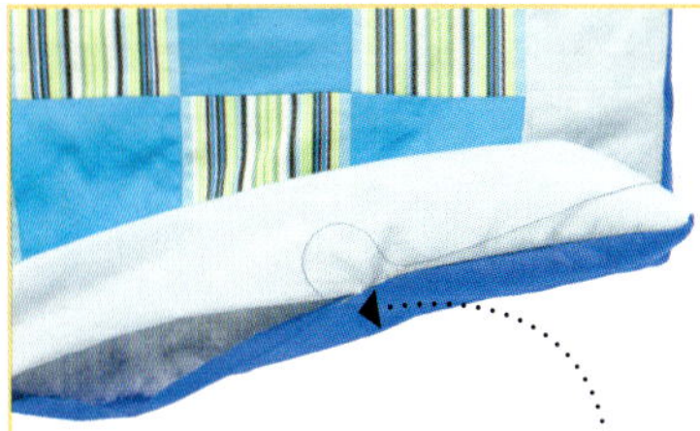

5 Level the edges on the inside. Pin or press lightly. Blind stitch the opening closed.

Making a bigger backing

Most bed quilts are wider than most fabrics, so it is often necessary to piece the backing. There are several ways to do this, but you should avoid having a seam down the vertical centre of the quilt.

1 Cut two full widths of fabric of the required length. Set one aside, and cut the other in half lengthways. Trim off all selvedges.

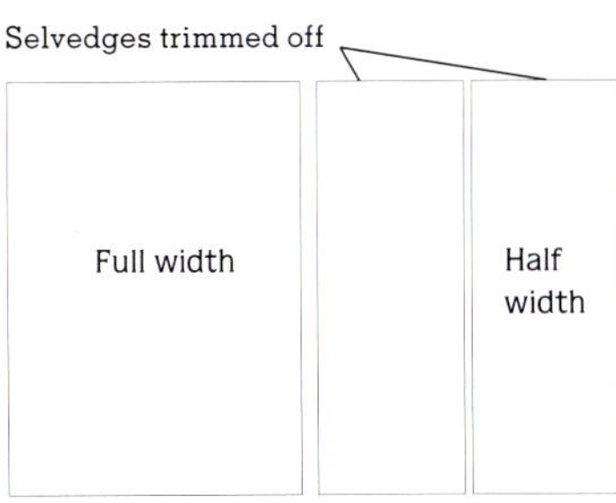

2 Add one half-width to each vertical side of the full width to achieve the required width.

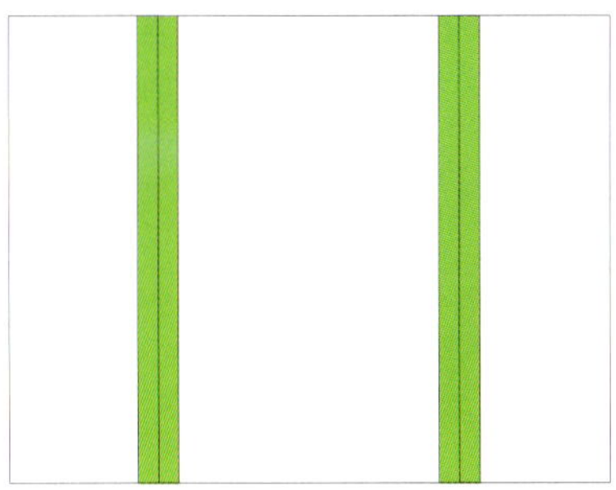

Hand quilting basics

Quilting by hand gives a soft look. Straight, even stitches are worked, ideally with the needle at an angle of 90 degrees, and the same stitch length on front and back. Because of the thickness of the quilt layers, the stitches are executed using a technique known as "rocking" the needle, which uses both hands. Use quilting threads and needles, and wear a thimble on your middle finger and a protective guard underneath.

KNOTTING TO BEGIN

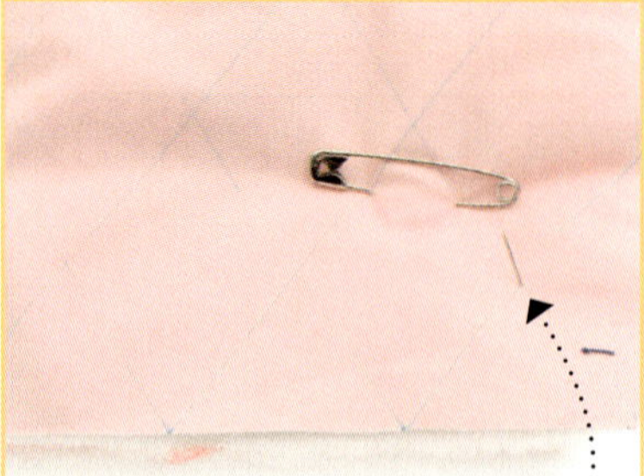

1 Knot a 50cm (20in) length of quilting thread. Take the needle down through the top layer of fabric, about 2.5cm (1in) away from where you wish to start stitching. Bring it out where you wish to begin.

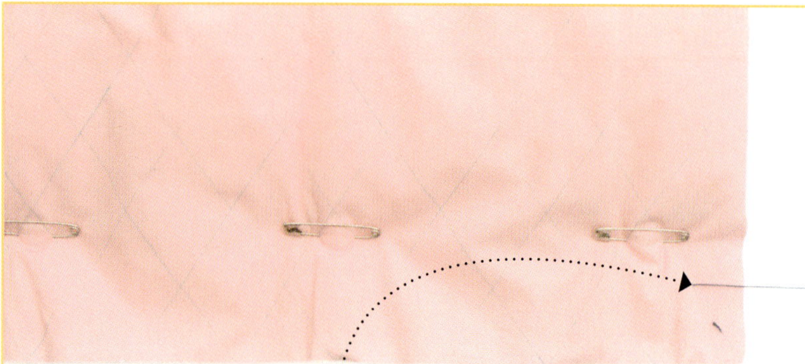

2 Pull the thread gently until the knot pops through the fabric but not hard enough to bring it out again.

3 The knot will bury itself in the wadding and be virtually undetectable.

FINISHING OFF

1 To secure the thread at the end, take a small back stitch through the top layer and pull the thread through to the top. Make a French knot, close to the end of the stitching. Secure the wraps with your finger and pull the knot tight.

2 Insert the needle point into the top layer only, next to where the thread emerges and in the opposite direction to the stitching. Slide the needle within the wadding and bring it out about 2cm ($\frac{3}{4}$in) from the end of the stitching. Gently pull the French knot through into the wadding.

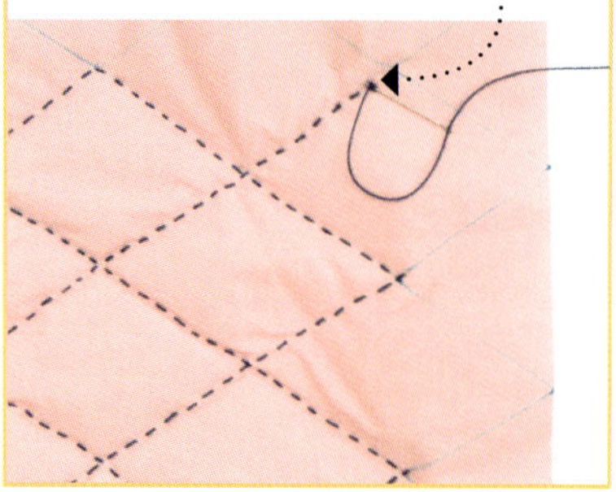

3 Carefully cut the thread close to the surface and let the tail sink into the wadding.

QUILTING OR ROCKING STITCH

1 Bury the knot as in knotting to begin (see opposite). Place one hand under the quilt where the needle should emerge.

2 With the needle between thumb and forefinger of your needle hand, push the needle with your thimbled finger straight down until you feel the point with your underneath hand. Stop pushing.

3 With your underneath finger, push up gently against the side of the needle and the quilt. At the same time, push down with your top thumb and make a bump in the layers while you push the needle to the top.

4 Stop when the length of the needle protruding on the top is the same length as the next stitch.

5 Use the thimbled finger to bring the eye of the needle upright again, while at the same time pushing in front of it with your thumb. When the needle is upright and the point breaks through the fabric, push down as in Step 1.

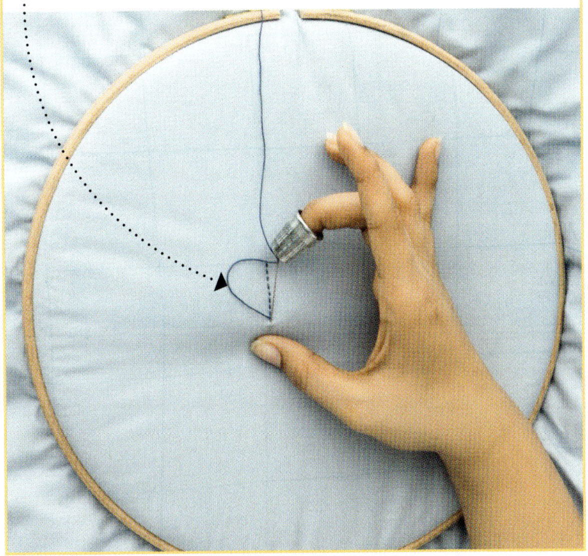

6 Continue this motion until the needle has as many stitches as it will hold. Pull the thread through. Repeat.

STAB STITCH

1 Stab stitch is an alternative way to work on thick quilts. Use a thimble on each middle finger. Bury the knot as in knotting to begin (see page 170). Push the upright needle straight down through all layers. Pull the needle and thread through to the back.

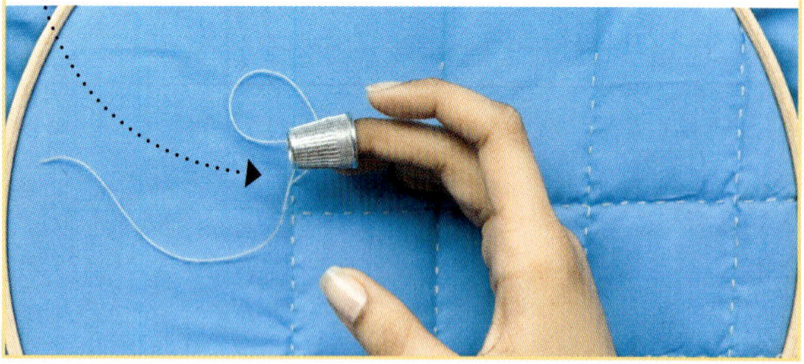

2 Push the upright needle back up through all layers, working a stitch length away from the previous stitch. Pull the needle and thread through to the top. Repeat.

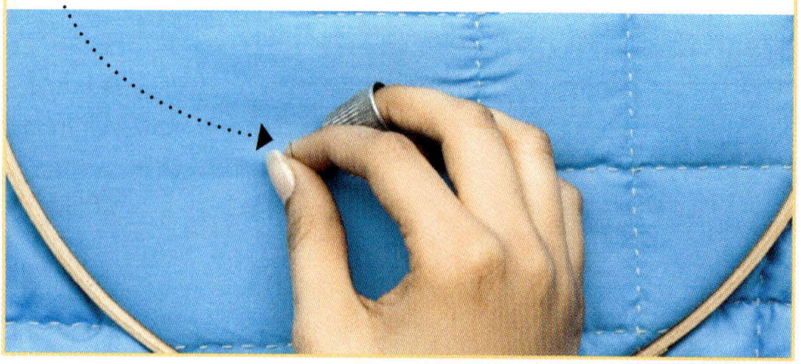

Concentric quilting

Concentric quilting lines can be worked by hand or machine. Outline quilting emphasizes a pieced or appliquéd design and requires minimal marking. Straight lines can be marked with 5mm (¼in) masking tape; curves can be drawn lightly. Echo quilting is similar, but consists of a series of evenly spaced concentric quilted lines. It is most often used in Hawaiian appliqué (see pages 138–139).

OUTLINE QUILTING

Follow the seamlines or outlines of the motif, working 5mm (¼in) away inside or outside, or on both sides of, the lines.

ECHO QUILTING

Make a row of outline quilting (see left). Then add evenly spaced rows to fill the background around the motif.

Seeding

Also known as stippling, this hand-quilting method uses small, straight stitches to fill the background.

1 Bury the knot (see page 170). Bring the needle and thread out near the motif. Take to the back and come up a short distance away from the first stitch.

2 Take another stitch straight down and pull the thread through and come up a short distance away. Work outwards from the motif. Keep the stitches small on the front and back and position them randomly to look like seeds.

Tying

Tying involves tying lengths of thread, lightweight wool, or ribbon through the layers of a quilt to hold them together. Cotton perle and stranded cotton both work well. You will need a sharp-pointed needle with an eye that is large enough to hold the thread but small enough to avoid making holes in the quilt. Space the ties according to the type of wadding, the block pattern, and the size of the quilt. Cotton and wool wadding shift easily and should be tied more closely than polyester. A general guide is 10–15cm (4–6in) apart.

1 Working from the centre out, take a stitch through all the layers and pull the needle and thread through, leaving a 10cm (4in) tail on the top.

2 Take a second stitch in the same place.

3 Tie the ends of thread in a reef knot. Cut the thread from the reel and trim the ends to the same length. Repeat, double-stitching and knotting over the entire quilt.

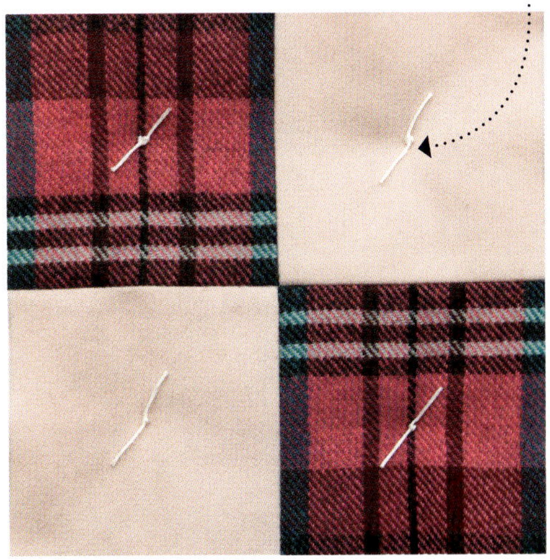

Corded quilting and trapunto

Corded quilting, or Italian quilting, and trapunto, or stuffed quilting, are techniques that can be used separately, but they work well together. Both involve stitching a design through a top and a thin backing layer, usually of butter muslin. The motif is then filled from the back with lengths of quilting, knitting wool, or soft cord, or with stuffing material. The outline is traditionally worked by hand.

1 Cut a background fabric and transfer the design to the right side, using a water-soluble pen. Cut a piece of butter muslin or similar fabric the same size. Tack them together around the edges.

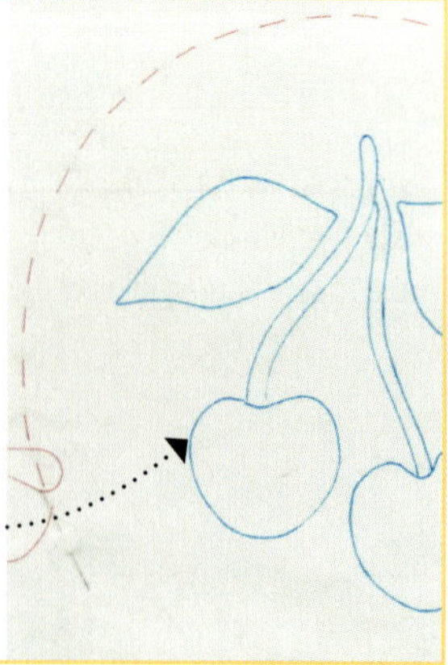

2 Outline the motif(s) with a small running stitch. Here we have used a contrasting colour thread for clarity. Where lines meet, keep stitches separate so they don't cross over.

3 When stitching is complete, remove the marking.

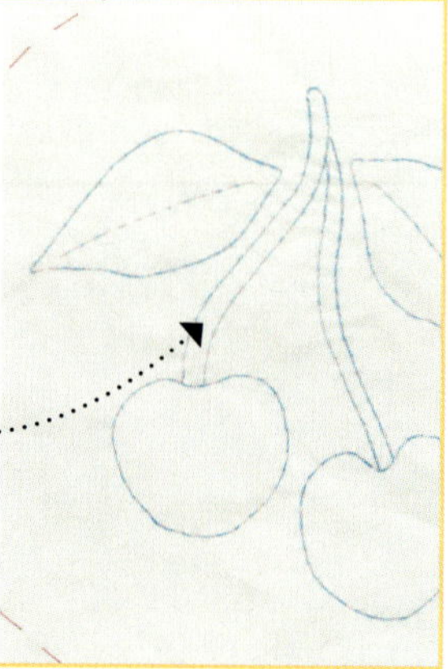

4 Thread a tapestry needle with quilting or knitting wool or cord. From the back, slip the needle through the first channel, leaving a short tail at each end.

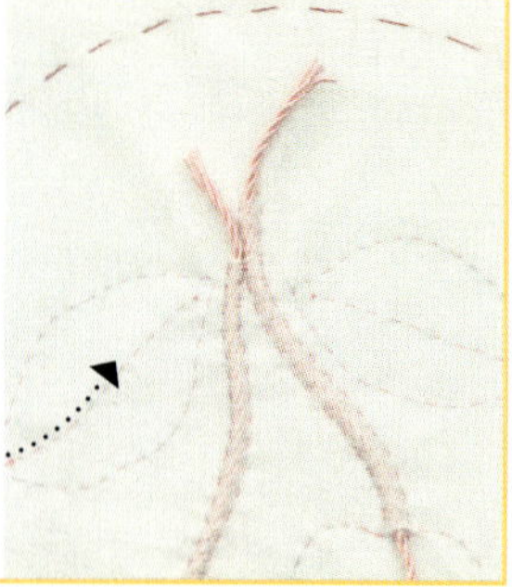

5 Make small slits in the centre of each element through the backing layer only and stuff small pieces of wadding between the top and the muslin.

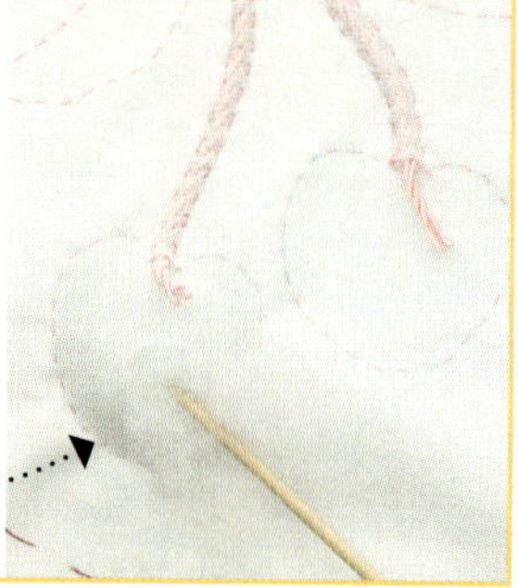

6 Close each slit in the backing with a crossed stitch, such as herringbone. Remove the tacking.

7 The completed motif. The cording and trapunto gives the motif a three-dimensional quality.

Machine quilting basics

Beautifully machined quilts are in no way second best to those worked by hand. Because the stitches are continuous, the finished product is usually flatter than a hand-quilted one. An even-feed, or "walking" foot, which feeds the layers through at the same speed top and bottom, is useful. Start and finish either by setting the stitch length to 0 and taking a few stitches before re-setting, or leave a tail of thread to tie off.

PREPARING A QUILT FOR MACHINING

1 To work on a small area at a time, roll up both sides of the quilt towards the centre, leaving 30cm (12in) open in between. Hold the edges with clips.

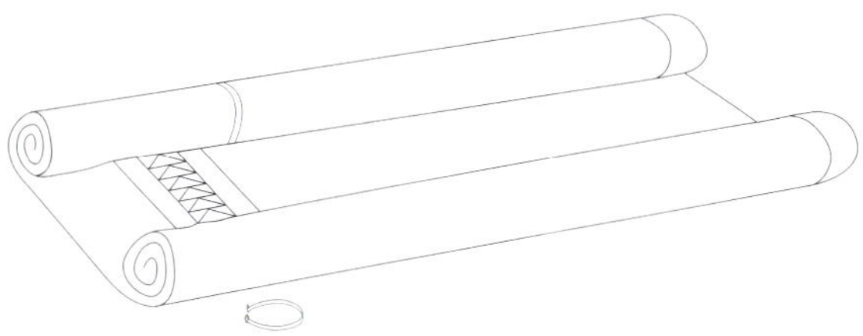

2 Fold or roll up the open ends of the piece and secure them using clips, leaving space to work on. Repeat the rolling and/or folding process as you work.

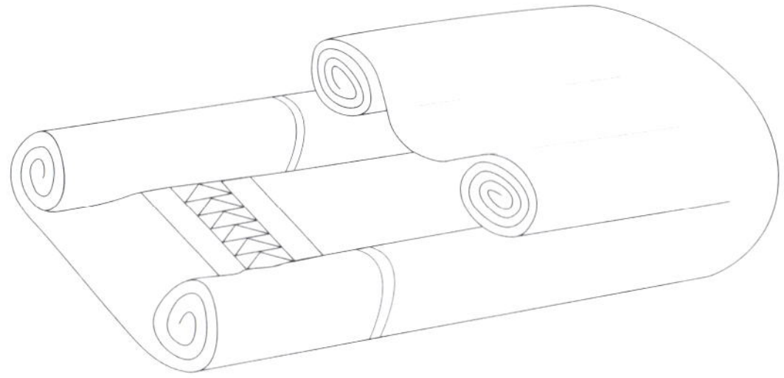

Freestyle quilting

Freestyle, or free-motion, quilting gives machine quilters a great deal of freedom to create their own designs. Mastering the technique requires practice, but the effort can be well rewarded with unique work. You need a darning foot or a free-motion foot and to know how to lower the feed dogs. If your machine has the option to stop work with the needle always down, use it.

1 With the presser foot down where you will start, take one stitch. Hold the top thread and use it to gently pull the bobbin thread to the top. Secure with a few very short stitches. Start slowly and take a few more short stitches. Cut away the thread tails.

2 Guide the fabric with your hands, moving the work in any direction. Position your hands in an open circle around the machine foot and press the layers gently. Keep a moderate speed and make the stitches the same length. Tie off with a few short stitches, as in Step 1.

Quilt as you go

If you work patchwork directly onto layers of wadding and backing fabric, you will end up with a finished piece that needs no further quilting. The technique works best when piecing strips or assembling a medallion quilt (see page 155) with a border. Borders can be pieced and added as strips.

1 Cut backing and wadding to size of finished piece plus 2.5cm (1in) all around. Tack together along all edges.

2 Cut a central medallion and the strips for the first border. Position the medallion face up in the centre of the backing and apply the first strip, right sides together, sewing through all layers. Add side strips first, fingerpress open, then apply top and bottom strips. Fingerpress the first round open.

3 Add strips in your chosen order. Trim backing and wadding to correct size and add binding (see page 182–183).

Quilting in the ditch

Here, the stitching follows the piecing lines on the quilt top and is hidden in the seams.

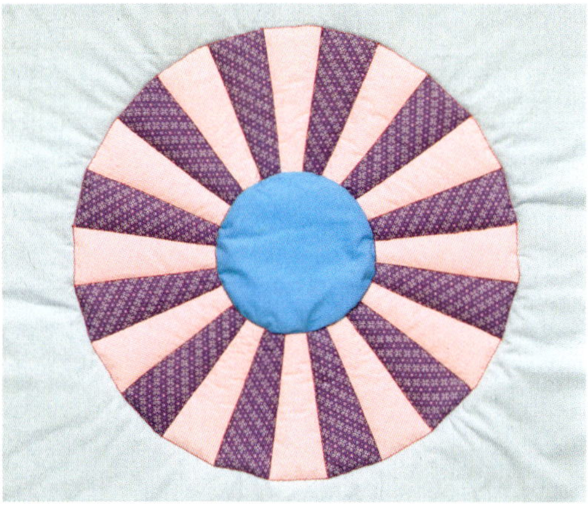

Secure the thread. Stitch along each row of piecing in turn. Stop and start as little as possible.

Grid patterns

Traditional gridded quilting patterns can be square or diamond shaped. Mark the grid by drawing the centre line in each direction, or use 5mm (¼in) masking tape. If you set a quilting guide on your walking foot, you can use it to measure the distance between rows as you work.

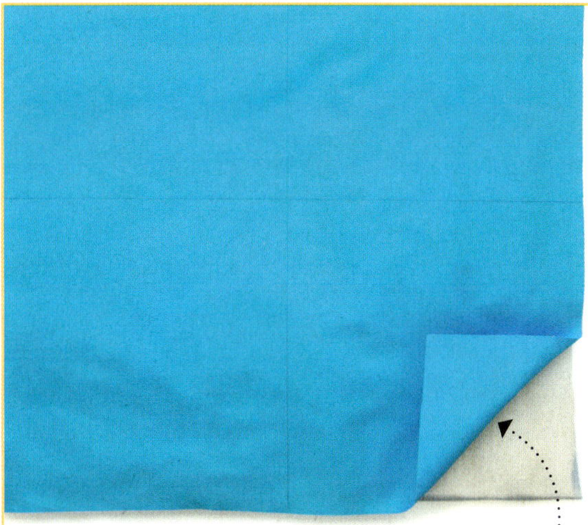

1 Take a few short stitches. Set the quilting guide to the correct distance on one side and stitch the first marked row from edge to edge. Turn the work and use the quilting guide to measure each vertical row in turn.

2 Repeat to work the horizontal rows.

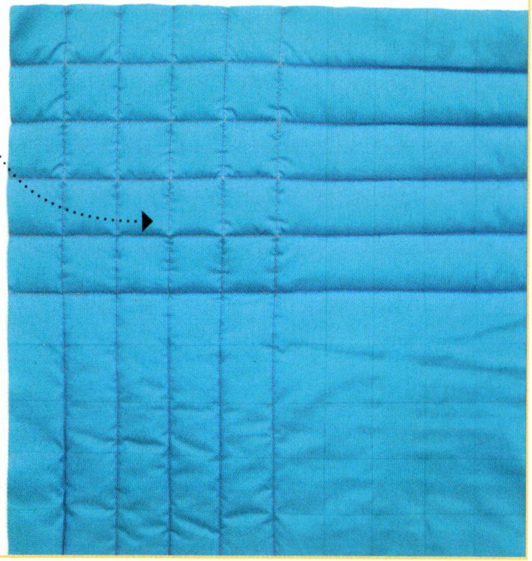

FINISHING

Finishing

Finishing the edges of a quilt is the final stage in its creation. Quilts must always be bound, either with an applied straight or bias binding (either single or double), by turning the backing to the front (or vice versa), or by folding the edges of both top and backing to the centre, a technique also known as creating a 'knife edge'.

Bindings

Bias binding is available in various colours and widths, or you can make your own. Bindings should be applied as a continuous strip. If possible, cut straight binding strips along the lengthways grain of the fabric or join pieces before applying (see page 159). Bias binding has more stretch than straight binding, making it suitable for binding work with curved edges.

MAKING A STRAIGHT BINDING STRIP

1 Measure the edges of the piece being bound and decide on the width of the finished binding. Cut strips twice this width plus 10mm (½in), allowing extra length for mitring corners and joining pieces.

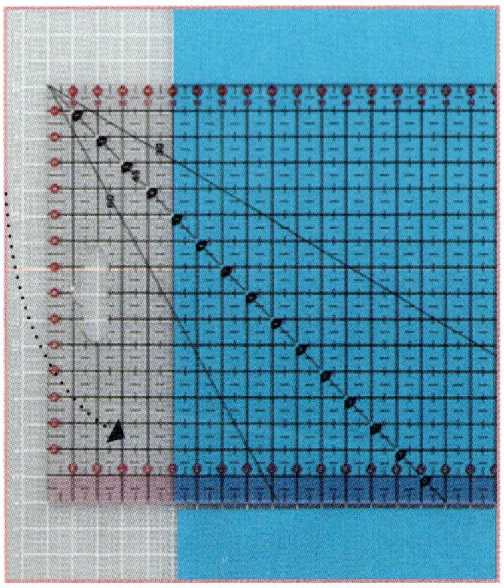

2 Ensure your edges are square and cut along the straight grain of the fabric. Add about 40cm (16in) to the length for full quilts, 30cm (12in) for baby quilts and wall hangings and 20cm (8in) for small works.

MAKING A BIAS STRIP

1 Buy at least 1.5m (1¾yd) of fabric so you can cut very long strips. Cut off selvedges and smooth the fabric flat. Straighten one corner of the fabric, then fold this edge back so that it aligns with the top edge and forms an exact 45-degree angle. Cut along this bias fold.

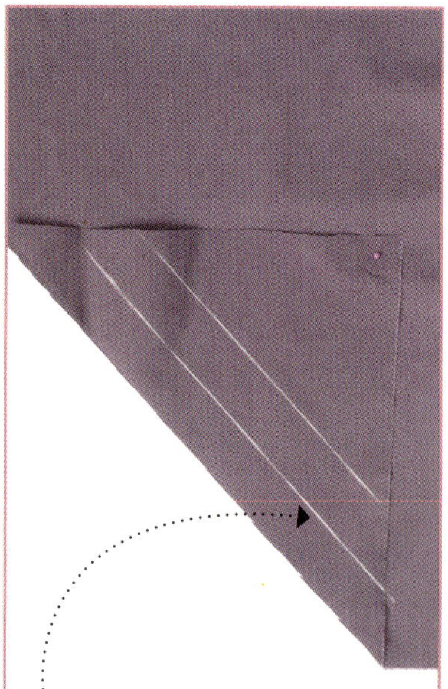

2 Using a metal ruler and a sharp piece of tailor's chalk, mark lines on the fabric parallel to the bias edge and 4cm (1½in) apart. Cut out the strips along the chalked lines. Cut as many strips as you need for your project plus a little extra.

3 Join strips together to make a continuous strip. Pin the strips together at a 90-degree angle with right sides facing and sew a 5mm (¼in) seam on the bias. The seam should run from edge to edge of each strip, with a triangle of fabric left at either end of the seam.

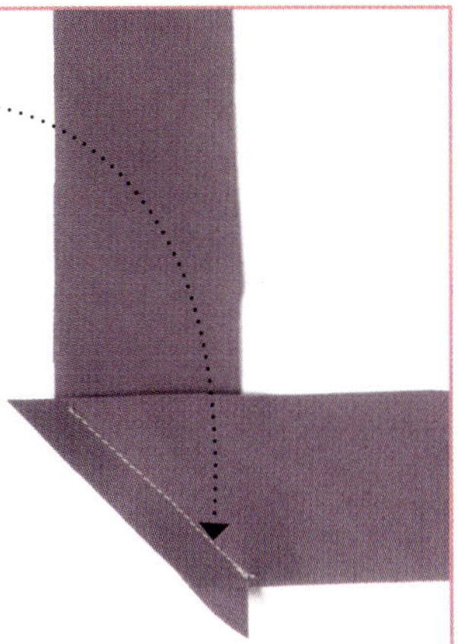

4 Press the seam open and trim off dog-ear seam allowances. Fold to the centre, wrong sides together, and press, or run the strip through a bias binding maker to prepare the strip for binding a quilt.

MAKING A CONTINUOUS BIAS STRIP

1 Cut a square of binding fabric with 90-degree corners. Mark two opposite sides as A and B and draw a diagonal line. Cut along the marked line.

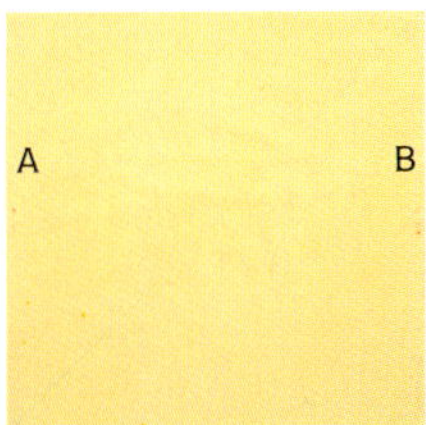

2 Place sides A and B with right sides facing and join them using a tight stitch length. Press seam open. Trim off the dog ears.

3 Mark lines parallel to the bias edges the desired width of the strip.

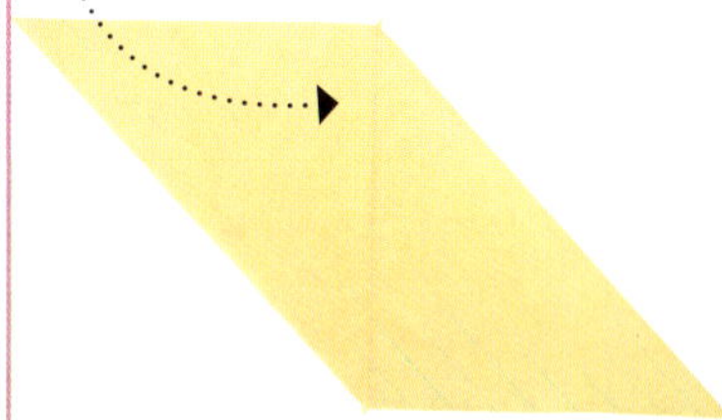

4 Bring the remaining two straight-grain edges together and offset the marked lines by aligning one tip of the fabric to the first marked line on the other side. Pin carefully to match the marked lines and sew together, right sides facing, to make a tube.

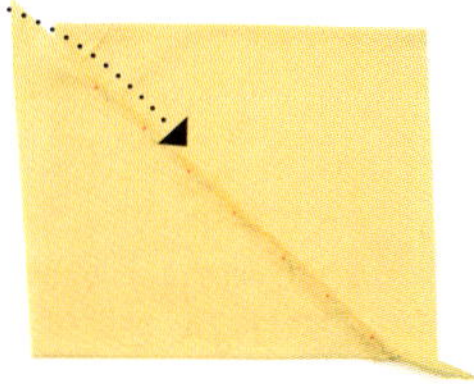

5 Start cutting at one end along the marked lines to make a continuous strip.

CALCULATING METERAGE

Multiply the length of two sides and divide by the width of the binding strip to calculate the length of a binding strip. For example, for a 5cm (2in) binding, from a 90cm (36in) square, 90 x 90cm = 8100cm (36 x 36in = 1296in). Divide by 5cm (2in) to get 1620cm (648in). You can make 16.2m (18yd) of binding, which should be sufficient for a king-size quilt. Always work in either the metric or imperial system.

SINGLE BINDING

1 Cut a binding strip to the desired width and press a 5mm (¼in) seam allowance along one long edge. Align the top of the binding strip with one corner of the piece and pin along the unpressed edge with right sides facing. Stitch the strip in place. Repeat on the opposite side.

2 Turn the strips to the wrong side, pin or tack in place and blind stitch along the folded edge, making sure the stitches don't show on the front.

3 Measure the remaining sides and cut two strips to that length, plus 10mm (½in) seam allowances. Turn under a 5mm (¼in) allowance at each end of each strip, and aligning the top and bottom, pin one strip to each of the remaining sides along the unpressed edge.

4 Stitch in place, then turn to the wrong side and repeat to blind stitch in place along the fold. Blind stitch the ends of these strips to finish.

DOUBLE BINDING

Double binding is stronger than single binding and is recommended for binding bed quilts. Quilted wall hangings and other small, layered items that won't get routine wear and tear can be single-bound.

1 Cut strips twice the desired width plus 10mm (½in) seam allowances. Fold in half lengthways, wrong sides together, and press. Mark each corner of the quilt top 5mm (¼in) from each side edge.

2 Align the corner of the binding strip to one corner of the right side of the quilt and pin with the doubled raw edges along the quilt edge. Repeat on the opposite side. The raw ends will be covered by the final strips.

3 Start and finish stitching from the marked seam allowance along the raw edges. Turn the folded edge of the binding to the back and slipstitch in place. Repeat on the opposite side.

4 Turn under a 5mm (¼in) allowance at each end of the two final strips and apply them in the same way.

Applying a flat trim

On some items a flat trim braid or ribbon is added for a decorative effect. This may be right on the hem or edge, or placed just above it. To achieve a neat finish, any corners should be mitred.

1 Pin the trim to the fabric, wrong side of the trim to right side of the fabric.

2 At the corner point where the trim is to be mitred, fold the trim back on itself and secure with a pin.

3 Stitch across the trim at 45 degrees from the edge of the fold, through all layers.

4 Remove excess trim from the corner.

5 Open the trim out and press.

6 Machine stitch the inner and outer sides of the trim to the fabric, close to the edge. Be sure the stitching at the corners is sharp.

Cording and piping

Cushion covers, home accessories, or bags made up in various needlework techniques often require a contrasting decorative edging of cording or piping. Cording is the easiest to apply; however, with piping your choice of colour is endless.

SEWING ON CORDING

Fabric edge on cording

1 Sew cording in between two layers of fabric, for example, along the seamline of a cushion cover. Align the fabric edge of the cording with the raw edge of the right side of the front piece. Tack in place along the cording.

2 Lay the back piece over the cording, with the right sides of the fabric pieces together, and machine stitch along the cording using a zip foot.

3 Remove the tacking and turn the fabric pieces right-side out. Press the fabric away from the cord so that the cord sits neatly along the seamline.

Piped edges

Piped edges can be single, double, or gathered. They add a stylish finishing touch to cushions and other home furnishings, and are very effective when used on borders and edges of quilts.

SINGLE PIPING

1 Just one piece of piping is used. Cut a bias strip 4cm (1½in) wide.

2 Wrap the binding, wrong side to wrong side, around the piping cord. Pin in place.

3 Machine along the binding close to the cord, using the zip foot.

4 Pin the raw edge of the piping to the raw edge of the right side of the work.

5 Machine close to the stitching line on the piping, using the zip foot.

6 Place the other side of the fabric over the piping, right side to right side.

7 Machine in place close to the piping, using the zip foot.

8 On the right side of the work, the piping can be seen at the edge. Press to finish.

DOUBLE PIPING

Different thicknesses of piping cord can be used for this. Make up single piping (see Steps 1–3, opposite).

1 Cut another bias strip, in a contrasting colour if you like.

2 Join the bias strip to the single piping, stitching next to the piping.

3 Place a second piping cord to the wrong side of the contrast strip.

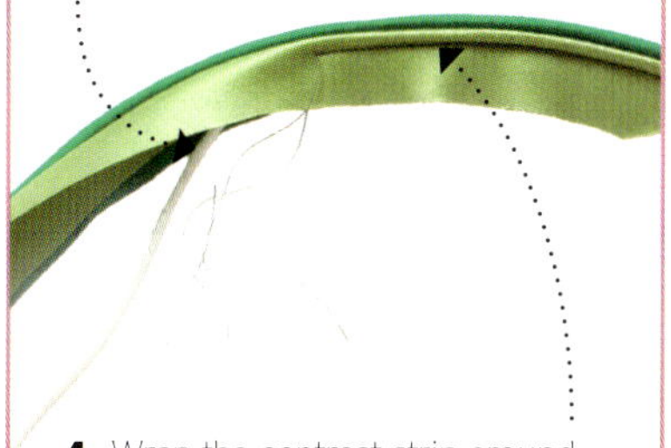

4 Wrap the contrast strip around the cord and stitch.

5 Attach to the edge of the work as for single piping (see Steps 4–7, opposite). On the right side, there is a double row of piping at the edge.

GATHERED PIPING

1 This is a great technique to try on cushions. Cut a bias strip 5cm (2in) wide. Stitch the bias strip loosely around a piece of piping cord. Secure the cord to the bias at one end.

2 Push the bias along the cord to gather.

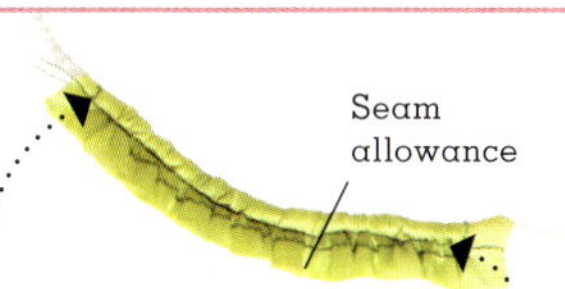

3 Machine the gathers in place. Secure the gathers at both ends of the cord.

4 Attach to the edge of the work as for single piping (see Steps 4–7, opposite).

Hemming needlework

Most quilted items are bound rather than hemmed, but sometimes a hem is needed instead. There is a choice of hems to use, depending on the fabric and the use of the finished piece, from simple turns to mitres.

DOUBLE-TURNED HEM

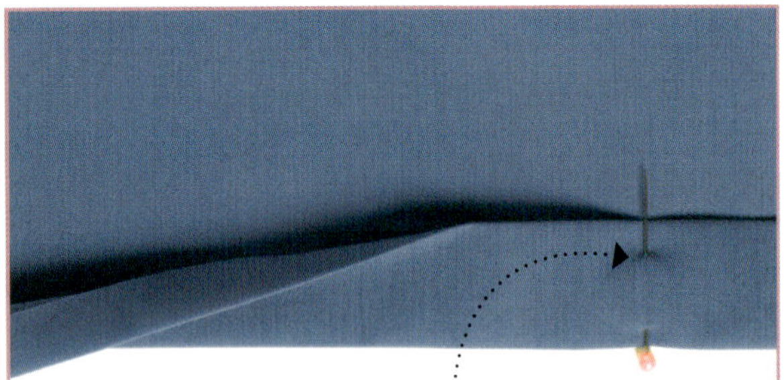

1 This method is suitable for most plain-weave fabrics. Turn under and press a 3–5mm (⅛–¼in) hem. For fine fabrics or those with a tendency to fray, tack and machine in place.

2 Turn under the hem to the desired width and pin in place.

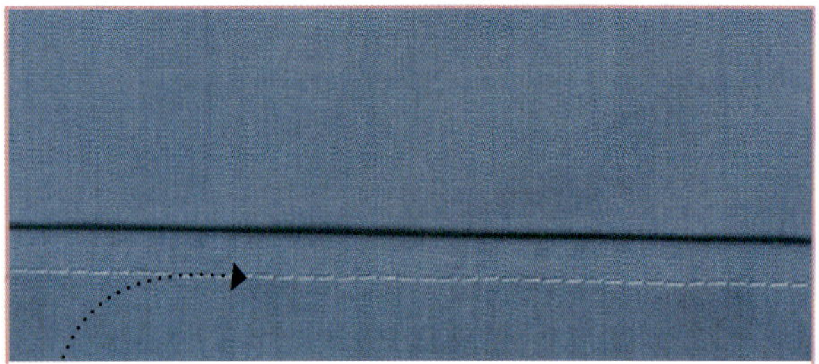

3 Blind stitch by hand, or machine using a straight stitch for a neat finish close to the upper fold.

SINGLE-TURNED HEM

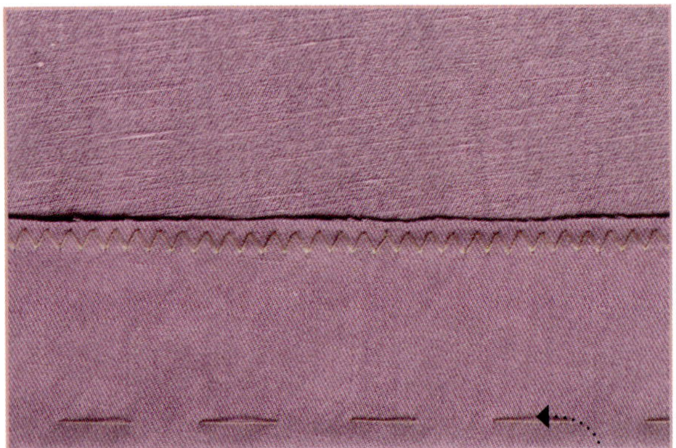

1 This method is best for heavy plain weaves. Finish the raw edge with a zigzag or overlocking stitch, or bind it with bias binding (see pages 180–181). Turn the hem to the wrong side, press lightly and tack in place.

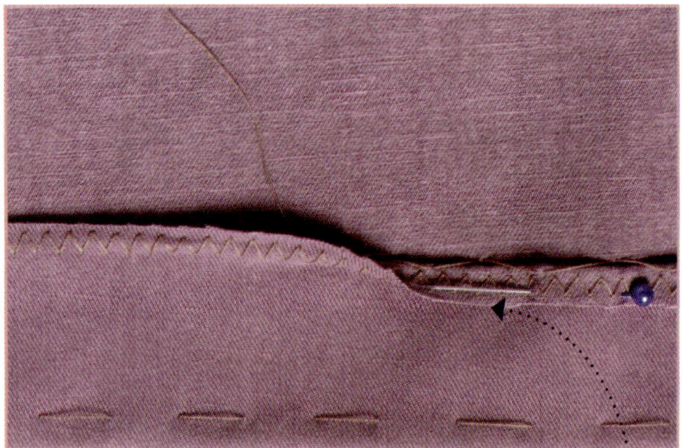

2 Either slip stitch in place by hand or blind stitch the hem in place by machine. Remove tacking.

Decorative facings

A faced hem can be decorative with scallops or points, or used for finishing a hanging or embellishing an edge on a cushion or a quilt.

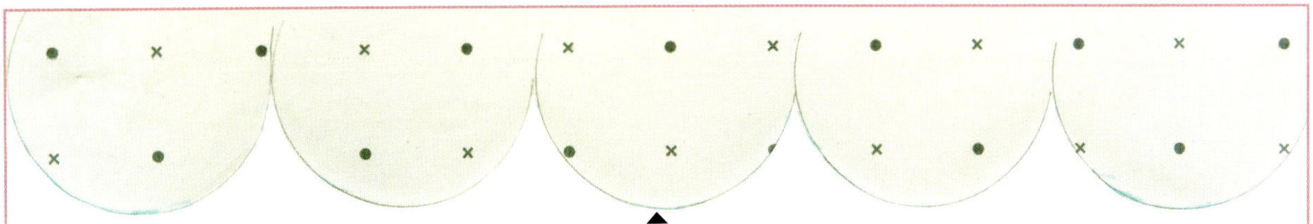

1 Make a template for the desired shape, either on pattern paper or card.

2 Cut a facing 10cm (4in) wide on the straight grain and finish one edge. Use the template to mark the shapes on the facing strip using the finished edge as the top edge and allowing 1.5cm (⅝in) between the bottom of the template and the raw edge.

3 Machine along the marked outline, pivoting the needle at the top of each scallop or point.

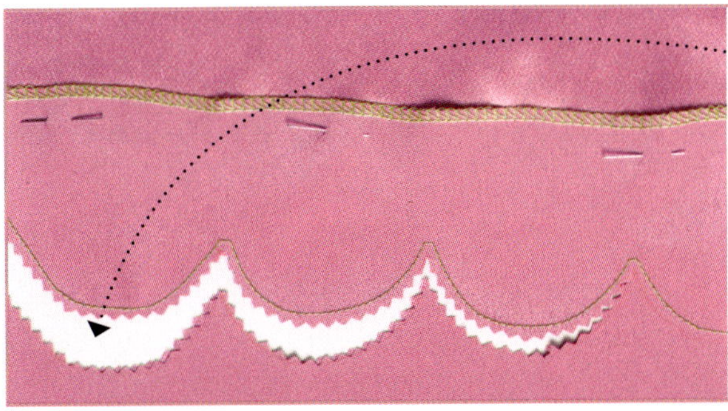

4 Use pinking shears to trim the fabric away from the bottom, cutting below the stitching line.

5 Turn through to the right side and press. Blind stitch the finished edge of the facing to secure it.

Ruffles

A plain ruffle is normally made from a single layer of fabric cut on the straight of the grain. The length of the fabric needs to be at least two and a half times the length of the seam into which it is to be inserted or of the edge to which it is to be attached. The width of the ruffle depends on where it is to be used.

1 Turn under one long edge 5mm (¼in), then turn under again by the same amount.

2 Pin in place, then machine with a straight stitch.

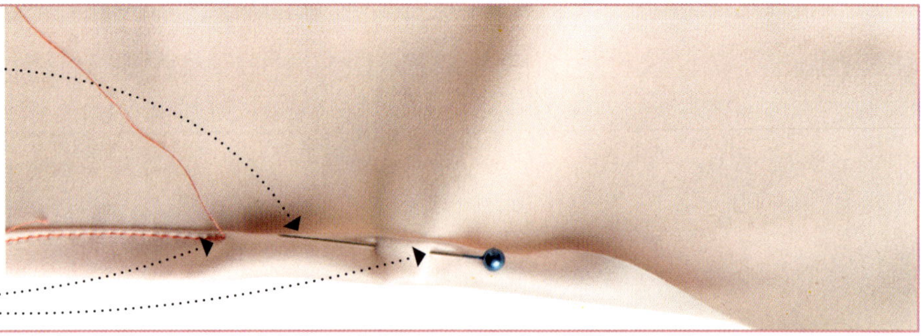

3 Press the machined edge flat.

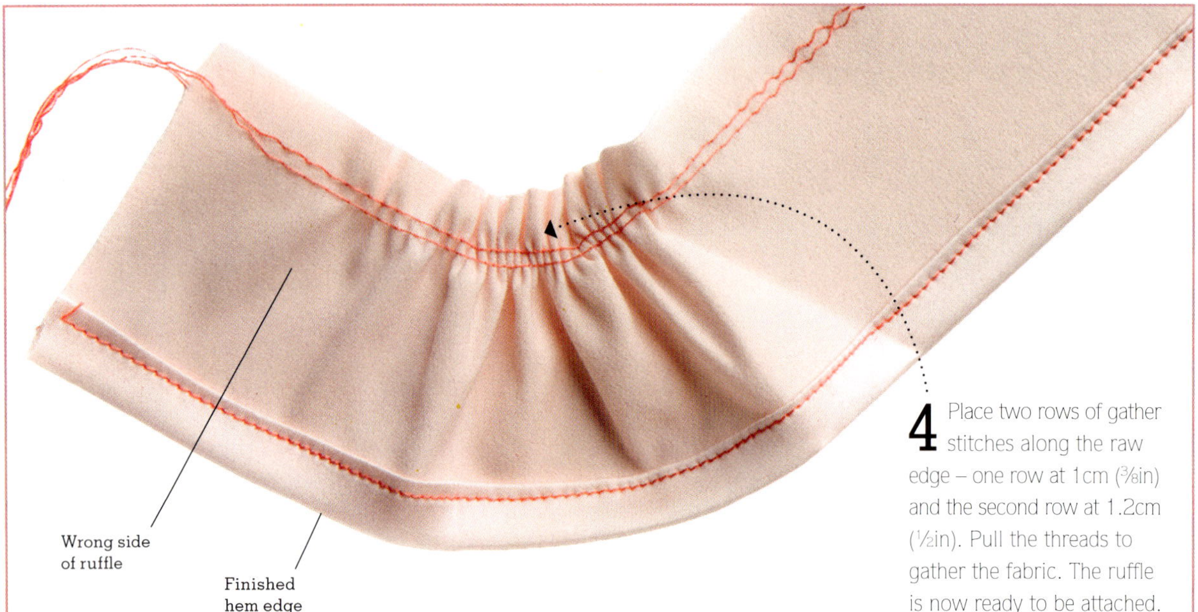

4 Place two rows of gather stitches along the raw edge – one row at 1cm (⅜in) and the second row at 1.2cm (½in). Pull the threads to gather the fabric. The ruffle is now ready to be attached.

Double ruffles

This is a useful ruffle on a fabric that is prone to fraying.

1 Cut the fabric for the ruffle twice the required depth.

2 Fold the fabric lengthways, wrong side to wrong side.

3 Pin the raw edges together.

4 Insert gathers along the raw edge.

5 Pull up the gathers to fit.

Ruffles with a heading

This type of ruffle can give a decorative effect on soft furnishings.

1 Neaten one long edge as for a plain ruffle (see Steps 1–3, opposite).

2 Turn down the other long edge – the amount of the turn down is the depth of the required heading plus a seam allowance of 1.5cm (⅝in).

3 Tack the heading in place.

Threads to pull up gathers

4 Insert the two rows of gather stitches.

5 Pull up the stitches to make the gathers.

6 After gathering, there will be gathers with a ruffle on one side of the stitch line and a short gathered heading on the other. Pull out the tacking stitches.

Stitching a ruffle to an edge

If a ruffle is not in a seam then it will be attached to an edge. The edge of the seam will require neatening, which is often best done by using a binding method as it is more discreet. A self-bound edge, where the seam is wrapped on to itself, is suitable for fine, delicate fabrics. For thicker fabrics, use a bias binding to finish the edge.

SELF-BOUND FINISH

1 Place the gathered ruffle on the edge of the fabric, right side to right side. Pin in place.

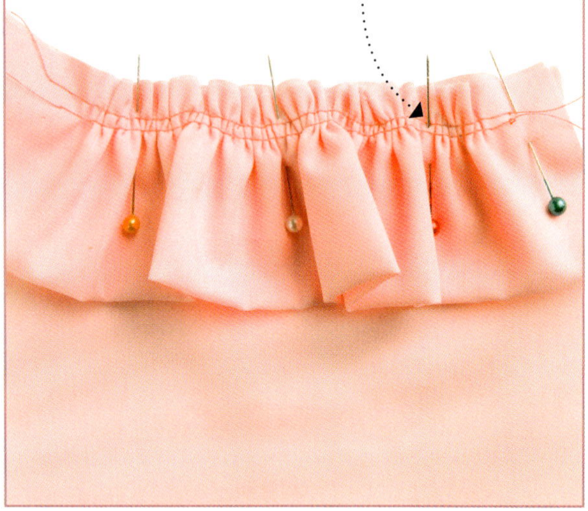

2 Machine the ruffle to the fabric using a 1.5cm (⅝in) seam allowance.

3 Trim the gathered side of the seam allowance down to half.

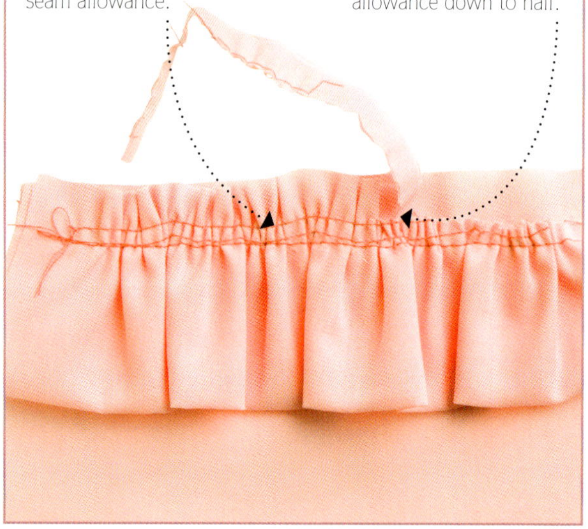

4 Wrap the longer, fabric side of the seam over the gathered seam, tucking under the raw edge. Pin in place.

5 Machine the wrapped seam to secure. Make sure it is attached to the seam only.

BIAS-BOUND FINISH

1 Machine the gathered ruffle to the edge of the fabric, right side to right side, using a 1.5cm (⅝in) seam allowance (see steps 1 and 2, opposite).

2 Use 2cm (¾in) wide bias binding. Stitch the crease in the bias over the machine stitching.

3 Trim back both sides of the seam allowance.

4 Wrap the bias over to the wrong side of the seam. Pin in place.

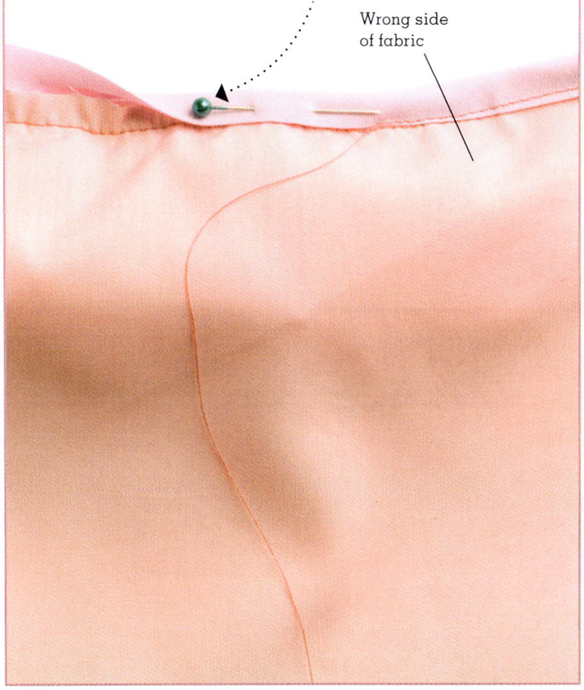

5 Machine stitch the other side of the bias close to the fold.

Stitching around a corner

It can be difficult to stitch a ruffle to a corner and achieve a sharp point. It is easier to fit the gathers into a tight curve, which can be done as the ruffle is being applied to the corner.

1 Pull up the gathers to fit along one side of the fabric seam and pin in place.

2 Fit the gathers into a tight curve at the corner.

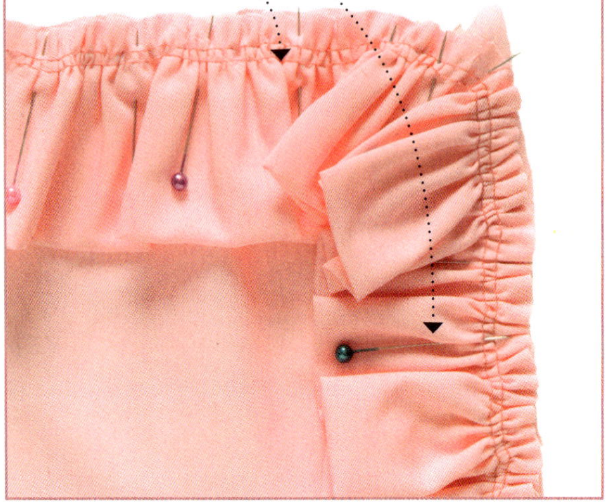

3 Machine the ruffle in place.

4 Attach the other piece of fabric and machine in place. Layer the seam.

5 Turn the fabric and ruffle through to the right side. The corner will have a tight curve.

Stitching into a seam

Once the ruffle has been constructed it can either be inserted into a seam or attached to the edge of the fabric (see page 190). The two techniques below apply to both single and double ruffles.

1 Insert two rows of gathers at the edge of the ruffle.

2 Pull up the gathers to fit along one side of the fabric seam and pin.

3 Even out the gathers and pin again.

4 Tack to secure.

5 Place the other piece of fabric over the ruffle, right side to right side.

6 Pin all the layers together.

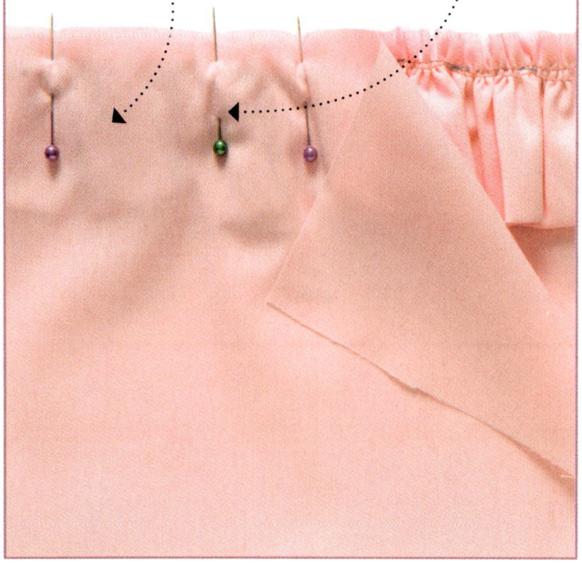

7 Machine through all the layers using a 1.5cm ($\frac{5}{8}$in) seam allowance.

8 Layer the seam.

9 Turn the fabric and ruffle through to the right side. Remove all tacking.

Fastenings

Many items other than quilts are made using patchwork, appliqué, and quilting techniques, from bags and soft furnishings to toys and garments. Sometimes they will need fastenings such as buttons or zips, and buttons of course need buttonholes or loops.

MAKING SIMPLE BUTTON LOOPS

1 Work simple button loops directly onto the seamline at the edge of the fabric so that the securing stitches are worked through four layers of fabric – the front fabric layer, the two seam allowance layers, and the back fabric layer.

2 Thread the needle with one strand of thick, strong buttonhole thread. Run it between the layers of fabric and out at the right of the loop position. Make three small stitches through the layers in the same place, close to the edge.

3 Insert the needle through the fabric to the left, leaving a gap the same width as the button's diameter. Create four loose strands of thread back and forth over this gap, making one stitch through the edge at each end of each loop.

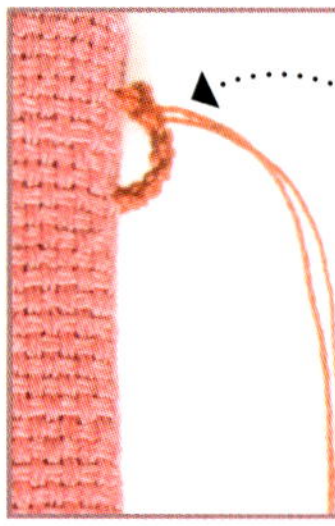

4 Working from right to left, cover the loose strands with closely made buttonhole stitches.

5 Once the strands are completely covered, secure the end in the same way as in Step 2.

HAND-STITCHED BUTTONHOLES

Practise on scrap fabric to improve your skills before stitching directly onto your needlework. Always work buttonholes through two layers of fabric that have an interfacing in between them.

1 Mark the desired finished length of the buttonhole on the right side of the piece, then machine stitch a rectangle 5mm (¼in) wide and as long as the required finished buttonhole length. Carefully cut a slit along the exact centre of this rectangle.

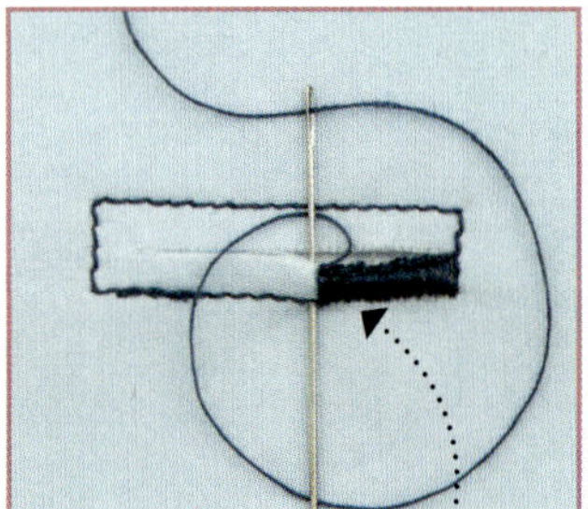

2 Using a thick, strong buttonhole thread, work tailor's buttonhole stitch (as shown) along both edges of the slit. Insert the needle through the fabric just outside the machine stitches, so that the stitches are 3mm (⅛in) long.

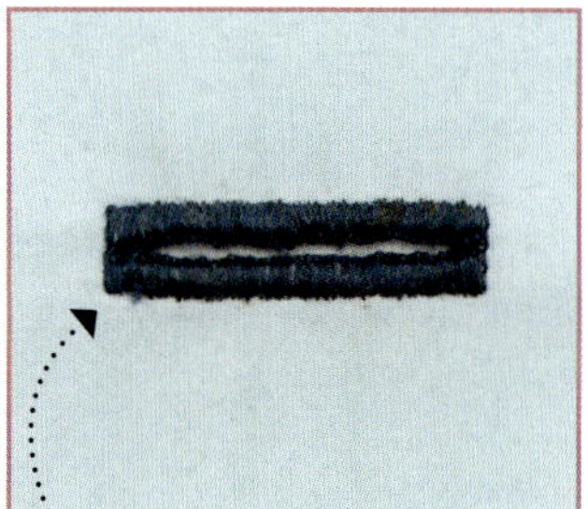

3 Finish each end of the buttonhole with three or four stitches that are the same width as the total width of the buttonhole.

ROULEAU BUTTON LOOPS

1 Cut a bias strip 4cm (1½in) wide from a lightweight cotton fabric (see pages 180–181). A strip 10cm (4in) long (excluding the pointed ends), is long enough for a loop for buttons up to 2.5cm (1in) in diameter. Fold the strip in half lengthways with right sides together and pin.

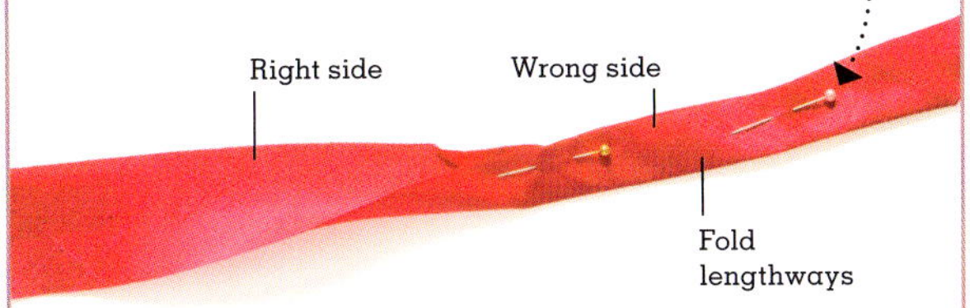

2 Machine stitch lengthways along the folded strip, 5mm (¼in) from the fold, leaving long thread ends. Then machine stitch along the seam allowance, 3mm (⅛in) from the first line of stitching.

3 Trim off the extra fabric close to the second line of stitches.

4 Thread the two long loose ends of thread at one end of the rouleau strip onto a blunt-ended needle and pass the needle through to pull the rouleau right-side out. Alternatively use a loop turner.

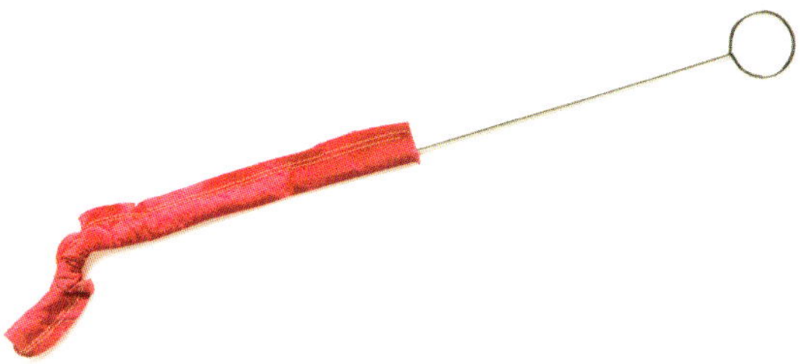

5 Press the rouleau strip flat, aligning the seamline along one edge. With the seamline along the inside of the button loop, fold the rouleau as shown. Ensure the folded loop is long enough to accommodate the button, with a sufficient seam allowance at the ends.

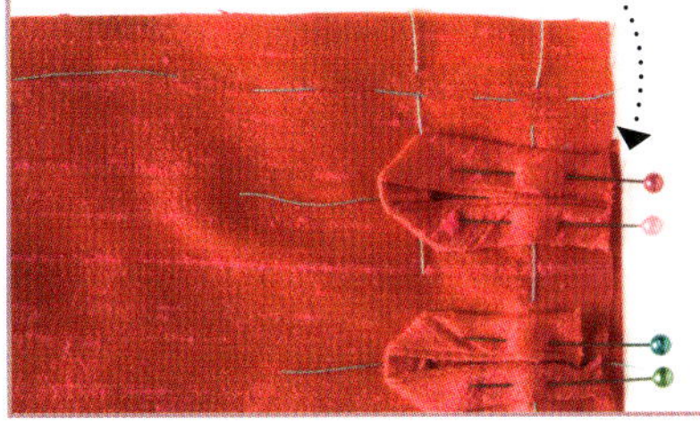

6 Machine stitch the folded rouleau loop face down to the right side of the piece with raw edges aligned.

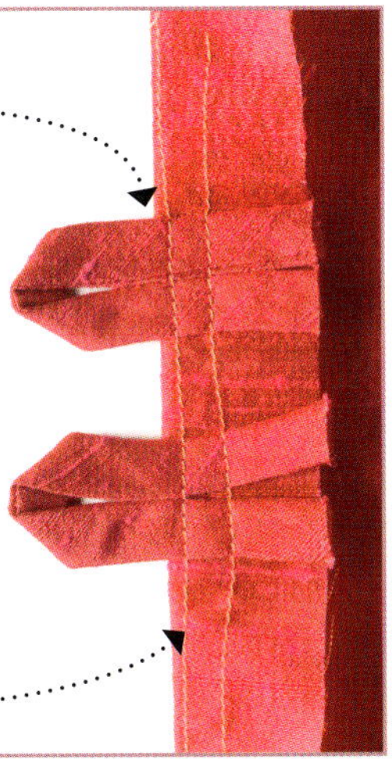

7 Machine stitch the first line inside the seam allowance just outside the seamline. Stitch the second line 4mm (3/16in) from the first.

8 Sew on the facing, catching the button loop in the seam. Turn right-side out and press.

SEWING ON BUTTONS

1 Thread your needle with a doubled strand of thread. Secure the thread to the fabric where the button is to be positioned. Pass the needle up through one hole of the button, down through the other hole to the back. Do not pull the thread taut yet – first insert a cocktail stick (or matchstick) under the button and between the button's holes. Then pull the thread taut.

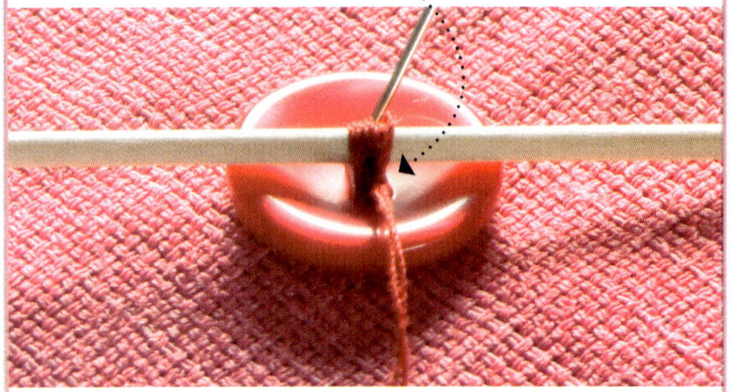

2 Continue working back and forth through the holes of the button and through the fabric, until at least five stitches have been worked.

3 Remove the cocktail stick. Wrap the working thread several times around the thread under the button to form a shank. Secure the thread end with three small stitches at the back.

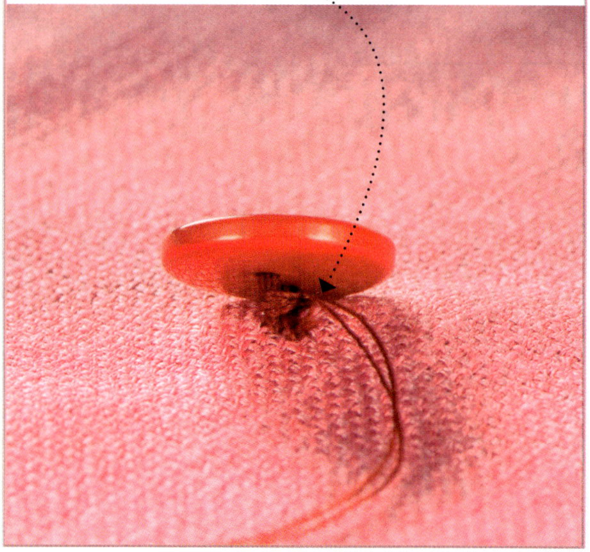

SEWING ON PLASTIC SNAPS

Although snaps or press studs are not visible, align them carefully when sewing them on. Use a doubled thread and work three or more stitches through each hole around the edge of the press stud pieces.

SEWING ON TIES

You can sew ties on a finished item with decorative stitching. Fold under the ends of the ties and tack them in place on the wrong side. Machine stitch a square with a cross at the centre over the end. Remove the tacking.

SEWING ON HOOKS AND EYES

Work a ring of straight stitches through the loops provided. Work the stitches only through the back layer of fabric and the seam allowances underneath. Ensure that the hook and the eye remain aligned by tacking the necks in position before stitching.

SEWING ON A ZIP

1 The easiest method for sewing on a zip is centring it on an opening in a seamline. To begin, machine stitch the seamline, leaving a gap in the stitches that is the length of the zip.

2 Tack the opening closed, working the tacking stitches along the seamline.

3 Open out the seam and press the seam allowance open on the wrong side. Open the zip and place it face down on top of the wrong side of the seam.

4 Centring the zip teeth carefully on top of the seam, tack one side of the zip tape in place 3mm (⅛in) from the teeth.

5 Close the zip and tack the other side of the zip tape in place. Using a matching thread, machine stitch the zip in place, stitching on the right side of the fabric and forming a rectangle around the zip just outside the tacking stitches.

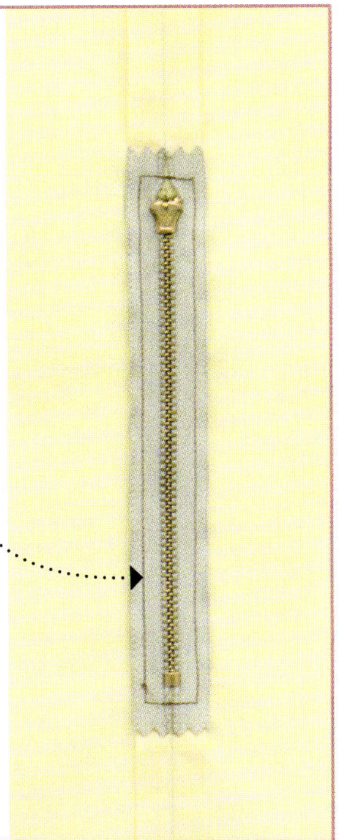

6 Remove the tacking around the zip tape and along the opening. Press.

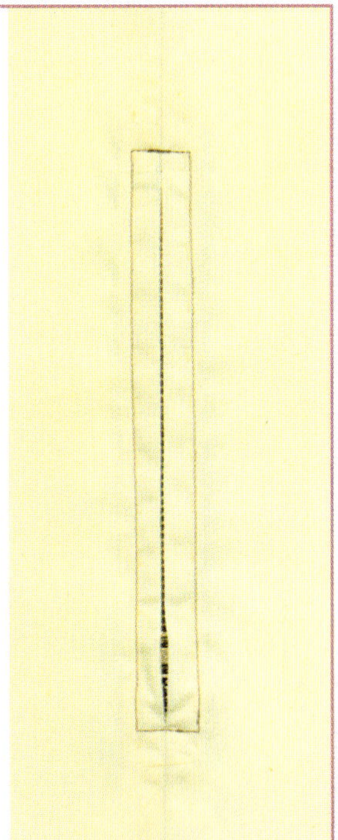

EMBELLISHMENTS

Embellishments

Finishing instructions sometimes involve the addition of simple handmade or ready-made embellishments. Here are some helpful tips for successfully applying these finishing touches.

Buttons

Buttons can be made from almost anything – shell, bone, coconut, nylon, plastic, brass, silver. They can be any shape, from geometric to abstract to animal shapes. A button may have a shank or have holes on the surface to enable it to be attached to fabric.

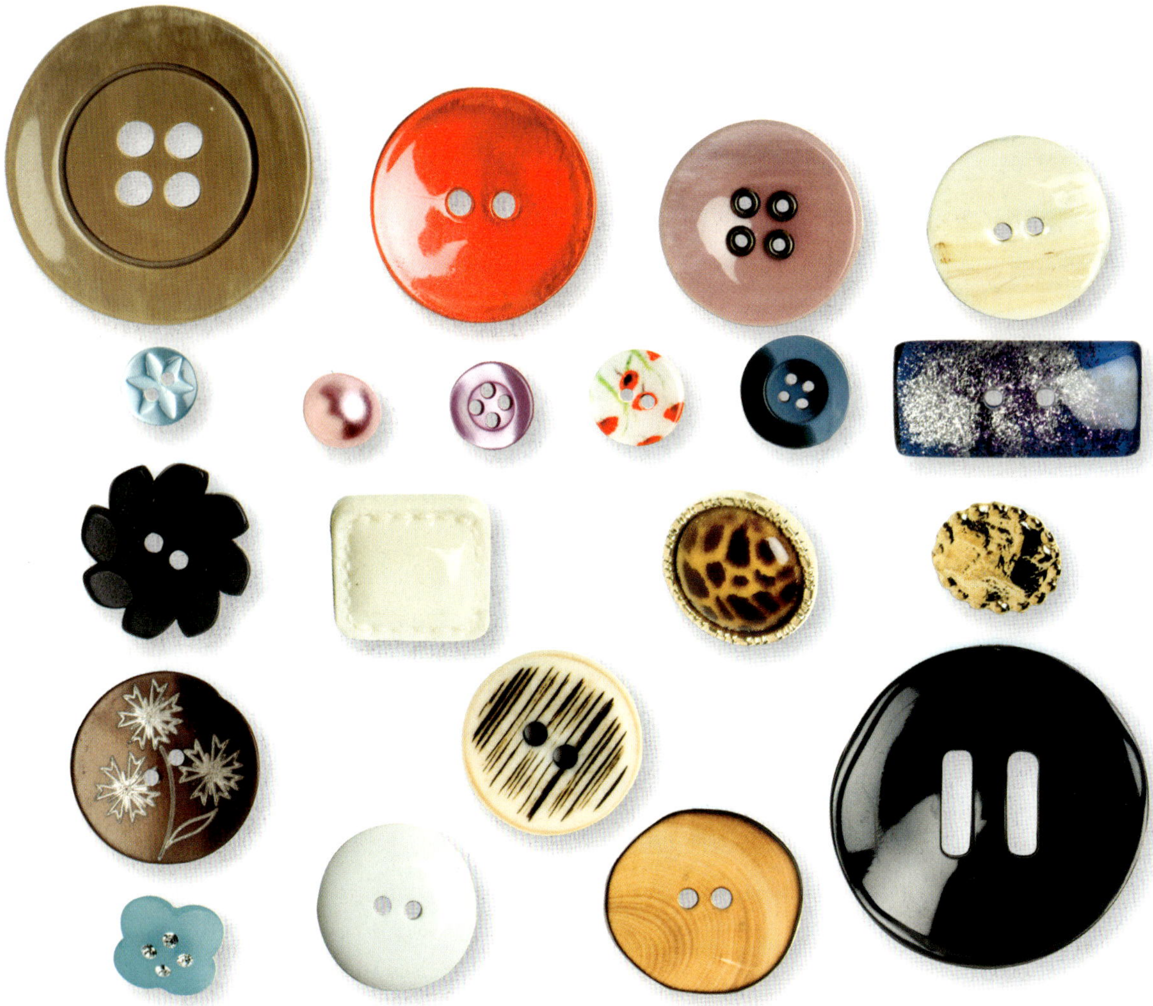

Trimmings, decorations, fringes, and braids

Decorative finishing touches – fringes, strips of sequins, ric-rac braids, feathers, pearls, bows, flowers, and beads – can add pizzazz and a flourish to quilted items, especially wall hangings and bags, and can personalize soft furnishings.

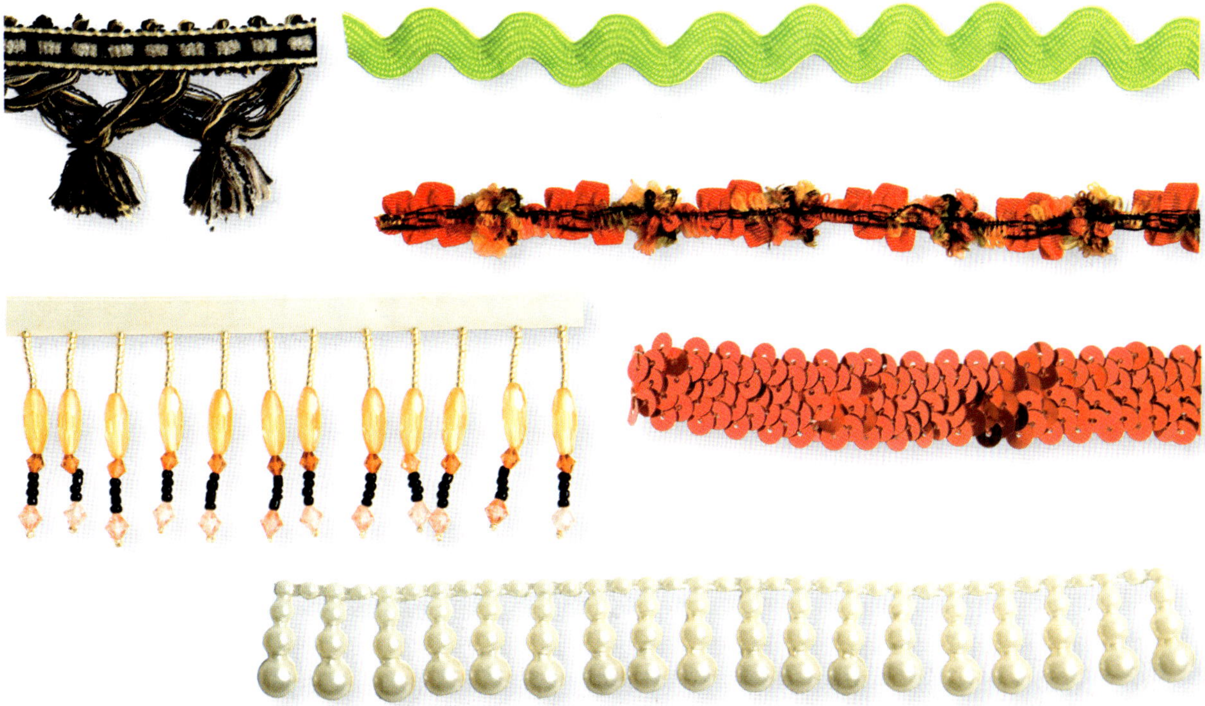

Ribbons

From the narrowest strips to wide swathes, ribbons are made from a variety of yarns, such as nylon, polyester, and cotton. They can be printed or plain and may feature metallic threads or wired edges.

Applying decorative edgings

A pretty decorative edging can bring a piece to life and add a professional touch. Sometimes trim is applied only along one of its sides. These trims usually overhang the edge, adding a lacy or frilly outline. Depending on the fabric and personal preference, the trim can be attached to the front or the back of the piece by hand or machine.

APPLYING SINGLE-EDGE TRIM TO THE FRONT

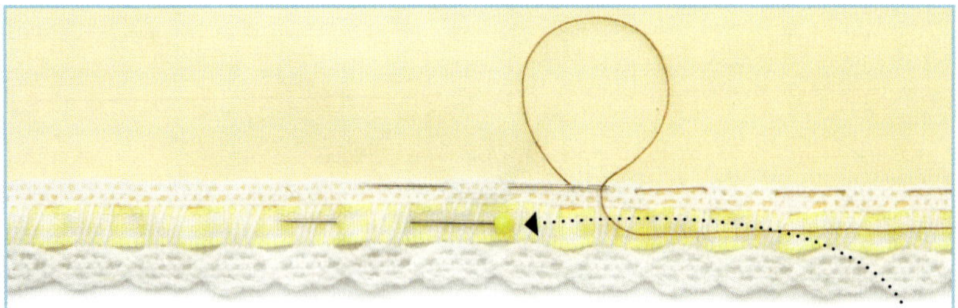

1 Measure the edge to be trimmed and allow an extra 10–15cm (4–6in) for the trimming to take account of any mitred corners or overlaps at joins. Hem the piece first (see page 186).

2 Pin the trim along the edge, starting in the middle of one side (or the bottom edge if there is a direction) as close to the edge of the trim as possible. Tack in place, removing pins as you work.

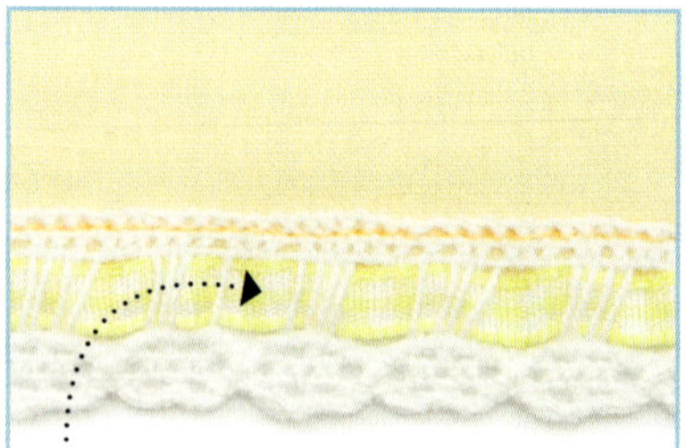

3 Turn under the end of the trim and fingerpress. Topstitch or blind stitch along the tacked edge using thread to match the trim.

APPLYING SINGLE-EDGE TRIM TO THE BACK

1 Turn under and tack a narrow hem (see page 186). Position the straight, top edge of the trim along the folded edge on the right side of the piece, with the decorative edge facing inwards.

2 Pin the trim along the edge, starting in the middle of one side.

3 Tack the trim in place, removing the pins as you work. Machine along the straight edge of the trim using matching thread, or hand stitch using a small back stitch to secure.

4 Turn the stitched edge to the wrong side and press.

5 Machine topstitch along the fold on the right side or hand whipstitch along the top fold on the wrong side. Use thread to match the fabric.

Applying other trimmings

There are many kinds of trimmings – ribbons, braids, beads, feathers, sequins, fringes, and so on – that can be applied to a fabric edge. If a trim is made on a narrow ribbon or braid it can often be inserted into a seam during construction. Other trims are attached after the item has been completed.

INSERTING A TRIM IN A SEAM

1 Place the trim to the right side of one piece of fabric, with the beaded or other decorative edge pointing away from the raw edge. The edge of the trim should be on the stitching line. Tack in place.

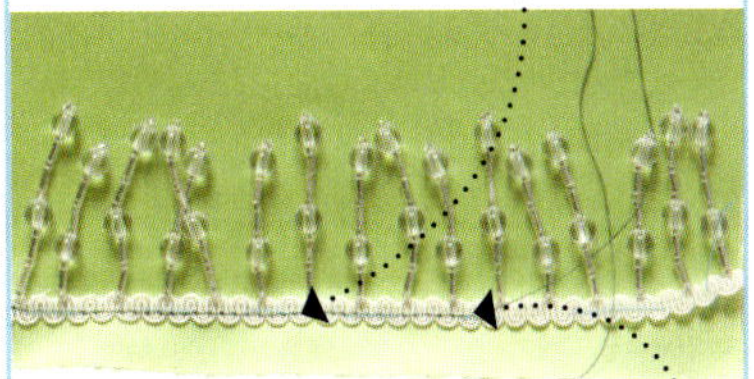

2 Machine along the trim using the zip foot.

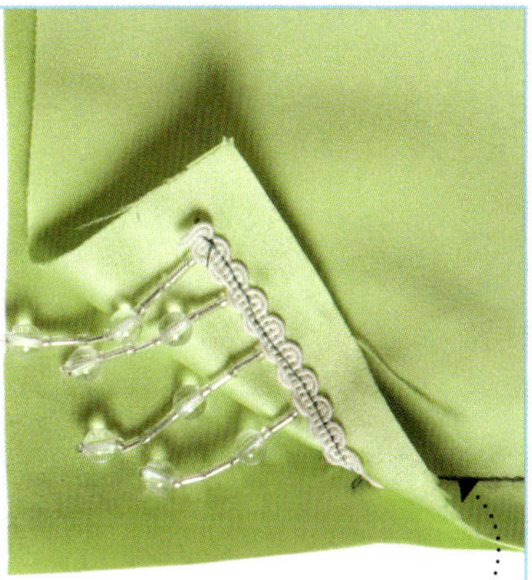

3 Place the other piece of fabric to the first one, right side to right side. Machine again to join them.

4 Turn to the right side. Press carefully. The trim should hang free.

ATTACHING A TRIM TO AN EDGE

1 Pin the trim in position along the finished edge of the work. Be sure the trim is aligned to the edge. Tack in place.

2 Using the zip foot, machine in place close to the upper edge, leaving the lower edge of the trim free.

HAND STITCHING A TRIM

Delicate trims are best hand stitched in place because machining the trim may damage it. Place the trim in position and carefully stitch down with a flat fell stitch.

Roses and bows

Fabric roses can add a lovely touch to quilted bags and soft furnishings, and create special 3-D effects on wall hangings and appliqued quilts, especially Baltimore album designs.

ROSE VERSION 1

1 Cut a bias strip 10cm (4in) wide. Fold in half lengthways, wrong side to wrong side.

2 Pin the raw edges together.

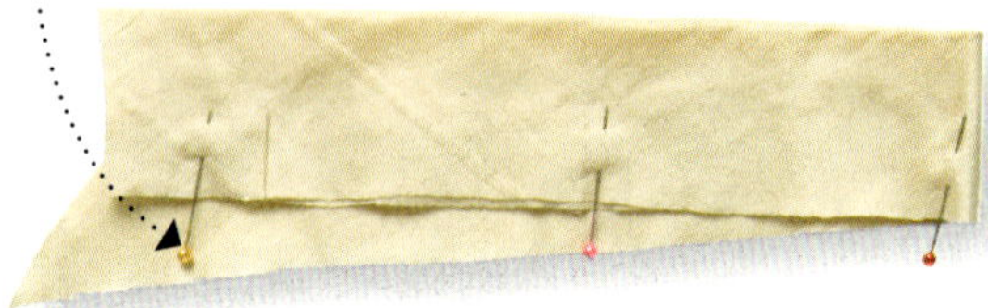

3 Insert two rows of gather stitches at the raw edge – one row at 1cm (3/8in) from the edge and the other row at 1.3cm (1/2in).

4 Pull up the gathers, grouping them together and leaving spaces between the groups. The groups and spaces will give the impression of petals.

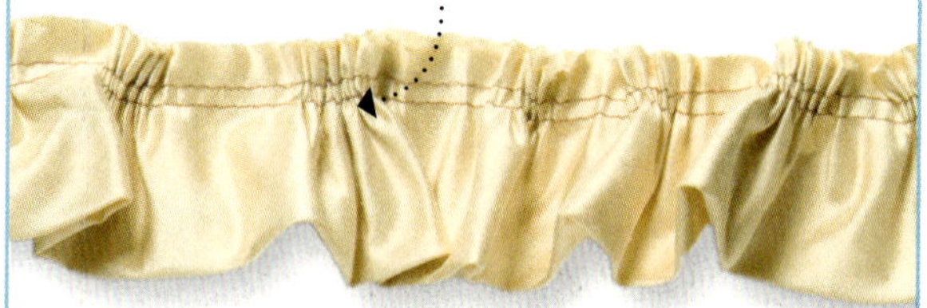

5 Hold the lower edge of one end in your left hand and loosely wrap the strip around.

6 When you have a rose shape, tuck any raw edges that show into the base.

7 Secure at the base edge with hand stitches.

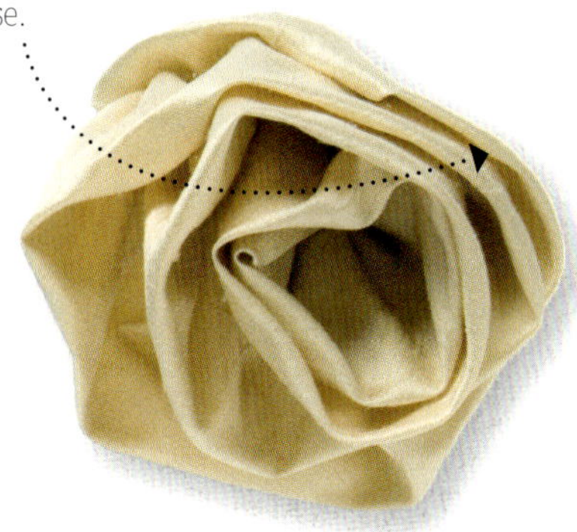

ROSE VERSION 2

1 Cut a bias strip 10cm (4in) wide.

2 Insert two rows of gather stitches along the centre of the strip. Leave a gap of 3mm (⅛in) between the rows of stitching.

3 Pull up the gathers into groups and spaces (see step 4, opposite).

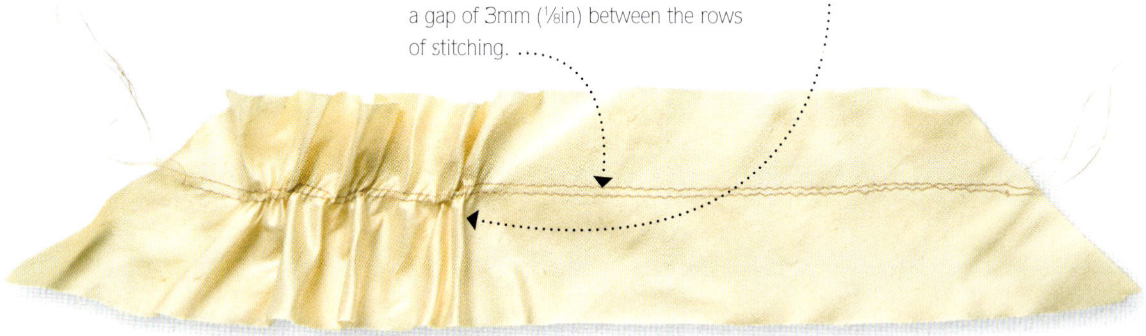

4 The groups and spaces will pull up to give a diagonal effect. Fold in half along the stitching lines.

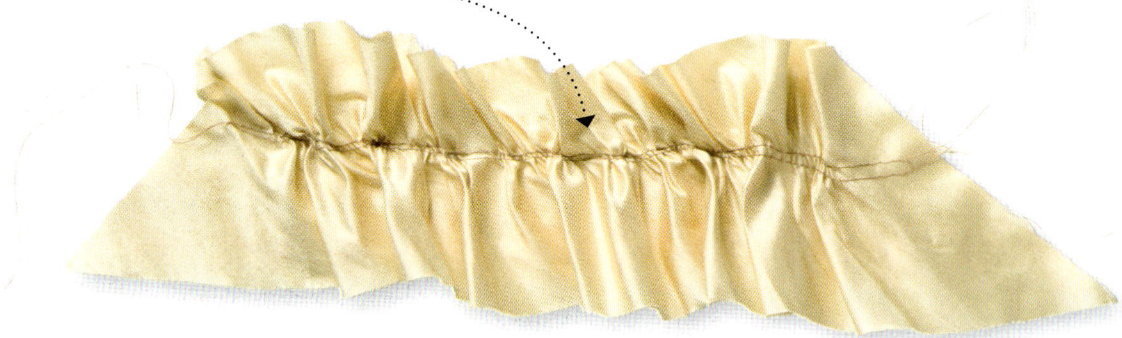

5 Hold the end of the gathers in your left hand and wrap the strip around loosely.

6 Secure at the base with hand stitches. Although the edge is raw, fraying is minimal as the strip has been bias-cut.

FANCY BOW

1 To make the loops, cut a piece of fabric that is four times the length of the loop required and twice the width plus seam allowances.

2 Interline with dress net to the wrong side. Tack the net around the raw edge.

3 Fold in half, right side to right side. Stitch along the raw edge leaving a 1.5cm (⅝in) seam allowance.

4 Turn through to the right side. Fold so that the seamline is in the centre.

5 Bring the short ends to the centre. Pin in place.

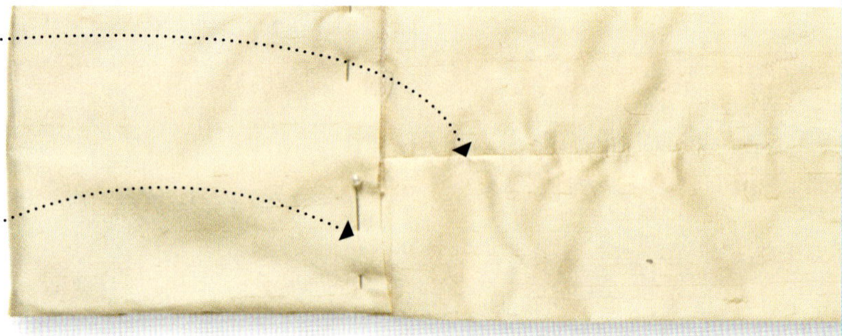

6 Tack through the centre, using double thread.

7 Pull along the tacking stitches to gather the centre.

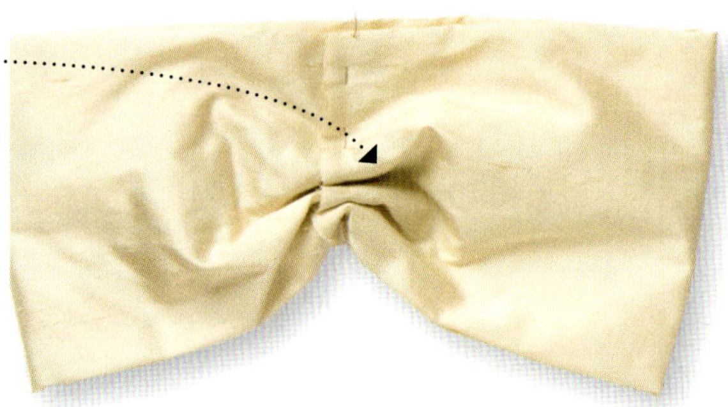

8 Next make the two ends. Cut two pieces of fabric the required finished length and twice the required width plus seam allowances.

9 Tack dress net to the fabric.

10 Fold each piece of fabric in half, right side to right side, and stitch along the long raw edge and at an angle at one end.

11 Remove bulk from the corners.

12 Turn through to the right side. Press. Make sure there are sharp points.

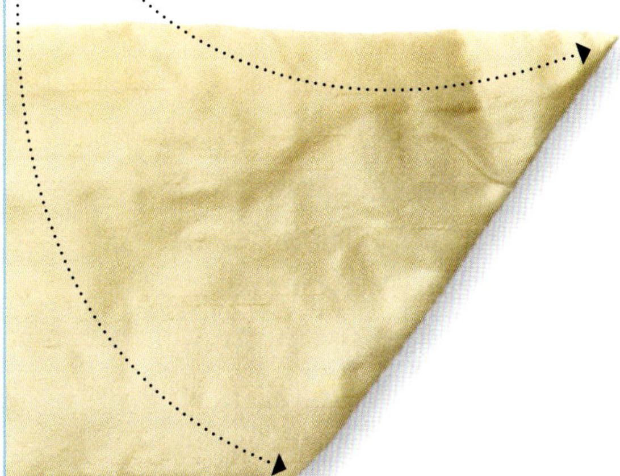

13 To assemble the bow, wrap a piece of fabric around the gathered centre of the loops and stitch in place by hand.

14 Scrunch the raw ends of the ends together and hand stitch behind the loop.

Beads

Beads can be used as accents or applied in rows in several ways. It is best to use a beading needle, which is thin enough to pass through almost any bead, and a polyester thread. Invisible nylon thread is ideal on plain-weave fabrics; alternatively, you can choose a thread that matches either the beads or the fabric.

SINGLE BEAD

Beads can be applied individually, either randomly or following a line. If the stitch is the same length as the bead, the next bead can be attached so they touch.

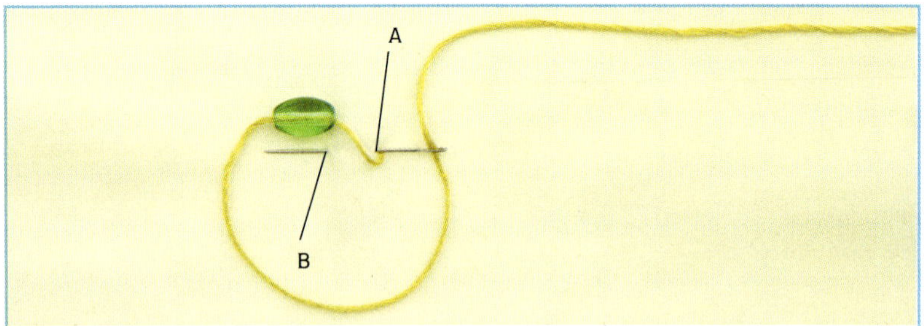

1 Knot the thread on the back. Bring the needle out at A and thread a bead on it.

2 Take the needle back in at A and come out at B. Repeat to secure the bead with a double stitch on the back.

3 Move to the next position and repeat to apply subsequent beads.

COUCHING

Couching beads is similar to couching threads (see Glossary). Cut lengths of thread that are longer than the line to be covered.

1 Knot the thread on the back and bring the needle out at A.

2 Thread on the required number of beads.

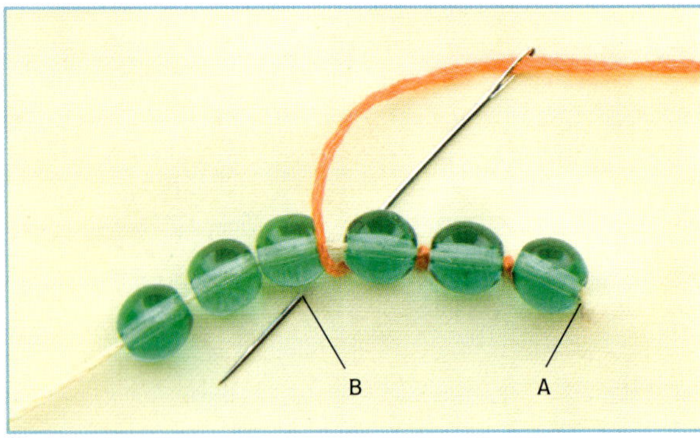

3 Position the first bead at A.

4 Bring a second needle out at B and make a couching stitch over the beaded thread.

5 Slide the next bead alongside the first and repeat. Continue until the row is filled. Take both needles to the back and finish off.

SPOT STITCH

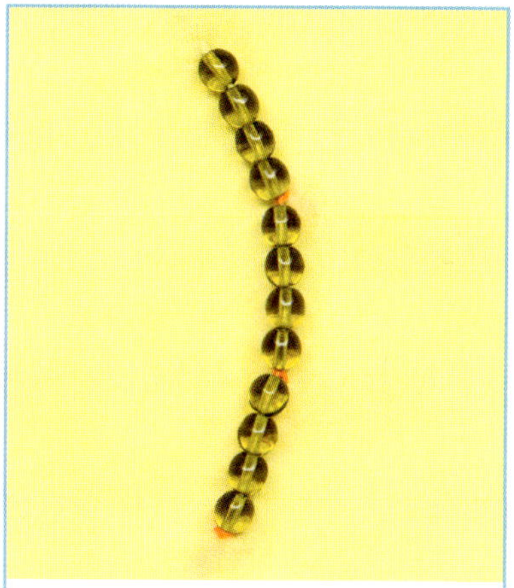

Spot stitch is another couching technique in which several beads are grouped between each couching stitch. It is quicker to work than individual couching, but it is also less secure.

1 Work as for step 1 of couching, then slide 3 or 4 beads down to A.

2 Bring a second needle out at B and couch over the thread holding the first group of beads.

3 Slide 3 or 4 more beads down to B and couch the beaded thread at C.

4 Continue until the row or line is filled, then take both needles to the back and finish both threads off securely.

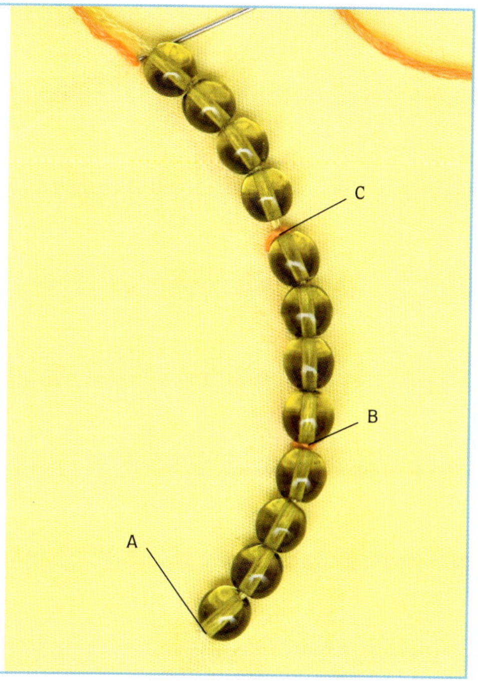

LAZY SQUAW FILLING

This is a quick method for filling an area with beads. Work in a hoop.

1 Mark guidelines on the area to be filled if necessary.

2 Cut a length of thread and knot it on the back.

3 Come out at A. Slide enough beads onto the thread to fill 1 row. Insert the needle at B, on the other side of the area. Come out at C, directly below B, to secure the beads. Repeat, working from side to side.

OJIBWA FILLING

This is a much more secure way of beading. Outline the area to be filled with tacking, which will be covered by the beads. Work in a hoop.

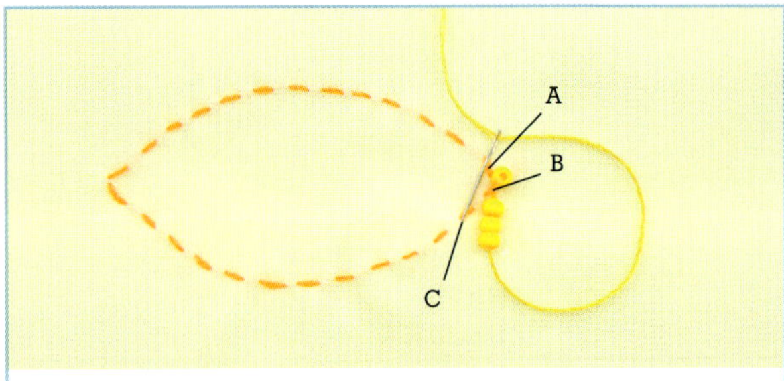

1 Knot the thread on the back. Come out at A, on the edge. Thread on one bead and apply as for a single bead (see page 208).

2 Come out at B and thread on three beads. Slide them next to the first bead. Insert the needle at C.

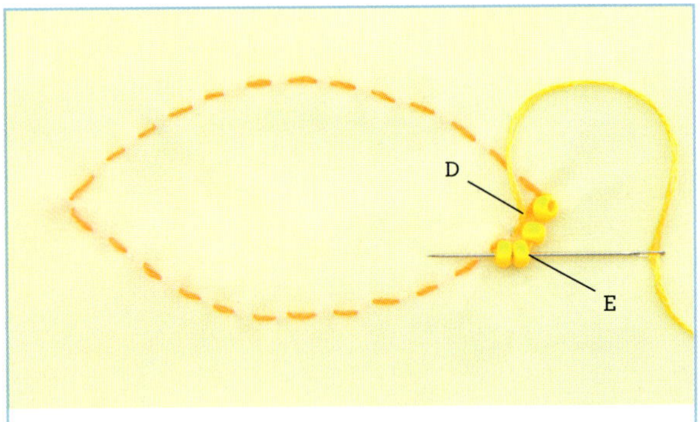

3 Take a stitch back to D, coming out between the first and second beads of group of three. Insert the needle at E, through the second and third beads in the group.

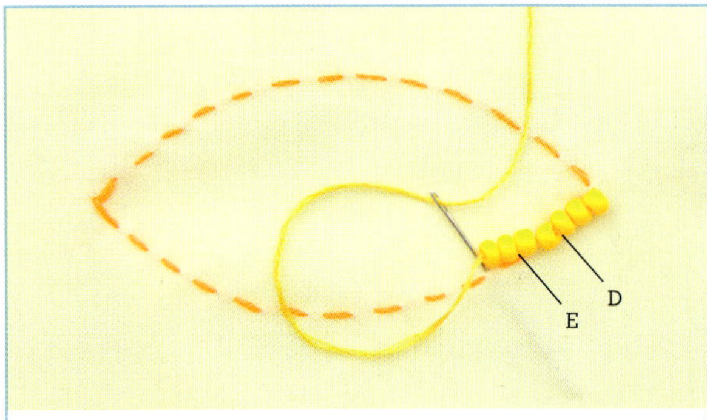

4 Add another three beads. Repeat to fill the shape from the outside in.

BEADED FRINGE

Use a strong thread that is thin enough to go through the holes in the beads.

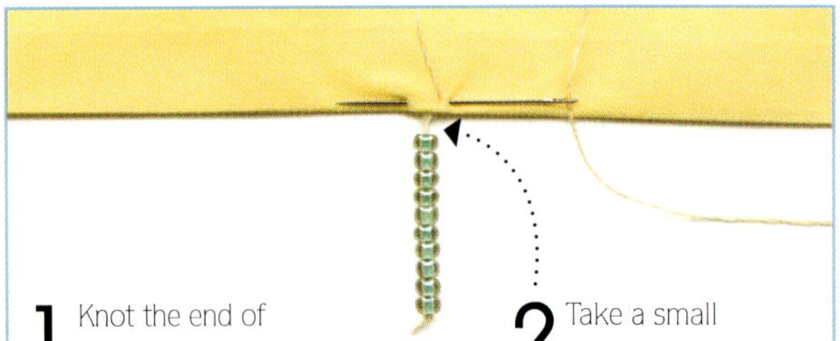

1 Knot the end of the thread. Slide the required number of beads onto the thread.

2 Take a small backstitch in the fold of the hem. Secure the thread.

LOOP FRINGE

This is a quick and easy way to embellish edges.

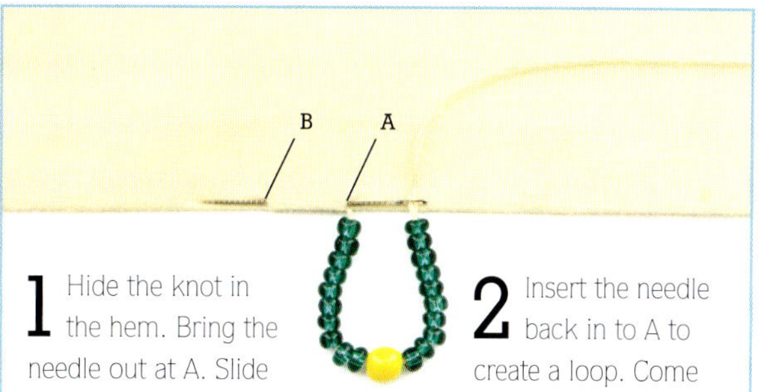

1 Hide the knot in the hem. Bring the needle out at A. Slide the required number of beads onto the thread.

2 Insert the needle back in to A to create a loop. Come out again at B to the left. Repeat.

Sequins

A sequin is a small disc of metal or plastic with a hole in the centre through which it can be attached to fabric. Traditionally sequins are round, but they are available in a myriad of shapes and colours. They can be attached individually, in groups, or rows.

SINGLE SEQUIN

Single sequins can be attached on one or more sides. Sequins can be placed edge to edge or scattered across the surface.

1 To secure individual sequins with a single stitch, knot the thread on the back and bring the needle out at A.

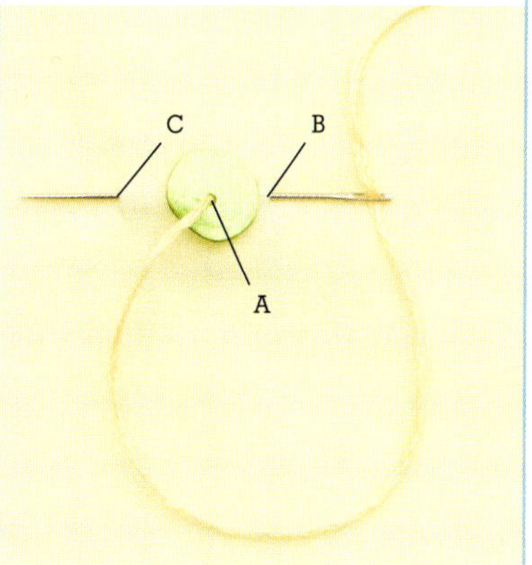

2 Slide a sequin onto it and, with the sequin flat on the background, take a backstitch at B on the right-hand edge of the sequin, coming out at C, where the next sequin will be placed.

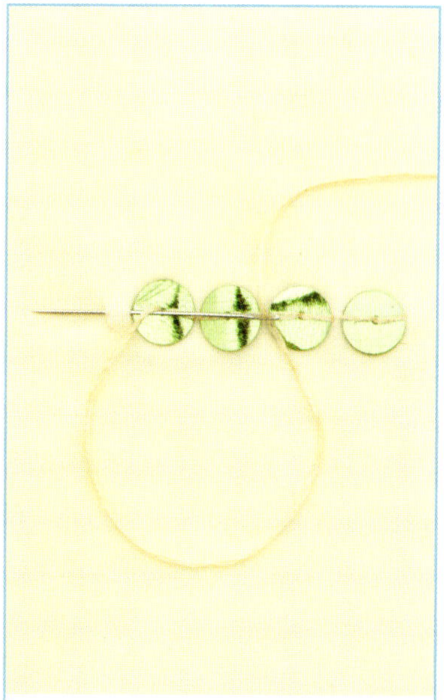

3 Slide another sequin on the needle and pull the thread through. Repeat the backstitch and come out at the next position.

SEQUIN CHAIN

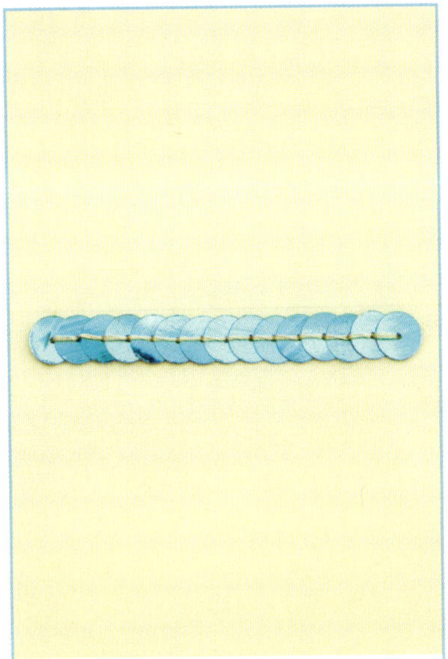

An overlapping chain of sequins can be worked to create many interesting effects.

1 Knot the thread on the back and bring the needle out at A.

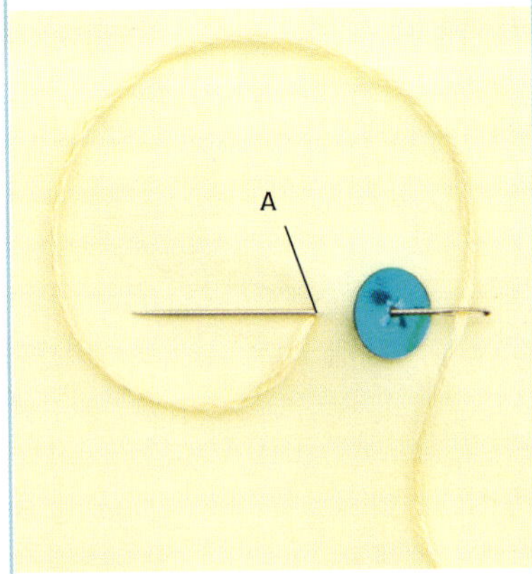

2 Lay the first sequin just to the right of the thread and backstitch into the hole.

3 Come out again at A. Slide the second sequin onto the needle.

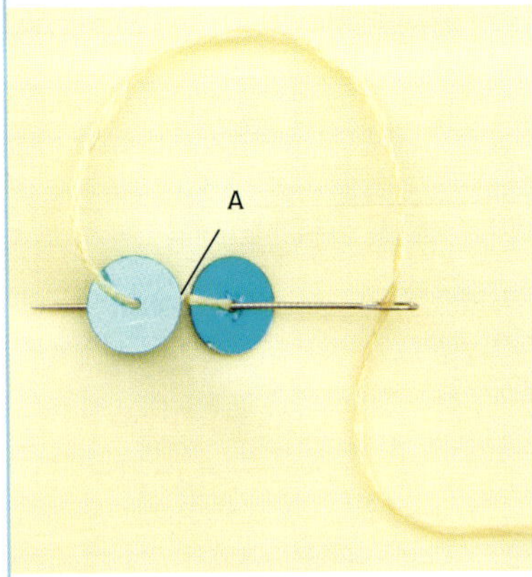

4 Backstitch into the hole of the first sequin and come out on the left-hand edge of the second sequin. Repeat to complete the chain. Secure the thread on the back.

BEADED SEQUIN

Sequins can also be anchored to the fabric by a bead.

1 Lay a sequin in position and bring the needle out through the hole.

2 Slide a bead onto the thread and insert the needle through the hole in the sequin again.

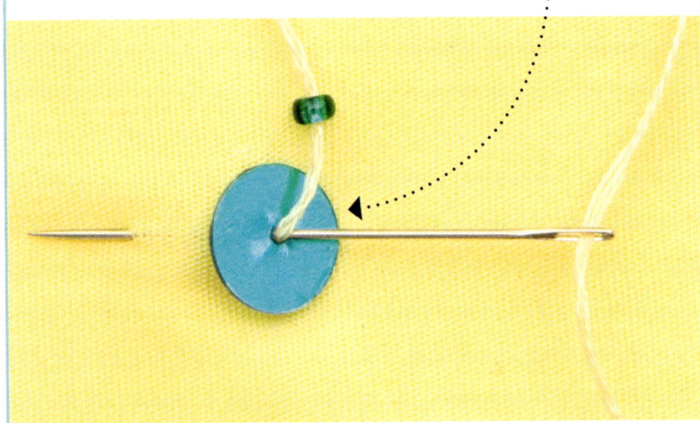

3 Pull gently to settle the bead on top of the sequin and secure the thread on the back.

Mirrorwork

Also called shisha work, mirrorwork is a traditional form of textile decoration from Central Asia. Shisha are small discs of mirror, glass, or tin that are held in place by a foundation framework on which a decorative edge is stitched. On plain-weave fabrics, use a crewel needle and a single-ply thread or doubled stranded cotton with enough body to hold the disc securely and give a firm edge.

SINGLE THREAD METHOD

This traditional shisha stitch shows off the mirrored surface well.

1 Hold the disc in place. Bring the needle out at A.

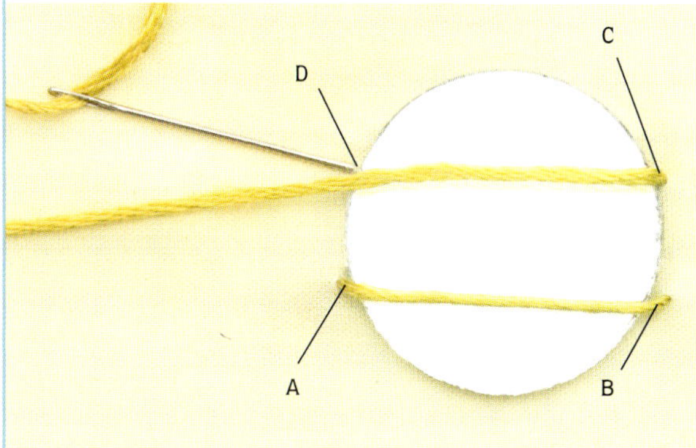

2 Insert the needle at B and come out at C. Insert at D to make two parallel stitches.

3 Bring the needle out at E and loop the thread under and over the bottom securing stitch, then under and over the top stitch.

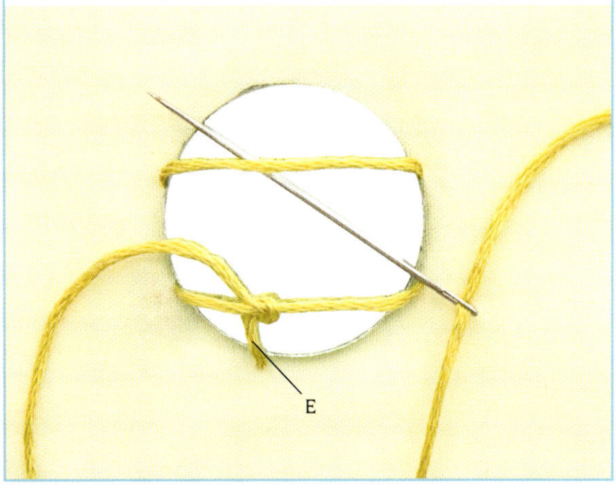

4 Insert the needle at F and come out at G.

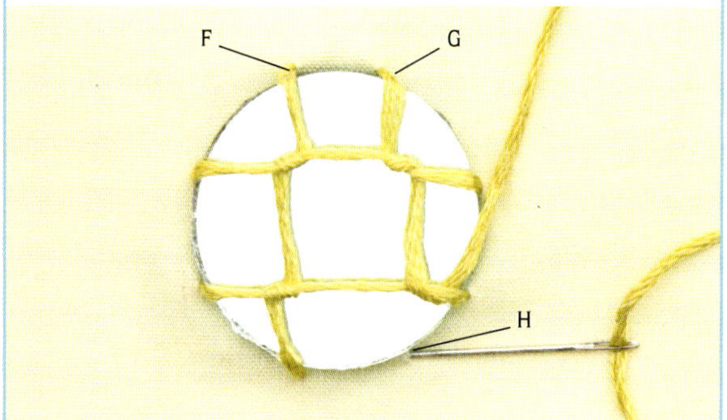

5 Loop the working thread around the horizontal stitches as before, to make a parallel vertical stitch. Insert the needle at H.

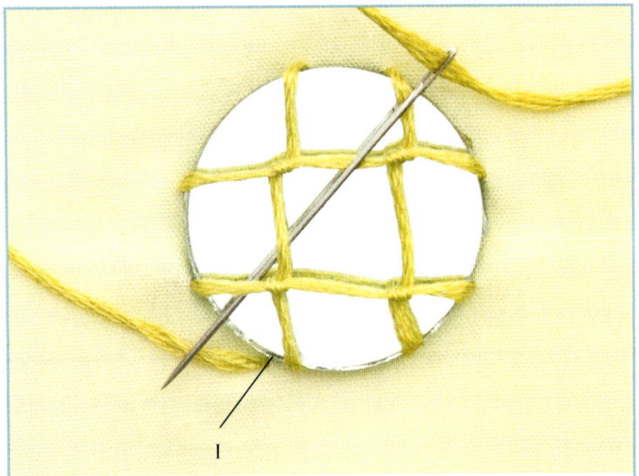

6 Bring the needle out at I and slide the needle under the crossed threads in the bottom left corner, keeping the thread left of the needle.

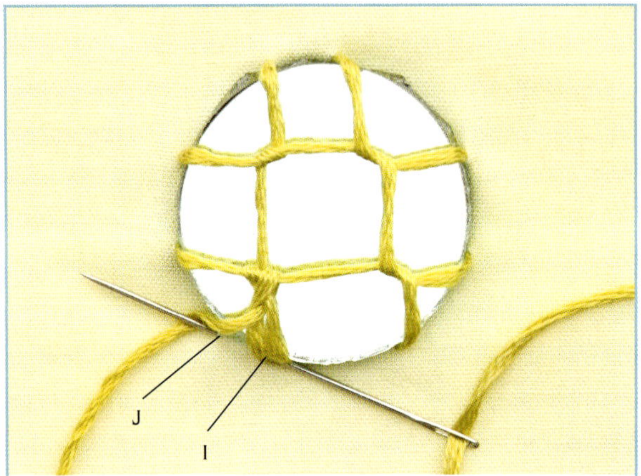

7 Insert the needle at I again and come out at J, with the needle on top of the working thread.

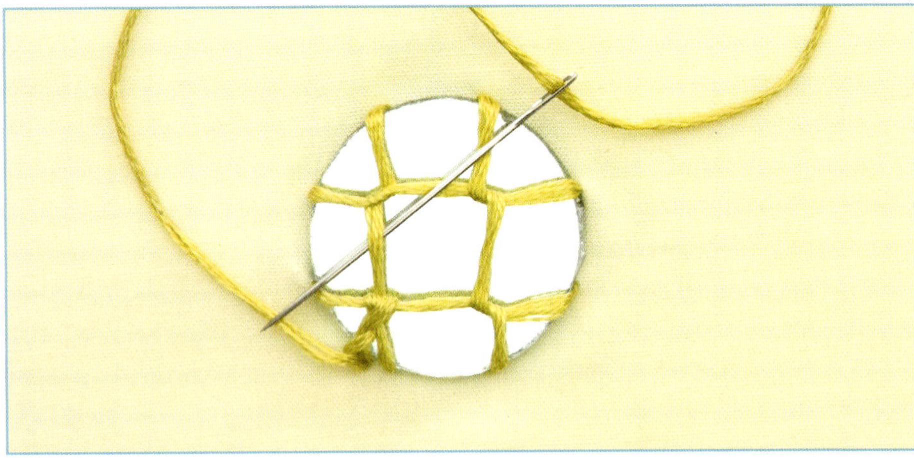

8 Slide the needle under the left-hand vertical thread and over the working thread.

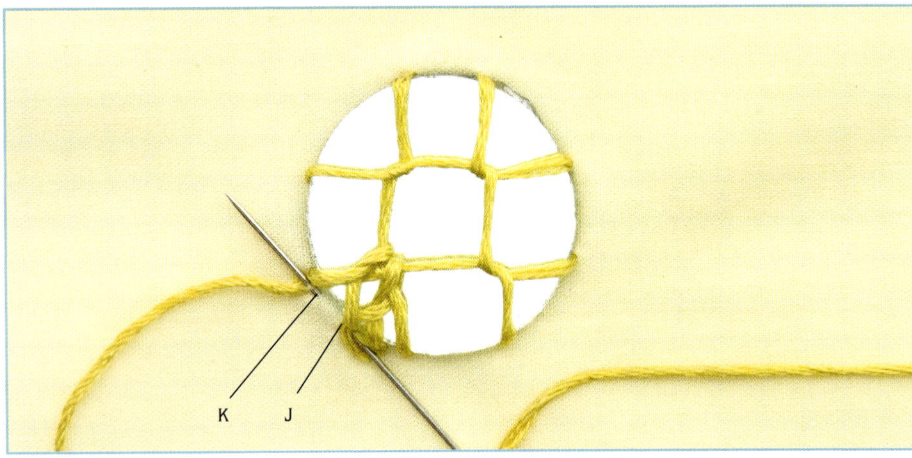

9 Insert the needle at J and come out at K, with the needle on top of the working thread.

10 Repeat the sequence of taking a small stitch through the fabric and a loop under the foundation threads to create a decorative edge.

DOUBLE THREAD METHOD

The mirror is held in place by a "frame" of four pairs of straight stitches. To keep the disc securely in place, work all the stitches as tightly against the edge of the mirror as possible, inserting the needle vertically against the edge each time.

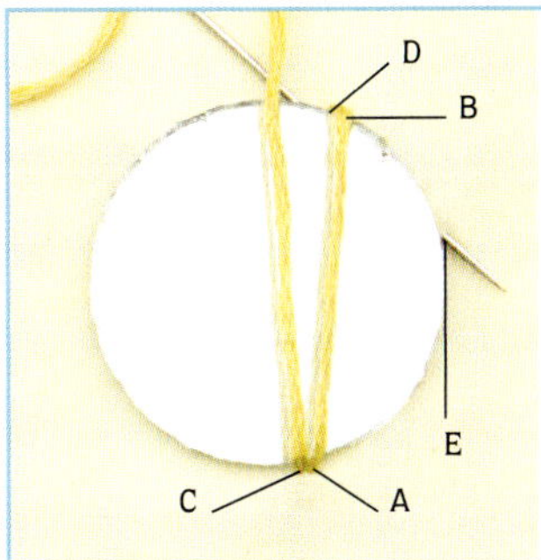

1 Hold the disc in place. Bring the needle out at A. Insert it at B and come out at C, next to A. Insert it at D, next to B, and come out at E.

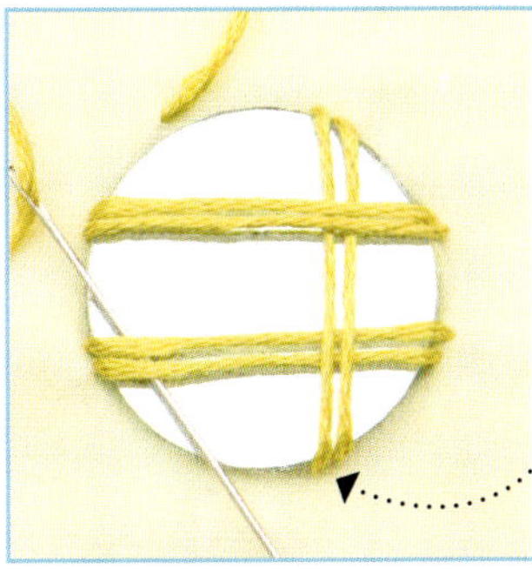

2 Repeat, making pairs of threads on all four sides. Each pair should cross on top of the previous pair; take the final pair under the first pair of threads.

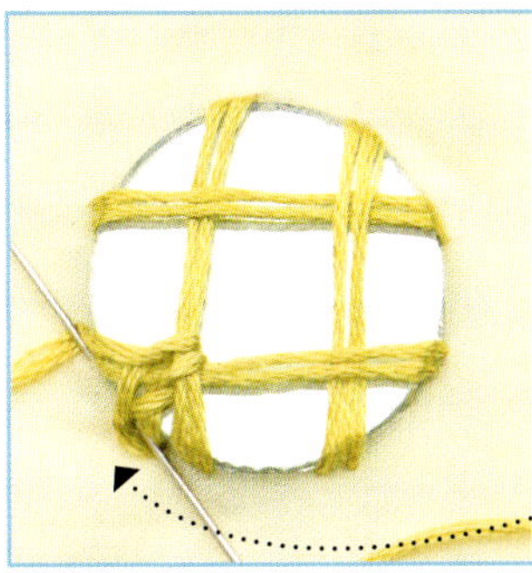

3 Working as close to the edge as possible, repeat Steps 4–7 of Single thread method (pages 213–214). If you prefer, you can work a simple buttonhole stitch.

LATTICE

This is a simple, non-traditional mirrorwork method. Make sure that the edges of the disc are smooth so that they don't cut into the thread.

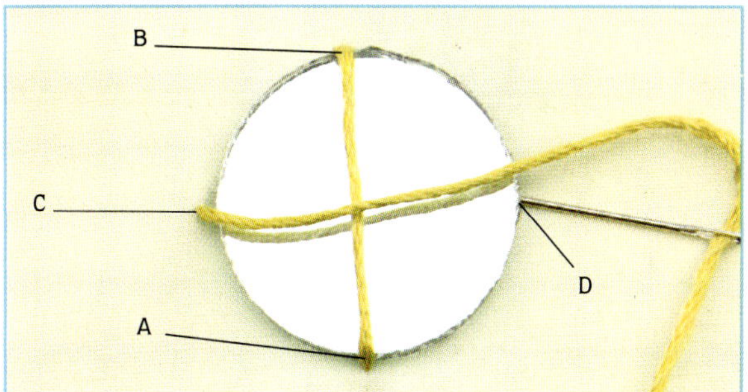

1 Work a lattice of at least three threads. Holding the disc in place, bring the needle out at A and take it across to B. Then take a stitch horizontally across the centre from C to D. Add a stitch in each direction on either side, alternating sides as you work.

2 Add lattice threads as desired, then outline the disc with chain stitch or one of its variations, worked as close as possible to the edge.

CARE OF PATCHWORK

Cleaning and storing quilts should be done carefully. Quilts of any size require an investment of time, energy, and patience to create, so they should be treated with care and respect. Start by taking account of the various textile components of the items, which will include fabrics and probably wadding, as well as trims, before attempting to wash any quilt.

Cleaning quilts

Modern quilts in everyday use will probably be made from washable fabrics such as cotton and filled with polyester or cotton wadding. Give a good shake when you change the bed and an airing outdoors, weather permitting. Dry-cleaning is not recommended for quilts.

Machine washing

If a quilt needs to be laundered, make sure there is no damage to the fabrics. Small items such as baby quilts can be laundered in the washing machine, as can bed quilts. Use a gentle cycle, a mild detergent, and lukewarm water.

Hand washing

Large quilts can be soaked in the bath. Run the water lukewarm, fold the quilt until it fits into the bath and leave to soak. Use a gentle washing solution if necessary, but bear in mind that it will need to be rinsed out completely. If the water looks murky, drain and refill the bath. Once the water remains clear, drain the bath and leave the quilt to continue to release water for several hours. Use a clean sheet to lift the quilt out.

Drying

Dry washed quilts flat. Spread a white sheet on the floor, lay the quilt flat on top, and cover it with another white sheet. When the top side feels dry, turn the "sandwich" upside down.

Vacuuming

Fragile quilts can be vacuumed with extreme caution. Set the vacuum on low and use an upholstery brush to work lightly over the surface, which should be protected by a clean nylon screen or a piece of fine netting.

Storing quilts

Store flat: a bed is an ideal place. Fold quilts as few times as possible and store them on a cupboard shelf or in a blanket box. Refold them occasionally if they will be stored for a long time. An alternative is to hang them as a wall display.

Glossary

APPLIQUÉ
From the French verb appliquer, meaning "to apply", a decorative technique in which shapes are cut from one fabric and applied to another, either by stitching them in place or by heat bonding with fusible bonding web.

BACK STITCH
A hand stitch used to seam patchwork. A more secure alternative to running stitch.

BAGGING OUT
A finishing technique that involves placing the quilt top and backing right sides together, on top of the wadding, and then stitching around the edges before turning the quilt through to the right side – thereby obviating the need for a separate binding.

BIAS
The diagonal grain of a woven fabric, at 45 degrees to the straight grain.

BINDING
A narrow strip of fabric used to cover the raw edges of a quilt to provide a neat finish and prevent it from fraying. For straight edges, the binding can be cut on the straight grain; bias-cut binding has more stretch, and should always be used for curved edges.

BLANKET STITCH
Decorative hand or machine stitch worked along the raw or finished edge of fabric to neaten it. Often used in appliqué work.

BLOCK
A single design unit in patchwork and appliqué. Patchwork blocks traditionally fall into one of four main categories: four-patch (two rows of two patches), nine-patch (three rows of three patches), five-patch (five rows of five patches), and seven-patch (seven rows of seven patches).

BUTTONHOLE
Opening through which a button is inserted to form a fastening. Buttonholes are usually machine stitched but may also be worked by hand or piped for reinforcement or decorative effect.

BUTTONHOLE STITCH
A hand stitch that wraps over the raw edges of a buttonhole to neaten and strengthen it. Machine-stitched buttonholes are worked with a special close zigzag stitch.

CHAIN PIECING
A method of piecing together patchwork units by feeding them through the sewing machine in sequence without lifting the presser foot or breaking the thread so that they form a chain with a short length of thread between each one.

COUCHING
An embellishment technique in which a thread, ribbon, or string of beads is laid over the surface of the fabric and attached by means of tiny "tying" stitches worked vertically or diagonally across it.

DOUBLE RUFFLE
Decorative trim made from doubled fabric. One side can wider than the other. Attractive on home furnishings.

ENGLISH PAPER PIECING
A traditional patchwork method for making a quilt of mosaic shapes by tacking the fabric pieces (all of which have some bias edges) to pre-cut paper templates the size of the finished element.

FACING
A separate layer of fabric placed on the inside of an edge of fabric to finish off raw edges. A useful way to finish off shaped bindings such as scallops.

FOUNDATION PIECING
A patchwork technique in which fabric pieces, or patches, are stitched to a foundation, either a lightweight fabric such as calico, or to paper which is removed once the design is completed.

FUSIBLE BONDING WEB
A non-woven material impregnated with heat-activated adhesive. Widely used in machine appliqué work.

FUSSY CUTTING
Isolating an individual motif on a printed fabric and cutting it out to use as a feature in a patchwork or appliqué block.

GATHERS
Bunches of fabric created by sewing two parallel rows of loose stitching, then pulling the threads up so that the fabric gathers and reduces in size to fit a specific space. Used to trim home furnishings, and to make trims like fabric flowers.

MEDALLION
A style of quilt in which a large central motif is surrounded by several borders.

MIRRORWORK
Also called shisha work, a traditional form of textile decoration from Central Asia and India that involves stitching around or over small discs of mirror, glass, or tin to hold them in place on the fabric.

MITRE
To finish a corner by stitching adjacent sides of fabric together at a 45-degree angle.

OVERCASTING
Also known as whipstitch, this is a hand stitch used particularly in English paper piecing.

PATCH
An individual piece of fabric used in making a patchwork design. Patches may be whole squares or rectangles, or sub-divided into triangle units, curved units, or combinations thereof.

PATCHWORK
The technique of stitching together small pieces of fabric to make a larger one.

PLAIN-WEAVE FABRIC
A tightly woven fabric in which the warp and weft form a simple criss-cross pattern. The number of threads in each direction are not necessarily equal. Examples of plain-weave fabrics include cotton, linen, and silk.

QUILTING
The process of stitching the three layers of a quilt (top, wadding, and backing) together. In addition to serving a practical purpose in holding the three layers together, the quilting stitch pattern often forms an integral part of the quilt design. It is normally marked out on the quilt top in advance and may consist of a geometric grid of squares or diamond shapes, concentric lines that echo shapes within the design, intricate shapes such as hearts, feathers, and swags, or a continuous meandering pattern.

RAW EDGE
Any cut edge of fabric. Raw edges are usually hidden in seams or turned under and hemmed or stitched in place, as in appliqué. Some techniques depend for their effect on leaving the raw edge unstitched.

REVERSE STITCH
Machine stitch that stitches backwards over a row of stitches to secure the threads.

RIGHT SIDE
The front of a piece of fabric, the side that will normally be in view when the piece is assembled.

ROCKING STITCH
The ideal stitch for hand quilting in which the needle takes several stitches up and down vertically before pulling the thread through.

ROULEAU LOOP
Button loop made from a strip of bias binding, often found on home furnishings.

RUFFLE
Decorative gathered trim made from one or two layers of fabric.

RUNNING STITCH
A simple, evenly spaced, straight hand stitch separated by equal-sized spaces, used for seaming and gathering.

SASHING
Strips of fabric interspersed between blocks when making a quilt top.

SEAM
The join formed when two pieces of fabric are sewn together.

SEAM ALLOWANCE
The amount of fabric allowed for on a pattern where sections are to be joined together by a seam. The standard seam allowance in patchwork is 5mm ($^1/_4$in).

SEAM EDGE
The cut edge of a seam allowance.

SEAMLINE
The line along which a seam should be stitched.

SELVEDGE
The rigid edge woven into each side of a length of fabric to prevent the fabric from fraying or unravelling. It occurs when the weft thread turns at the edge of the warp threads to start the next row.

SET OR SETTING
The way the blocks that make up a quilt top are arranged. Blocks may be straight set (stitched together edge to edge, with each block oriented the same way), or set "on point" (turned on the diagonal so that they appear as diamonds rather than squares). Pieced and appliqué blocks may be alternated with plain "spacer" blocks, or blocks may be rotated to create secondary patterns.

SETTING IN
In patchwork, sewing one shape or patch into an acute angle formed when two other shapes have been joined together.

SLIP STITCH
A hidden stitch used mainly in appliqué work.

STAB STITCH
An alternative hand quilting stitch used particularly on thicker fabric layers. The needle is taken up then down to make individual stitches.

STRAIGHT GRAIN
The parallel threads of a woven fabric running at 90 degrees to either the lengthways (warp) or crossways (weft) direction of the weave.

STRAIGHT STITCH
Plain machine stitch, used for most applications. The length of the stitch can be altered to suit the fabric.

STRING PIECING
In patchwork, similar to strip piecing, but the strips can be of uneven width.

STRIP PIECING
A patchwork technique in which long strips of fabric are sewn together and then cut apart before being reassembled in a different sequence. The method is used to create many popular blocks, including Log cabin and Seminole patchwork.

TACKING
A temporary stitch used to hold pieces of fabric together or for transferring pattern markings to fabric. It can be worked by hand or machine and can be a straight line or individual doubled stitches.

TENSION
The tautness of the stitching in a seam.

TOP-STITCH
Machine straight stitching worked on the right side of an item, close to the finished edge, for decorative effect. Sometimes stitched in a contrasting colour.

TOP-STITCHED SEAM
A seam finished with a row of top-stitching for decorative effect on soft furnishings and garments.

TYING
A utilitarian quilting method in which thread, string, cord, etc., is stitched through the layers and tied in a secure knot.

WADDING
Also called batting, this is a layer of filling made from polyester, cotton, wool, or even silk and used to provide warmth and give body to a quilt.

WARP
The vertical threads of a woven fabric, also known as the lengthways grain.

WEFT
The horizontal threads of a woven fabric, also known as the crossways grain.

WRONG SIDE
The reverse of a piece of fabric, the side that will normally be hidden from view when the piece is made up.

YO YO
A type of quilt made from rounds of fabric that have been gathered and joined together.

ZIGZAG STITCH
A machine stitch used to neaten and secure seam edges and for decorative purposes. The width and length of the zigzag can be altered.

Index